IMAGES
of America

LEEDS

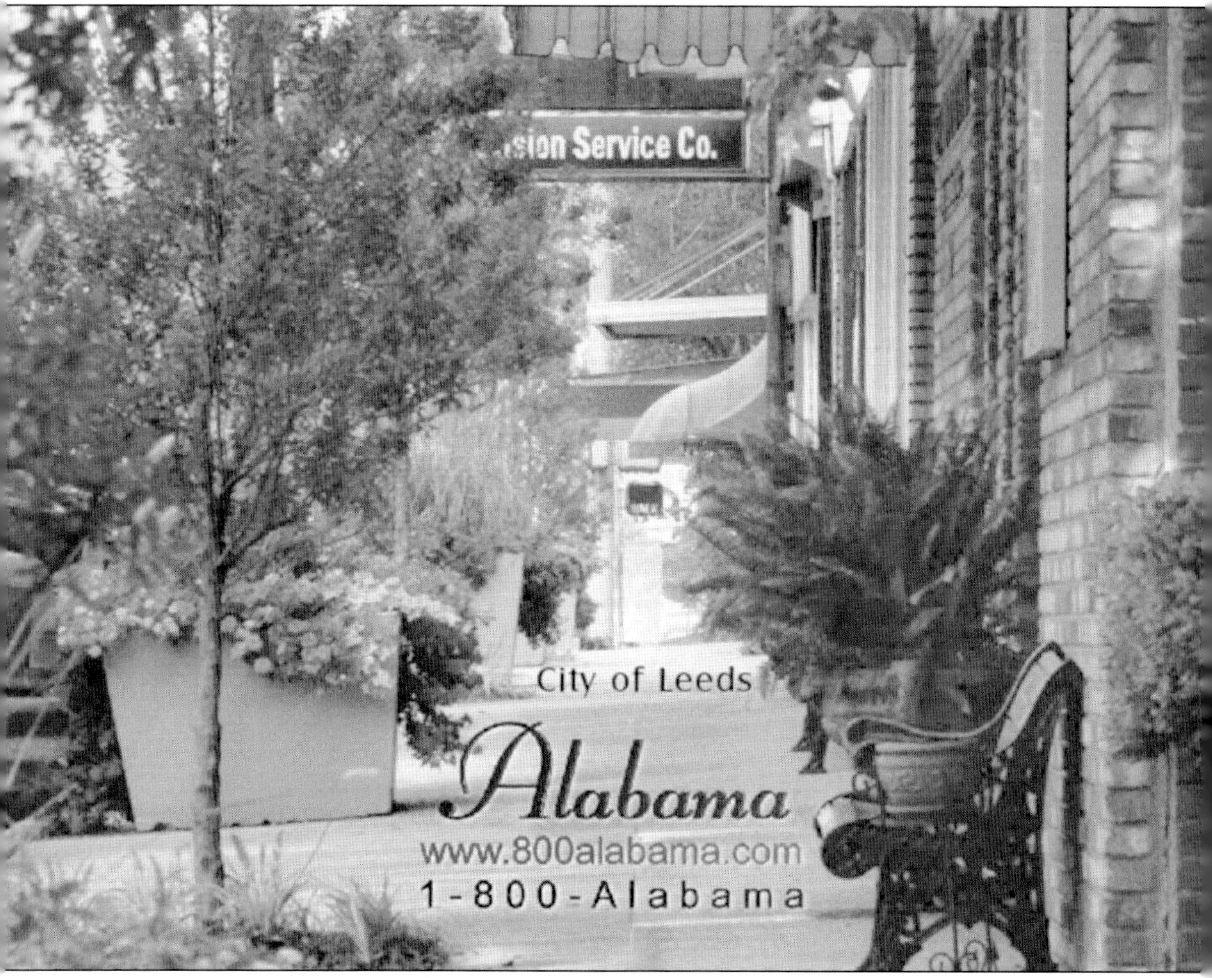

Historic, yet progressive, Leeds is the primary population center of an area known as the Cahaba Valley, a region of fertile bottomland nourished by the Cahaba and Little Cahaba Rivers. Leeds remains a small Southern town settled by European immigrants, African Americans, and Native Americans. It was a walkable city from its inception, and the sidewalks of Leeds link decades of Appalachian heritage. The first residents brought their pioneer spirit with them when they came to the Leeds area by path, road, and rail to form one city from three cultures. Today, a sound and growing commercial and industrial base provides livelihoods for many residents, while offering a small-town atmosphere convenient to big-city services and cultural and social events in Alabama's largest metropolitan area. Now, almost 200 years since the town was settled, the pioneer spirit prevails among natives and new residents.

On the Cover: In 1910, Leeds State Bank was incorporated under Alabama law. The bank was housed in a building on the corner of Ninth Street and Parkway Drive and anchored shops and other businesses south of the Southern Railway. A.W. Bell became the first president, and bank shares sold for $8. Employees included Ruth Jones Teal, Lillian Poe Payne, and Clarence Roberts. (Courtesy of Jeff Falletta.)

IMAGES
of America

LEEDS

Pat Hall and Jane Newton Henry

ARCADIA
PUBLISHING

ISBN 978-0-7385-9125-4

Published by Arcadia Publishing
Charleston, South Carolina

Printed in the United States of America

Library of Congress Control Number: 2011937368

For all general information, please contact Arcadia Publishing:
Telephone 843-853-2070
Fax 843-853-0044
E-mail sales@arcadiapublishing.com
For customer service and orders:
Toll-Free 1-888-313-2665

Visit us on the Internet at www.arcadiapublishing.com

To Jane Culbreth, champion of Leeds history, who led the efforts to restore the Southern Railway Depot and to create the Ninth Street Historic District.

Contents

Acknowledgments

This book is the story of the people of Leeds, from the first generation to the present one, and their many accomplishments that continue to make the city a pleasant place to live.

The authors wish to thank the past and present members of the Leeds Historical Society, who made this book possible through their enthusiasm for local history and hours upon hours of volunteer work to preserve the cornerstones of our past.

We express our appreciation to the Jefferson County Historical Commission, the St. Clair Historical Society, and the Shelby County Historical Society for providing information during interviews with the authors and for contributions from *Cherish*, the newsletter of the St. Clair Historical Society.

We are grateful to the Leeds Scenic Byway management team for its contributions and to Andy Harp and Jerry Noel for their help with the book. Thanks to the City of Leeds Archives for its project work.

Special thanks go to Sandra McGuire at the Leeds Area Chamber of Commerce for suggesting this project and to Judy Isbell for her work to establish a permanent memorial for the City of Valor.

Special thanks to our editors at Arcadia Publishing for their guidance and patience during the editing and printing processes. From Pat Hall, special thanks to my family: Tom, George, Anna, Daniel, Grant, and Michelle. You are my inspiration. From Jane Newton Henry, special thanks to my dear friends for their support. You know who you are.

Throughout these pages, the reader will note the names of families who have shared stories and photographs. Thanks to past and present members of the Leeds community for their help and encouragement.

Unless otherwise noted in the text, images appearing in this book were provided courtesy of Pat Hall. Other images were provided by Jeff Falletta, Frank Little, Carl Marbury, Dan Marbury, Bob Moore (BM), the Birmingham Library Department of Archives and Manuscripts (BL), the Leeds Historical Society (LHS), the Leeds Jane Culbreth Library (LL), and the Leeds City Schools (LCS).

INTRODUCTION

Geography, geology, and the War of 1812 brought pioneers to Leeds, and that same rich geography and pioneer spirit guide today's community. The war and its politics brought people to Leeds by path and road to form one city from three cultures. After the war, soldiers who served under Gen. Andrew Jackson settled the Cahaba Trail at Leeds. Most paid for their property, obtaining it on a preferential basis because of their military service.

Cherokee Indians came to Leeds on the Cahaba Trail. One of the first settlements in the southern end of St. Clair County, east of downtown, was at Ohanafeefee—the site where John Ingram Paschal Stewart, a Cherokee English teacher and American veteran of the War of 1812, lived before the Trail of Tears. He left descendants who remain chiefs of Alabama's Cherokee tribes. The Cahaba Trail became a road when Jackson and his Tennesseans widened it to accommodate their mule-drawn wagons. The wagons laid the way for European immigrants to settle Leeds.

Early European settlers included Col. James Hamilton, a Scots-Irish American veteran of the War of 1812, who was the first sheriff of Shelby County. He settled in Cedar Grove, Shelby County, in 1818. Before Hamilton died, his land became part of Jefferson County when county lines were changed to add more counties in Alabama. Hamilton and his contemporaries were first-generation Americans, whose parents had declared independence as a sovereign nation in the first decade of the country's history.

Around 1821, a group of Europeans settled at Oak Ridge and formed Shiloh Cumberland Presbyterian Church. They became the first Cumberland Presbyterian Church congregation in central Alabama, and the church building served as the first school in Leeds.

The Civil War divided the people of Leeds as it did the nation. Although the war did not come to Leeds, the town's citizens went to war. Carved in headstones at Shiloh Cemetery on Ashville Road (US Highway 411) are the epitaphs of divided philosophies among neighbors.

The offspring of Hezekiah Moor (also spelled Moore) wrote of the gallantry of the Southern cause, while Thomas Rowan, a justice of the peace, recorded his loyalty to the federal government. Andrew Jackson Hamilton left papers in the National Archives explaining his conviction that the cotton economy would destroy the South. African American slaves freed by the Scott, Rowan, Little, and McDanal families started a farming community that still keeps its sense of neighborhood.

The population and economy grew as railroads were built in Alabama. Railroad pioneers came to Leeds in the 1880s by rail and brought hard-working African American railroad men. One railroad man, Ciscero Davis, moved to Leeds with his family; they became the first African American family to settle in Leeds. The city was incorporated in 1887.

Leeds's geology and geography brought the Industrial Revolution to this farming community in 1907, literally putting Leeds on the map. Like the railroads 20 years earlier, the Standard Portland Cement Plant brought a new population. The principal survey of Leeds was entered into Jefferson County Mapbook No. 7 in 1908.

Members of the Marbury family, who were descendants of Ciscero Davis, were working, going to church and school, and sharing stories about John Henry when Eddie Marbury left for France with the US Army during World War I. He served with the 372nd Infantry at the Argonne Forest battle. This family had sent solders to the Spanish American War, so it was no surprise that their son left home to serve his country.

In 1934, at the height of the Great Depression, the children of Dwight Blair Sr. lived in the Farley-Blair House on Montevallo Road (Alabama Highway 119), which was the first paved road in Leeds. Its paving was sponsored by the Kiwanians in 1927. Carolyn Blair remembered that despite the Depression, life was good. She recorded the joy of barefoot children following the sprinkler wagon down district streets on a hot summer's day "in order to let the cold water stream across their legs."

Almost everyone was without work when the Works Progress Administration launched an effort during the Depression that provided jobs to pave the small city and build sidewalks and a park for its citizens. Their work made Leeds a walkable city.

Congressional Medals of Honor were conferred during World War II on Leeds native 1st Lt. William Lawley and Leeds resident S.Sgt. Henry Eugene Erwin. A few years later, during the Korean War, Leeds native PFC Alford Lee McLaughlin received a Congressional Medal of Honor as well. Of the three Leeds Congressional Medal of Honor recipients, two were direct descendants of the pioneers who came to Leeds after the War of 1812.

A B-17 pilot in the Army, Lawley responded to an attack on his aircraft by enemy fighters over Europe. After the attack crippled the plane, killed the copilot, and wounded eight crewmembers, Lawley flew the remaining crew to safety.

Erwin, a member of the Army Air Corps, served as a radio operator on a B-29 bomber that left Los Angeles, California, for Japan. Erwin dispatched smoke bombs to signal that his plane had reached the launching point. One phosphorescent bomb was faulty when he launched it, and he knew it would crash the plane. Blinded by the 1,300-degree bomb, Erwin clutched it to his body and threw it out of the aircraft.

McLaughlin became a Marine in 1945 and volunteered for duty a second time during the Korean War. Under a barrage of enemy artillery and mortar fire in August 1952, he fired two machine guns alternately, even though his hands became blistered from the guns' heat. When the guns became too hot to hold, he used a carbine (a short, lightweight rifle) and grenades until some 200 Chinese soldiers lay dead or wounded in front of him.

Because of the heroic actions of these three men, Leeds is known as the City of Valor.

Modern-day Leeds harkens back to the Cahaba Trail, now called the Stagecoach Route Through Leeds. The Alabama Scenic Byways Commission and the state of Alabama announced in 2007 that Leeds was again on the map—the roadmap of America—for its historic stagecoach route that remains as it was in 1812, a crossroads leading to the rest of Alabama. With that announcement, the Stagecoach Route Through Leeds became Alabama's newest scenic byway.

In the new millennium, in addition to the Leeds Downtown Historic District, more than 33 historic homes, businesses, churches, and cemeteries appear on the eight-mile byway. They display historic markers that capture the pioneer spirit of Leeds's early settlers. Historic buildings on the byway listed in the National Register of Historic Places include the Jonathan Bass House Museum, owned and operated by the Leeds Historical Society; the Southern Railway Depot, owned by the city and operated by the historical society; and a 100-acre national historic district, including 22 buildings listed together as the Leeds Downtown Historic District.

The people of Leeds greet neighbors and tourists alike twice a year during two festivals in the community. The Creek Bank Festival takes place in April; the Leeds Downtown Folk Festival and John Henry Celebration takes place in September. The Creek Bank Festival is held on the banks of the Little Cahaba River along the stagecoach route. The folk festival, first held in 2008, is an annual observance of the historic and cultural qualities along the Cahaba Trail at Leeds and is celebrated on the scenic byway in Leeds's Downtown Historic District.

Ultimately, Leeds is "Central Park" to largely urban Jefferson County. It is a getaway for those who love nature and a small-town atmosphere but also enjoy the cultural and social events of a large city with arts, a zoo, museums, theaters, and more. The scenic byway threads itself through the landscape, knitting together a history of citizens with diverse ancestries, stories of heroism, and the area's natural beauty.

One

Soldiers of the Second Revolution

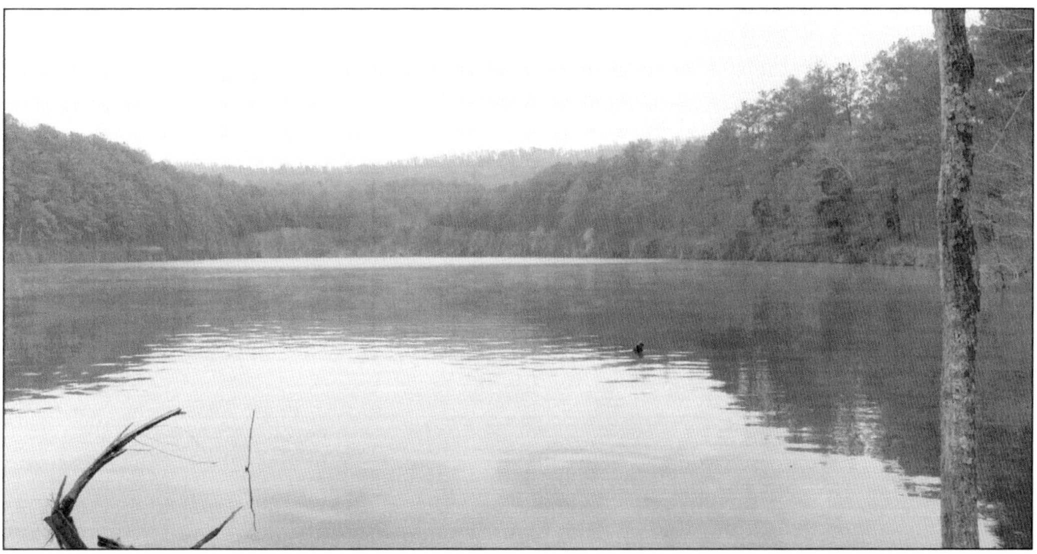

The raw wilderness across the Cahaba Valley lured settlers to the area as early as 1810. Local archaeologist Chris McLaughlin places Leeds on primitive Native American trails that include artifacts from early European culture. European names in Shelby County are now on mailboxes along trails that became streets in Leeds. McLaughlin, Whitmire, Scott, Little, Hamilton, and Lee are some of the surnames of settlers who came early and left descendants.

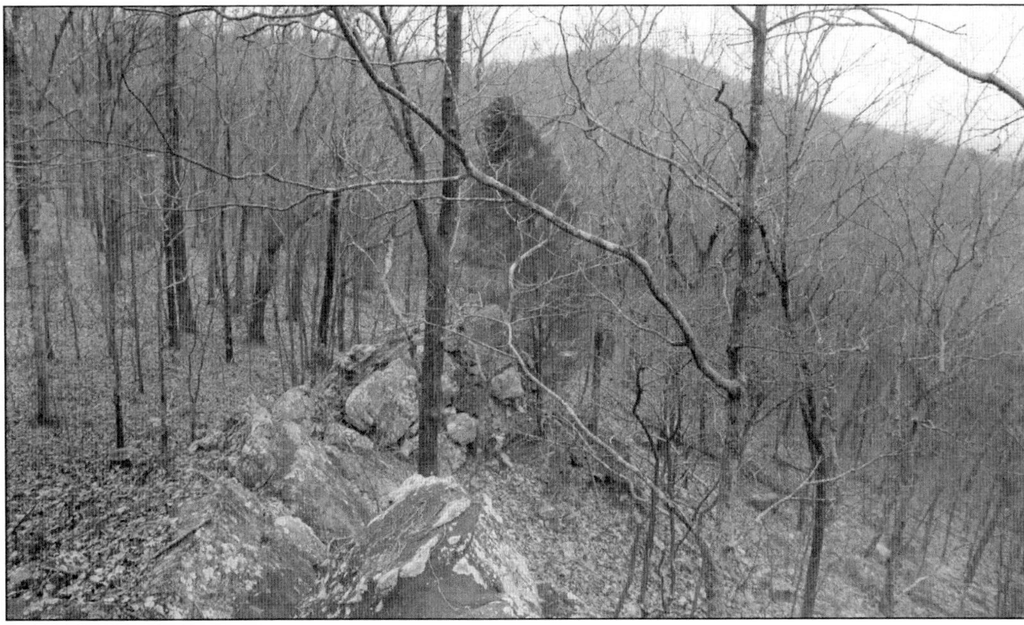

John Richard Ingram Paschal Stewart, a Cherokee English teacher and American veteran of the War of 1812, came to Leeds on the Cahaba Trail, an Indian path. He settled at the village of Ohanafeefee around 1840 to avoid the Trail of Tears. The village was on Oak Mountain, east of what is now downtown Leeds. Stewart is buried within the shadow of this timeless ridge with rock outcroppings.

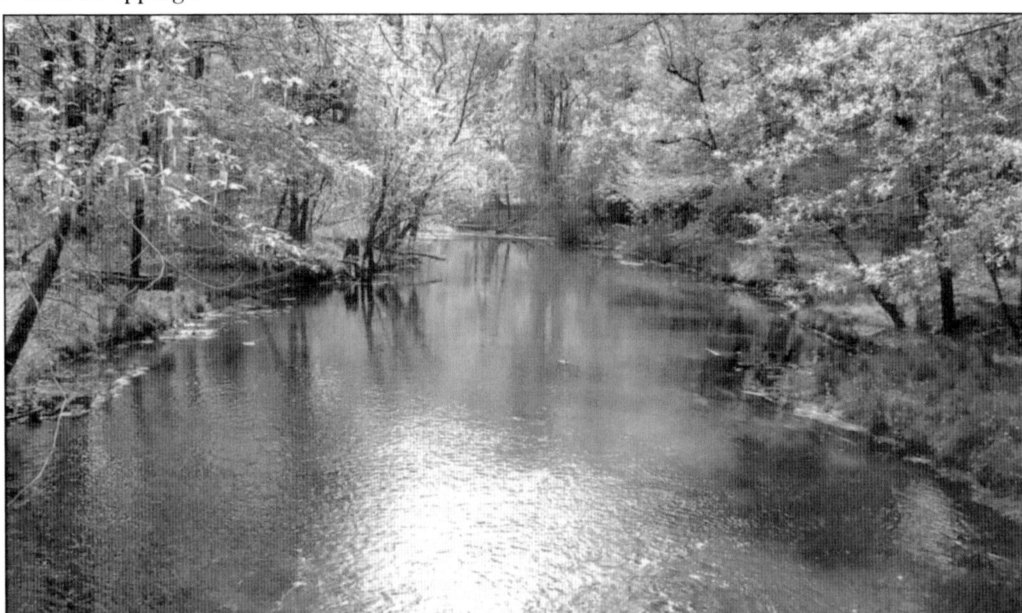

The Little Cahaba River provided transportation and drinking water for early settlers in the Leeds area. The Stagecoach Route Though Leeds still follows the river when not crossing it. Nature enthusiasts enjoy the scenic setting with activities that include bicycling, canoeing, horseback riding, nature photography, and fishing. Leeds's parks offer picnic sites on the Little Cahaba River, where monuments, flags, and interpretive exhibits tell stories of Leeds's history.

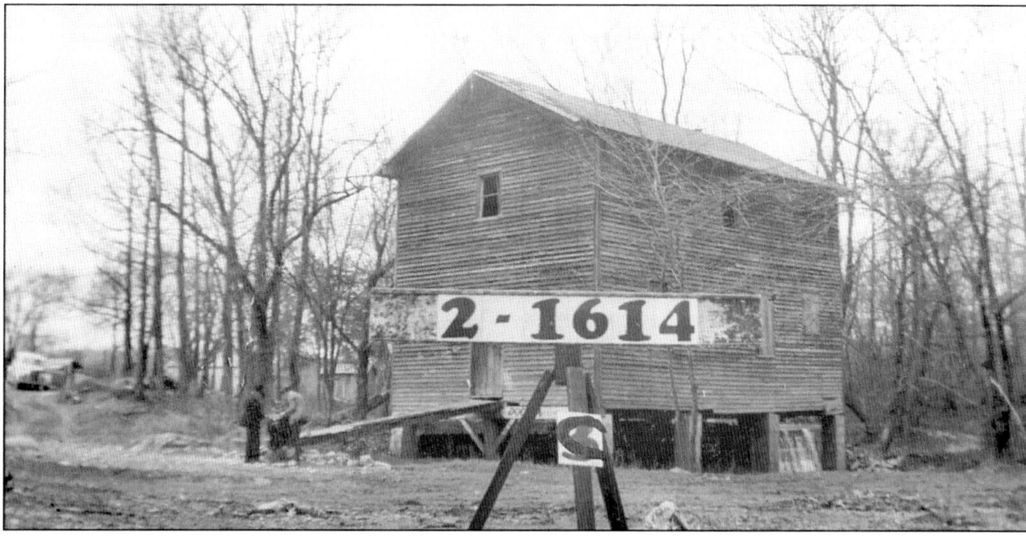

Pictured here is Fuller's Mill, a gristmill on the Little Cahaba River. Henry Little built his mill on an old mill site after settling in the southern Cahaba Valley in 1819. Sloan Fuller purchased the mill in 1923, and replaced its pine-plant dam and overshot waterwheel with a concrete dam and turbine waterwheel. The Bearden family purchased the mill in 1926 and operated it into the 1930s. (BL.)

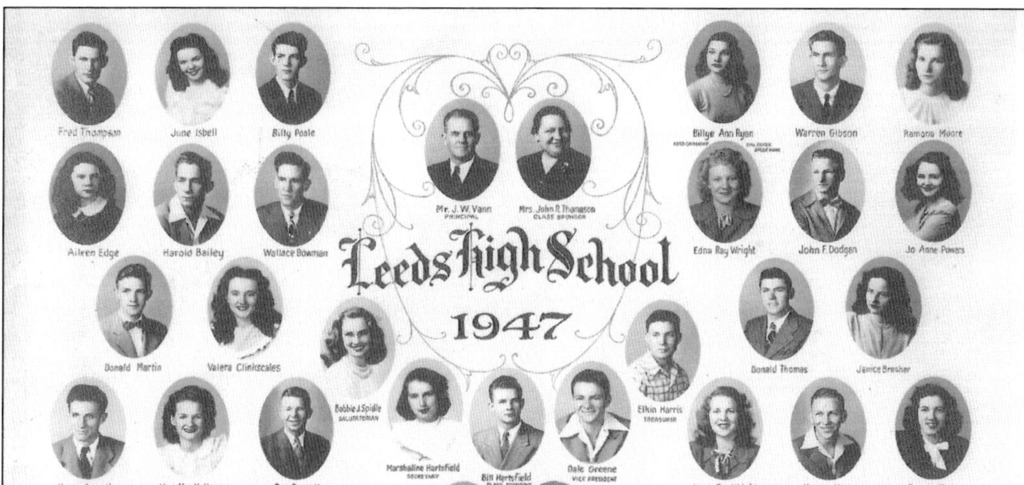

The family names of the members of this 1947 graduating class at Leeds High School are still heard in Leeds today; one of those is Isbell. The Marian Isbell family moved from nearby Vandiver to Leeds around 1906 and operated a chair-making shop. Marian's wife, Nancy Collins Isbell, gave birth to the first set of twins born in Leeds. Members of the Isbell family remain in Leeds today. (LHS.)

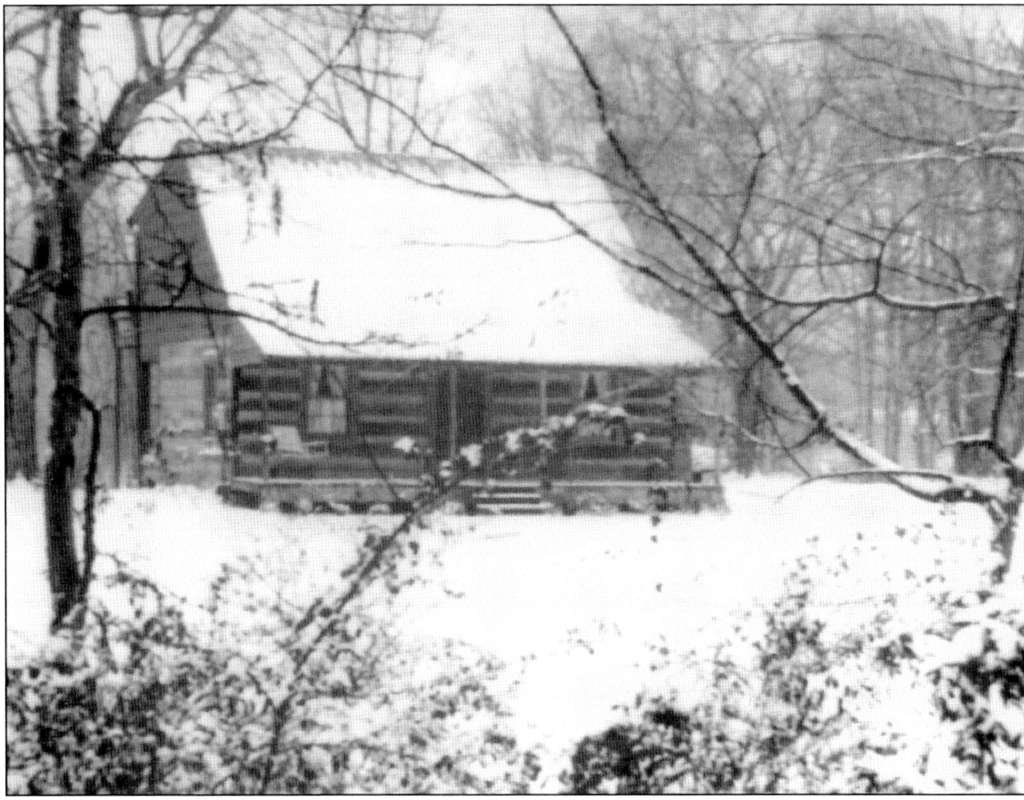

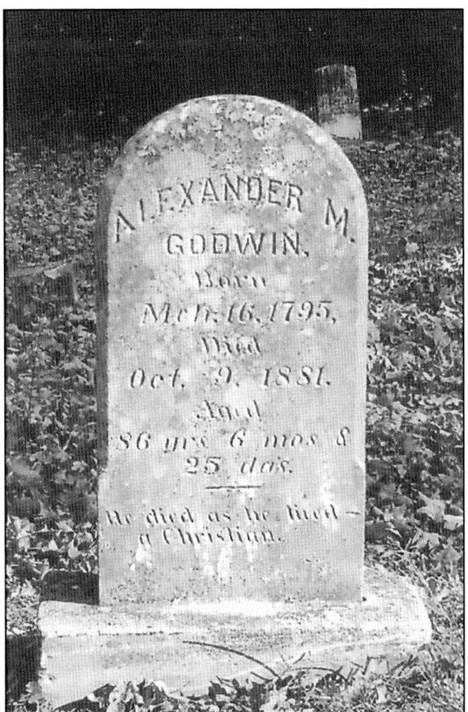

The Henry Little Log Home, pictured after a snowfall, has remained at this location since 1820. Little, who was named for an uncle killed in the Revolutionary War, settled in the Cahaba Valley after Gen. Andrew Jackson's Creek Indian campaign, which followed the War of 1812. Little and his neighbors valued the sovereignty of the young American government and sought to keep it from being overcome by European powers. (LHS.)

Pictured here is one of the oldest graves in Shiloh Cemetery, located in Oak Ridge. This cemetery was the burial site for members of the first Shiloh Cumberland Presbyterian Church in central Alabama. Shiloh Cemetery and Shiloh Church began operating in about 1820. Oak Ridge's first settlers were Scots-Irish. Many were Gen. Andrew Jackson's soldiers during the War of 1812, and many of their fathers fought in the American Revolution.

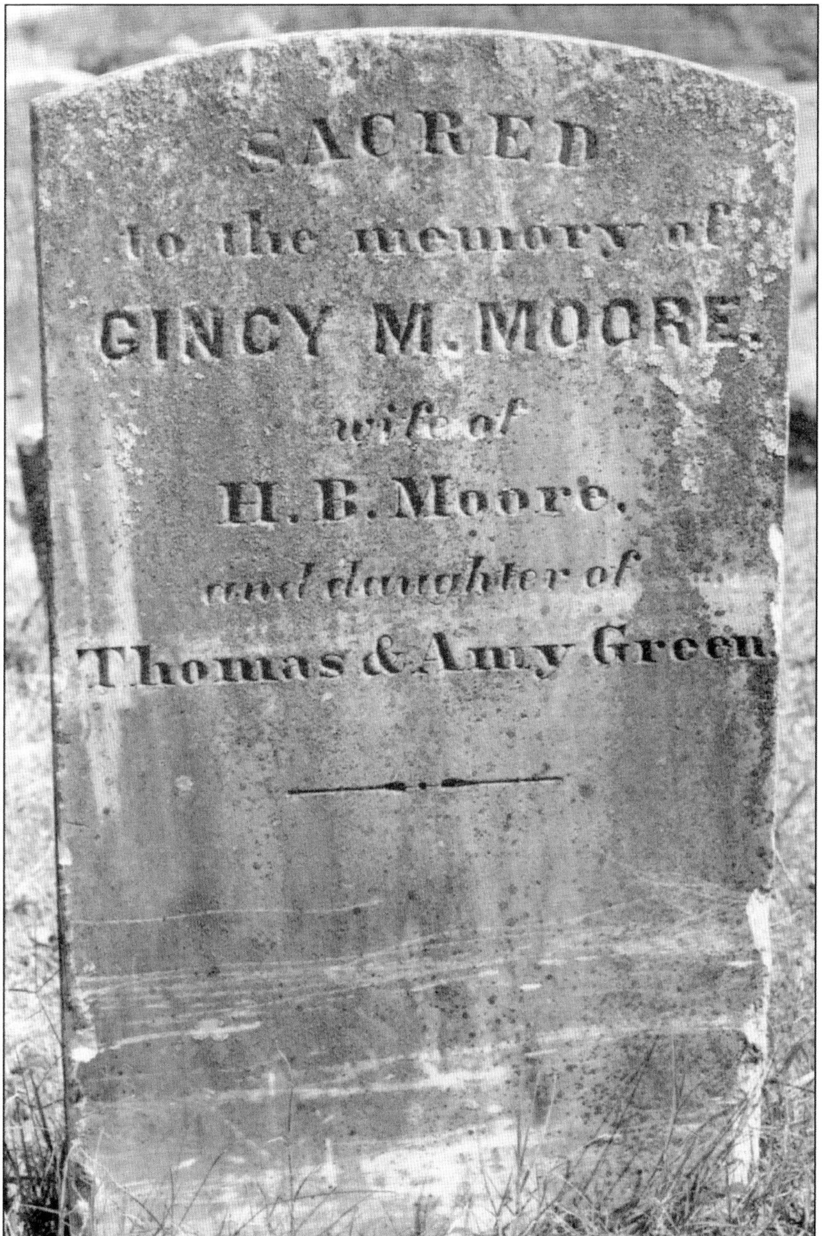

Gincy Moor's grave is the oldest in Cedar Grove Cemetery in the Oak Ridge community. The land originally set aside for the cemetery was a gift to Cedar Grove Church from Gincy's husband, Hezekiah Moor. He had settled the northern Cahaba Valley with William McLaughlin and Speers Jones and was awarded land grants for his medical service in the War of 1812. Later, the Civil War would make casualties of five of the Moors' sons and five of their grandsons. For Appalachian Alabama, the American Revolution and the Tidewater Revivals set the stage for the War of 1812, which called on the sons of Revolutionary War soldiers to defend the sovereignty of a young nation against European interests. William McLaughlin, Speers Jones, and John Stewart, a Cherokee, came to Leeds with common interests, including family, English-speaking culture, and a common book of faith. (BM.)

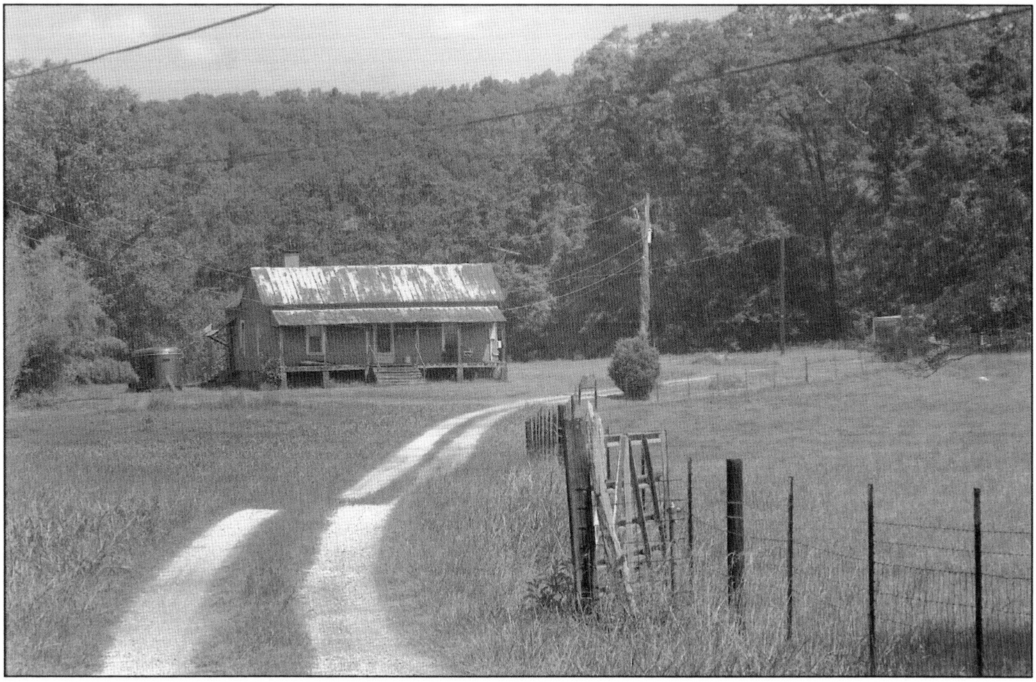

The Mitchell Pool (also spelled Poole) Century Farm is recognized as a working cattle farm that has been in the Pool-Poole family for 100-plus years. Mitchell Pool acquired the land in about 1819. Archaeological artifacts from the farm and private cemetery tell of a family that attended Shiloh Cumberland Presbyterian Church. Buried here are direct descendants of John Witherspoon, the only clergyman to sign the Declaration of Independence.

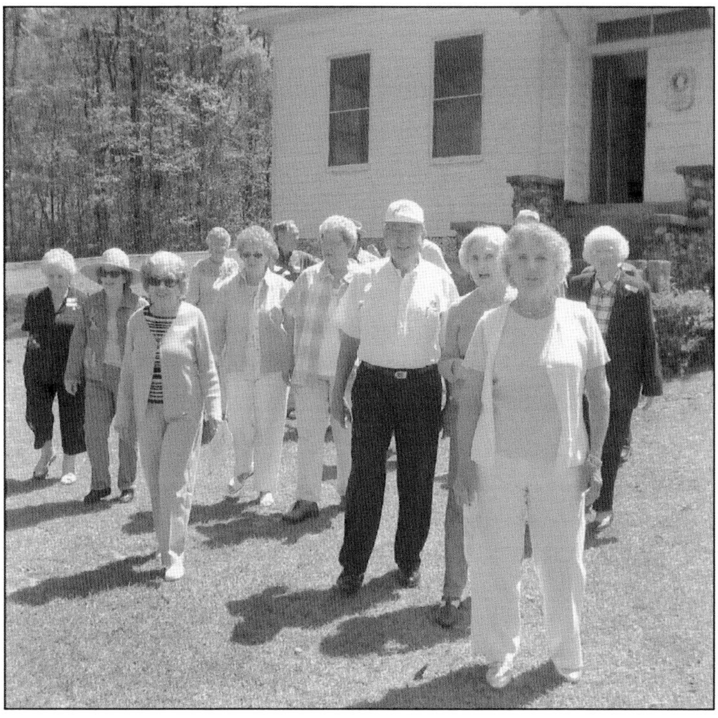

Former students at the Mount Hebron School, a 1919 Queen Anne one-room schoolhouse, gathered for this photograph during a 2005 homecoming. During Leeds's early days, schoolchildren attended one of four schools, depending on where the Little Cahaba River crossed Alabama Highway 119. Many of the former students pictured here are descendants of Henry Little, Hezekiah Moor, William McLaughlin, and Speers Jones.

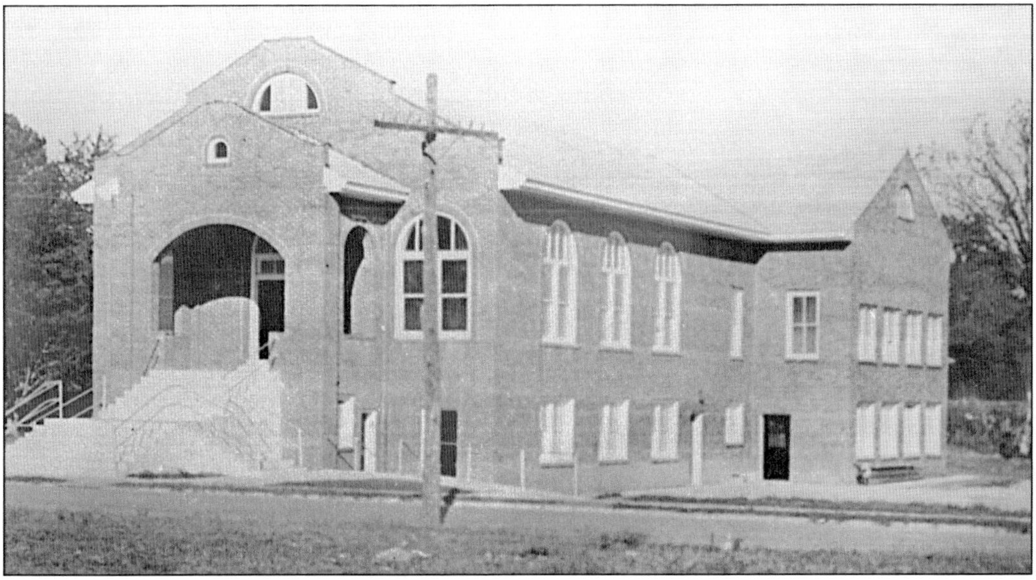

The second building that housed First Baptist Church, shown here, was constructed at the site of Shiloh Cemetery and Shiloh Cumberland Presbyterian Church. It was dedicated in 1938. Shiloh Church, built in 1821, was used as the first church school in Leeds. The land on which Shiloh Church was built was set aside by Alabama for schools. Shiloh Cemetery is located behind the site on which Shiloh Church was built. (BM.)

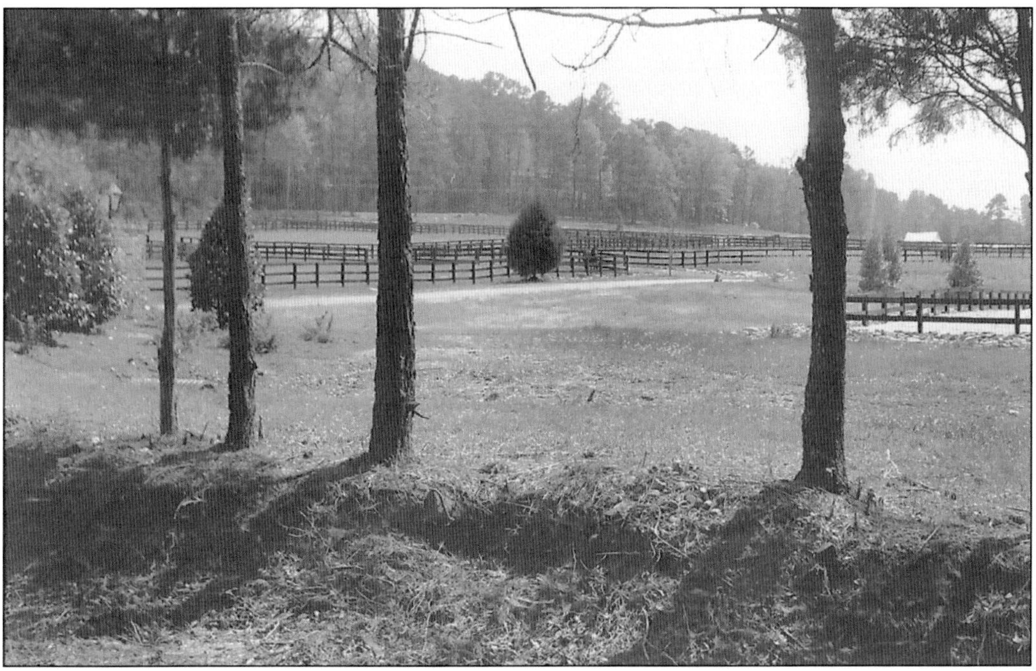

Land along the Cahaba Trail at Leeds still exhibits noticeable pastures. The Indian trail and stagecoach road in southern Leeds became known as the Cahaba Trail in the Cahaba River Valley of urban Alabama. This stretch of Montevallo Road (Alabama Highway 119) blends into the scenery to make road and scenery almost one, becoming a greenway that has been Alabama's Scenic Byway at Leeds since 2006. (BM.)

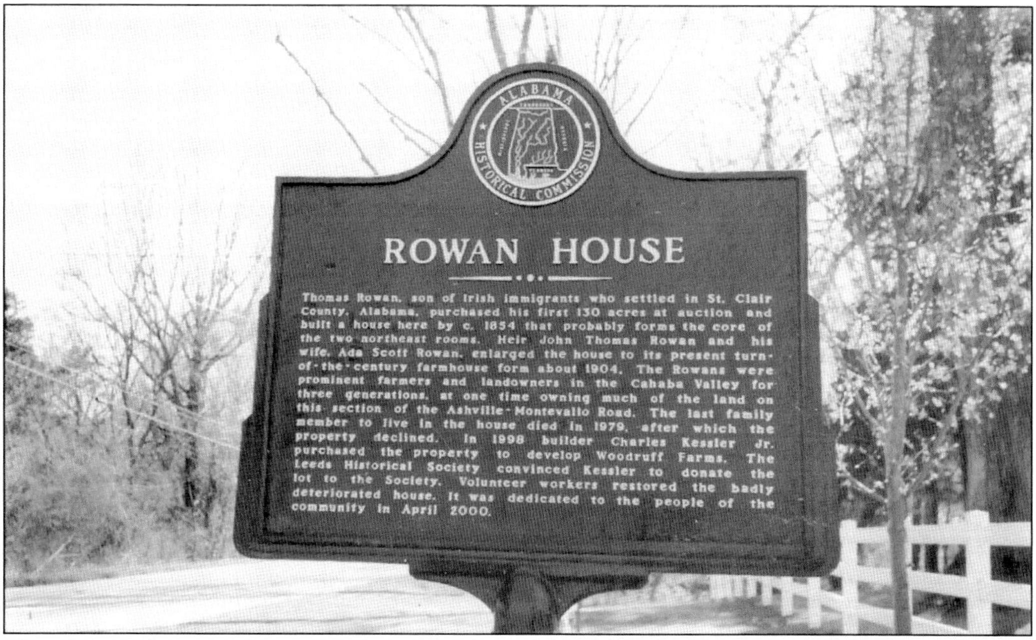

The carriage house at Rowan Oaks Historic Home holds the Leeds Historical Society's replica of a stagecoach that delivered mail along the Cahaba Trail through Leeds. When the Ashville, Alabama, courthouse was built in 1844, stagecoaches were traveling the Ashville-Montevallo Road. Daniel McLaughlin's Inn and Stagecoach Stop is thought to have been located near the Rowan house, where the Little Cahaba River could provide water for horses and stagecoach riders.

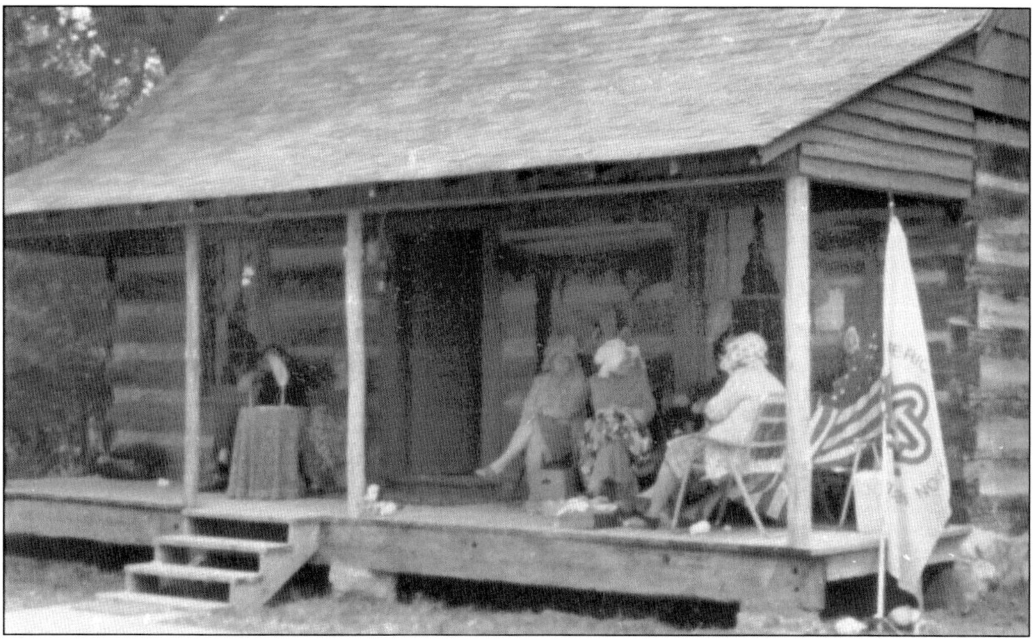

Starting just south of the Henry Little log home (shown here) on Montevallo Road (Alabama Highway 119), the stagecoach route stretches all the way to the John Looney House, a log home in Ashville, Alabama. Both of these well-built homes were constructed about 1820 and are excellent examples of a uniquely American architectural style. (LL.)

Two

Sheriff before Statehood

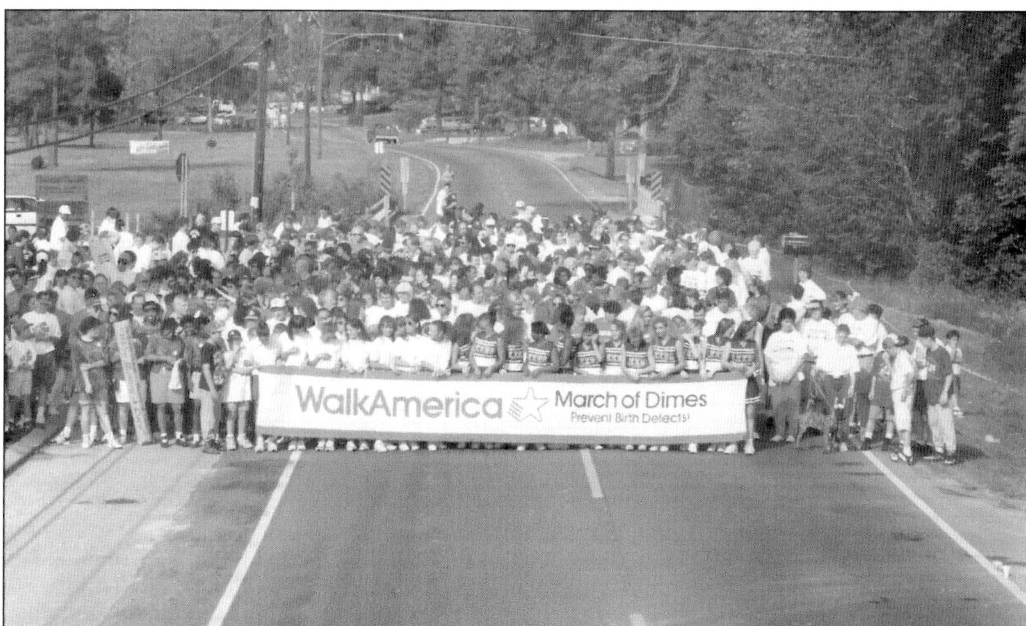

A gathering at Leeds Memorial Park spills out onto the Leeds Scenic Byway. The park, along with adjacent Leeds Historical Park, is located on land included in an 1821 land grant that belonged to Capt. James Hamilton. A soldier in the War of 1812, he came to the Cahaba Valley looking for bottomland near water, where he could farm and also protect, raise, and educate his children. He was the first high sheriff of Shelby County, serving from 1818 to 1820.

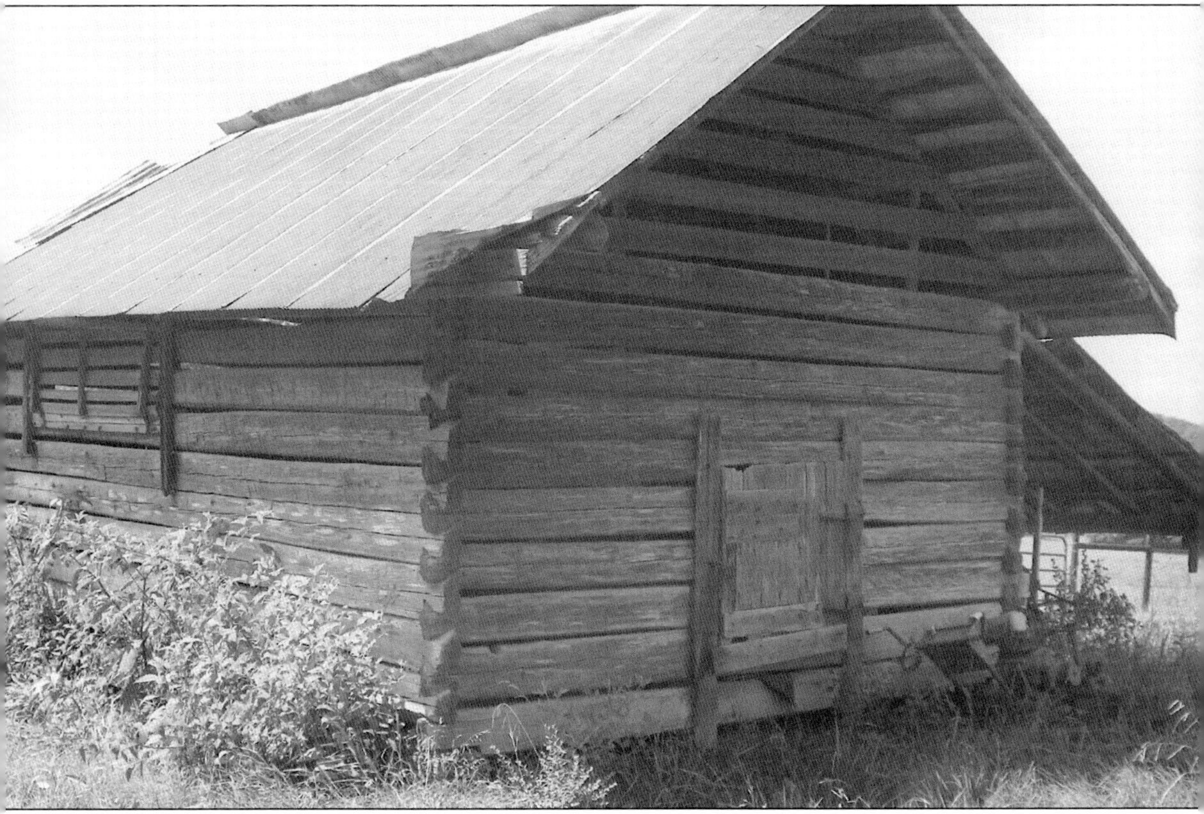

Cedar Grove had a post office by 1828. One of Henry Little's neighbors, William Cameron, was the second postmaster at that location on Alabama Highway 119. When Little, whose old log home still fronts this road, decided to rebuild a gristmill near his property, Cameron sold Little the land across the road to the southwest of the Mitchell Pool Century Farm. The corn crib shown here remains on the farm today. Around 1814, when Andrew Jackson brought his Tennessee Volunteers to Fort Strother, located at Ten Islands on the Coosa River near Ashville, Alabama, his supply wagons needed road space to accommodate their width. The Cahaba Road was formed from an original wilderness path to facilitate horse-drawn wagons. When the first European settlers arrived, the Cahaba Road was widened further into a busy stagecoach road, where a village grew along the banks of the Little Cahaba River.

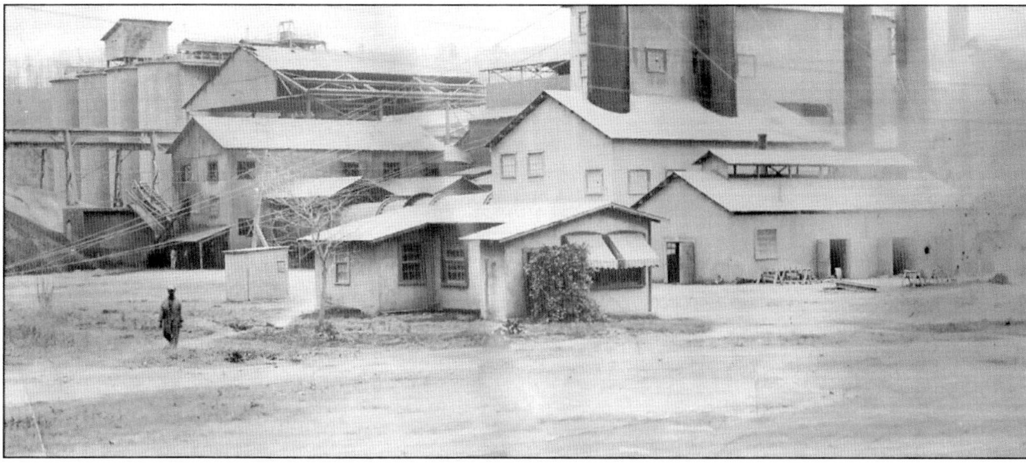

Improvements were made in 1907 to Joseph Ray's original land grant, where Portland cement has been produced for 100-plus years. Ray settled in the area in 1818, and, after he left, all of the minerals needed to make cement were discovered on that land. E.M. Tutwiler, who owned the land in 1905, exchanged it for stock in Leeds Improvement Company, which deeded the land to Standard Portland Cement Company. (LL.)

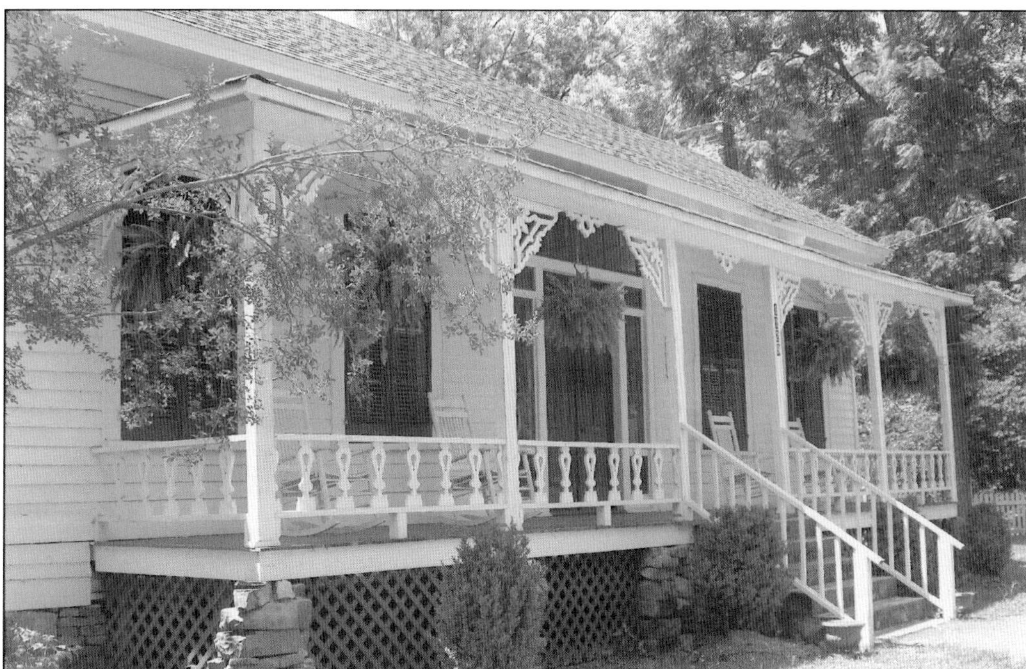

Jonathan Washington Bass, born on January 30, 1837, acquired the land where he built the Bass House on Montevallo Road (Alabama Highway 119), near the Little Cahaba River. The property was carved from portions of the original 1819–1821 land grant properties of James Hamilton, Joseph McLaughlin, and John McLaughlin. The Leeds Historical Society purchased the Bass House in 2003 and began restoration efforts.

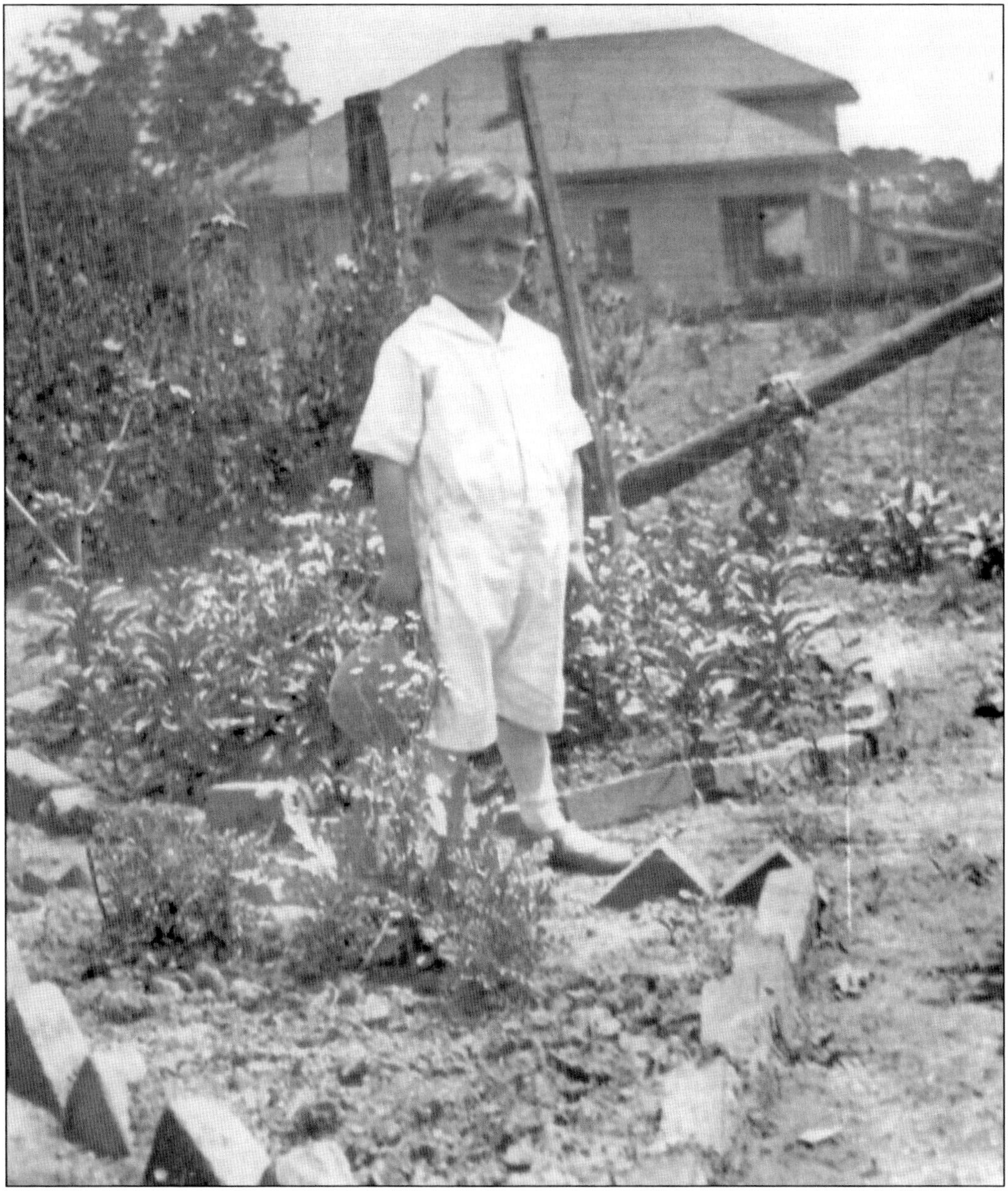

The Falkner-Nelms House, located on John McLaughlin's original land grant, is pictured shortly after being built in 1919, when incorporated Leeds had a growing population on Montevallo Road (Alabama Highway 119) south from the Southern Railway towards the present-day Bass House Museum. The boy shown here stands in a prominent vegetable garden that continued to be farmed as late as the 1980s. Among Leeds families, this house belonged to Falkners, Abercrombies, Farleys, and Nelms-Nelems. In the 1940s, it served as a flower shop. Like other historic homes in Leeds, the house was occupied continually through the 1940s, 1950s, and 1960s. It was redecorated in the 1920s, the 1930s, and the 1950s. During the Cold War, the Nelms family added a bomb shelter in part of a basement. The house's charm centered on the sunroom, the wide front porch with a swing, and a trumpet vine climbing a nearby power pole. On warm Southern nights, one could smell the trumpet vine and see its orange blooms from the porch swing.

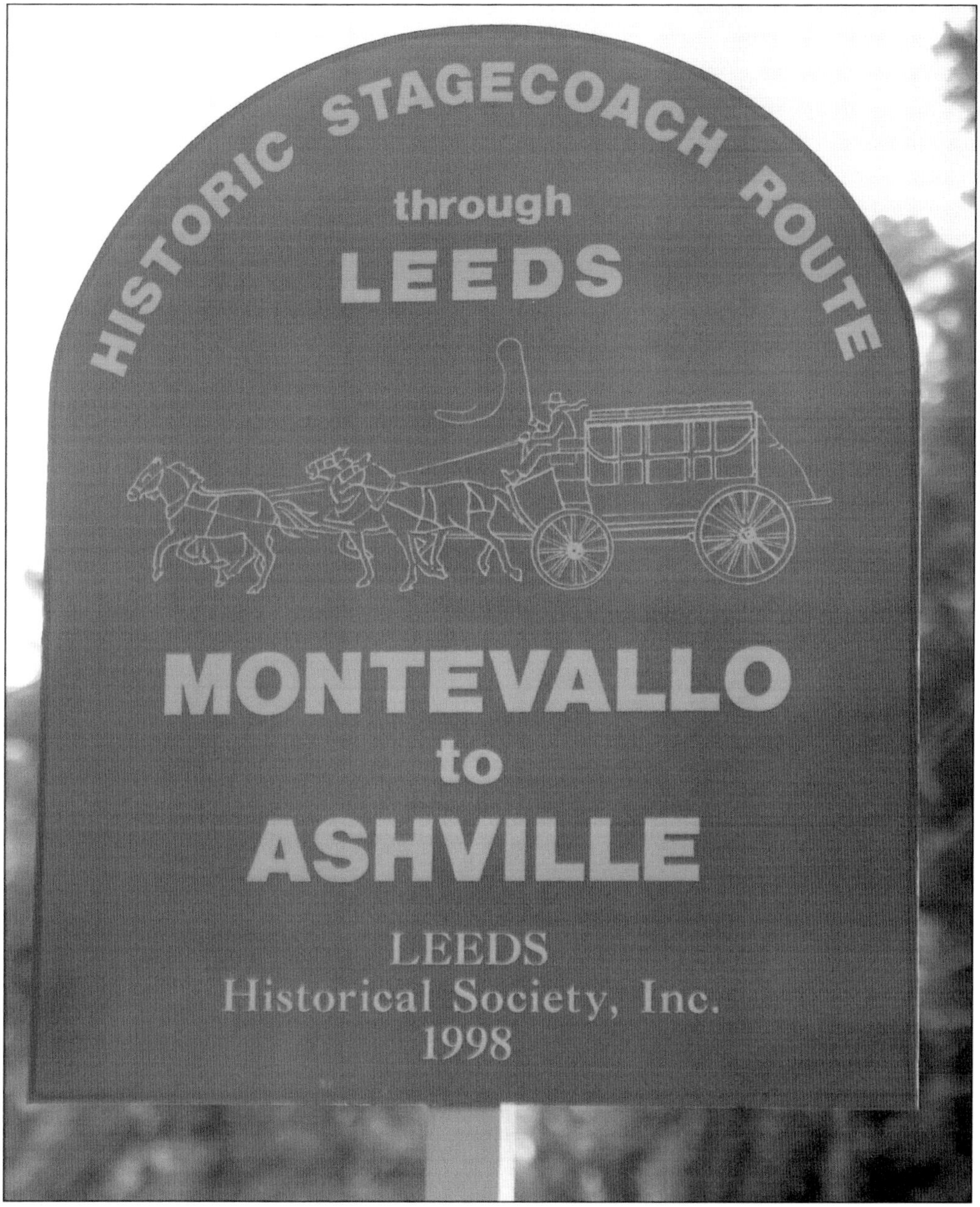

The descendants of Abner Dorough (also spelled Dorrough) chronicled the Cahaba Trail stagecoach line, indicating it existed at the end of the War of 1812. When the Ashville, Alabama, courthouse was built in 1844, it took 15 hours for a stagecoach to travel the road from Ashville to Montevallo. The stagecoach road at Leeds was busy with postal runs and lively with news from stagecoach drivers. It was the longest-lived stagecoach route in central Alabama. The entire Leeds Stagecoach Route runs through a mixture of rural and urban areas in north central Alabama; it passes through parts of Jefferson and St. Clair Counties and the city of Leeds. Beginning southwest of Leeds at the intersection of Alabama Highway 119 and Grants Mill Road, near Lake Purdy, the route continues through the Cahaba Valley. As it passes through Leeds, the route moves to US Highway 411 and terminates at the intersection of US 411 and Interstate 20.

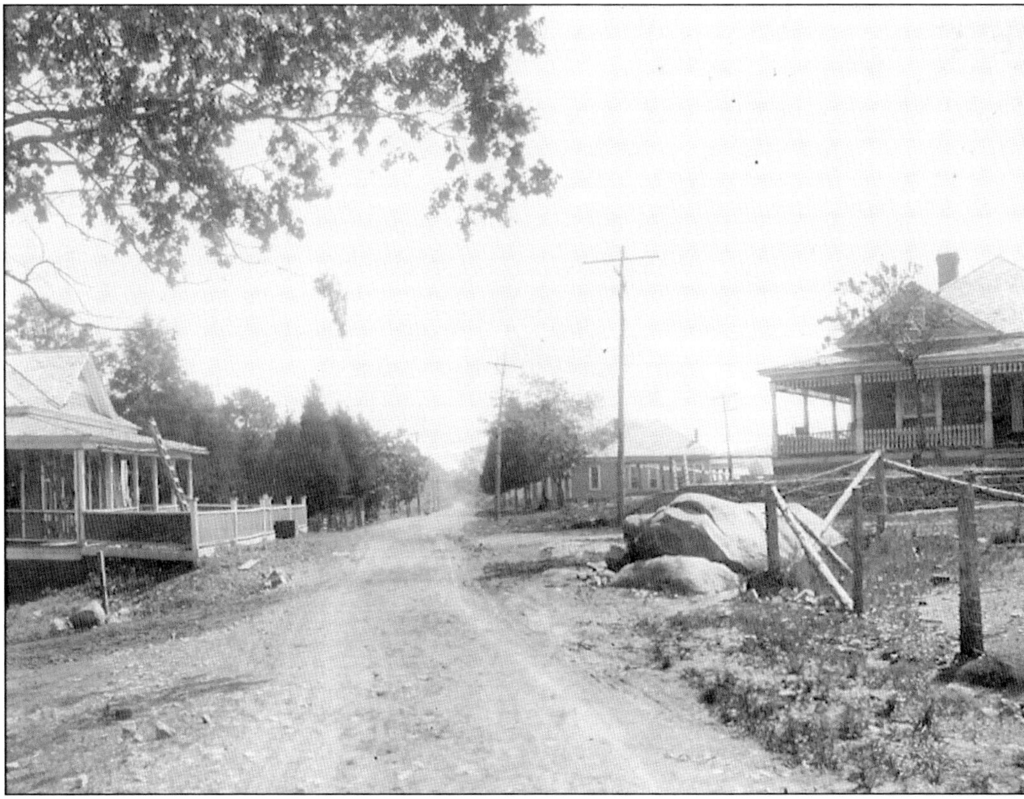

Crossing conditions at Lane Street and Ashville Road (US Highway 411) in the early 1900s look much as they did around 1819 when the Shiloh Cumberland Presbyterian Church was built one block north. The houses were built in the early 1900s by William Washington Whitmire's descendants, but the wagon marks on the road are reminiscent of the original settlement at Oak Ridge, which included an early home of Hezekiah Moor.

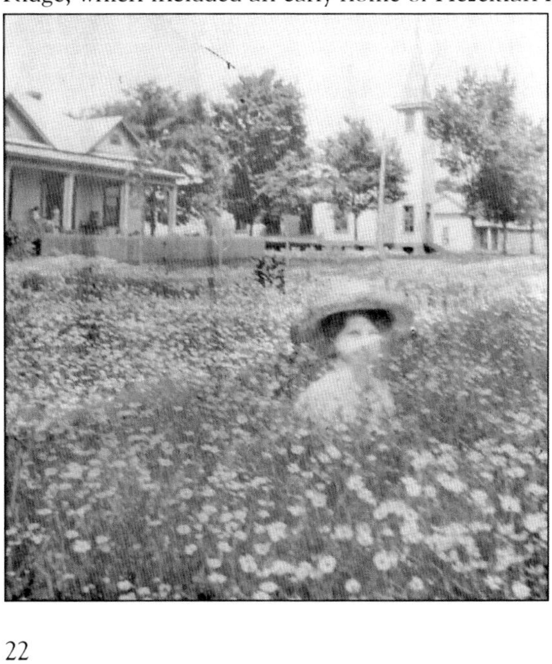

In 1907, the Birmingham (Alabama) Water Works evacuated and purposely flooded a small settlement at Bridgeton, located southeast of Leeds, to create a new reservoir known as Lake Purdy. The descendants of Needham Lee and John DeShazo, who had lived in Bridgeton, relocated to the Leeds area and became members of Leeds Presbyterian Church, pictured here, in about 1911. Lee's progeny descended from Revolutionary War colonel Thomas Lee. Era Jones Owen is pictured in the foreground. (LL.)

Three

SOLDIERS OF DIVISION

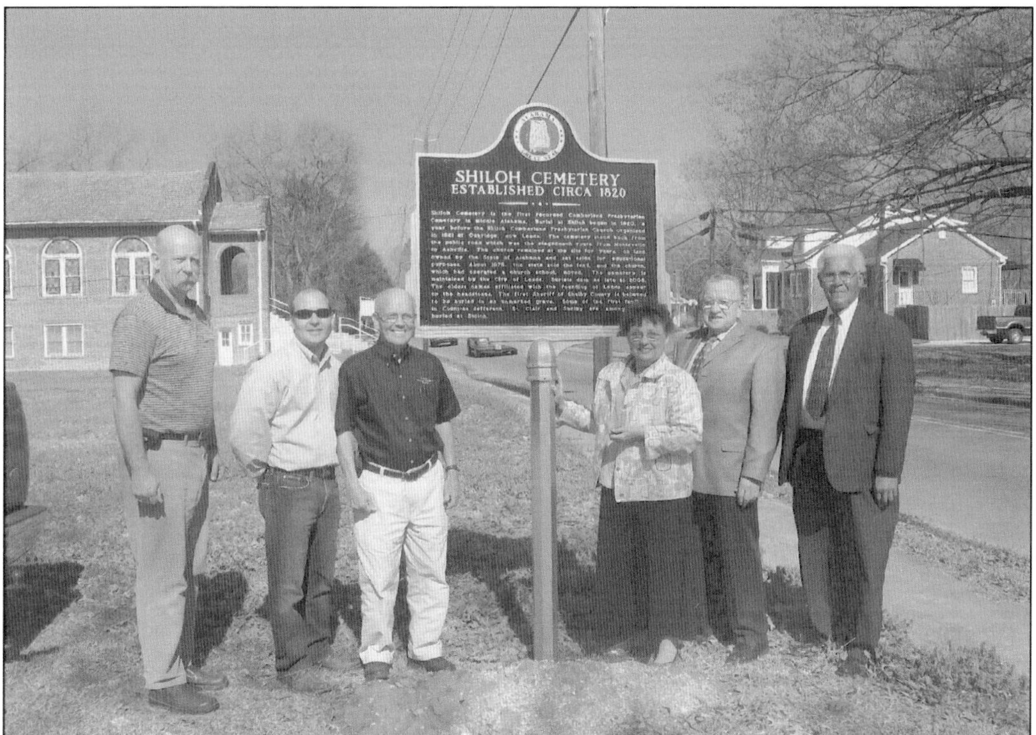

Descendants of Civil War soldiers and dissenters are buried in Shiloh Cemetery near busy Ashville Road (US Highway 411) in Leeds. Beside the cemetery's historic marker stand the modern progeny of the people of the early community, including a councilman, mayor, and state senator. Grave markers and decorations tell of a community that early Moor-Moore family letters describe as tense: "not knowing who is with us and who is not."

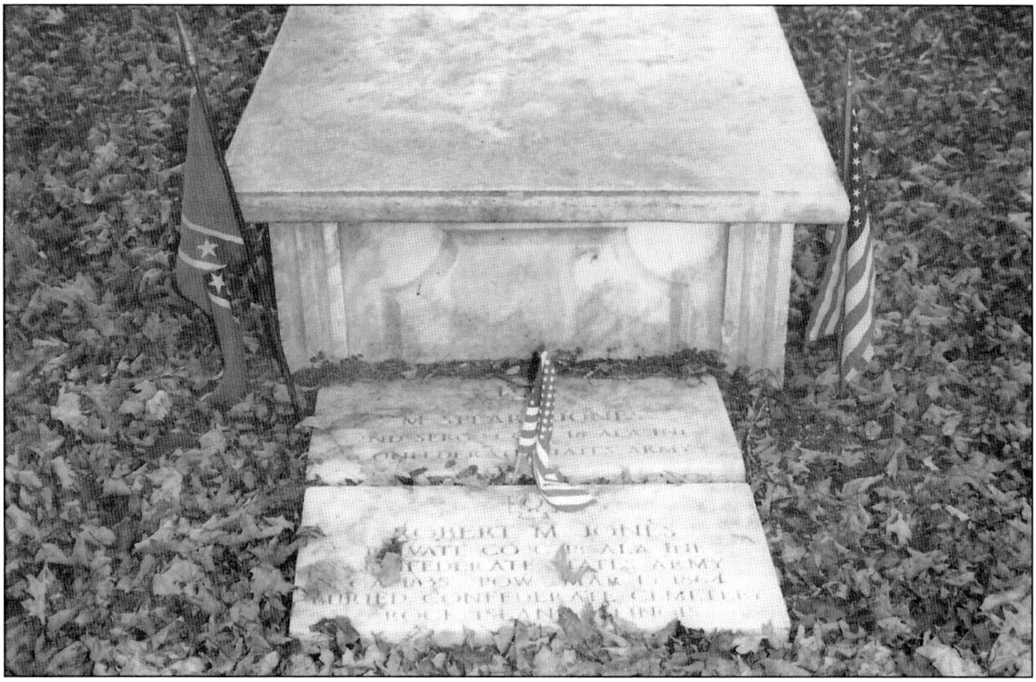

Speers Jones's family tomb in Shiloh Cemetery shows flags of the Confederacy and the United States. His grandfather, Thomas Jones, fought in the American Revolution, and his son, Robert, fought for the Confederacy. A prisoner of war, Robert Jones was buried at Rock Island, Illinois. He also is remembered at the foot of the family tomb in Leeds with a Confederate soldier's gravestone.

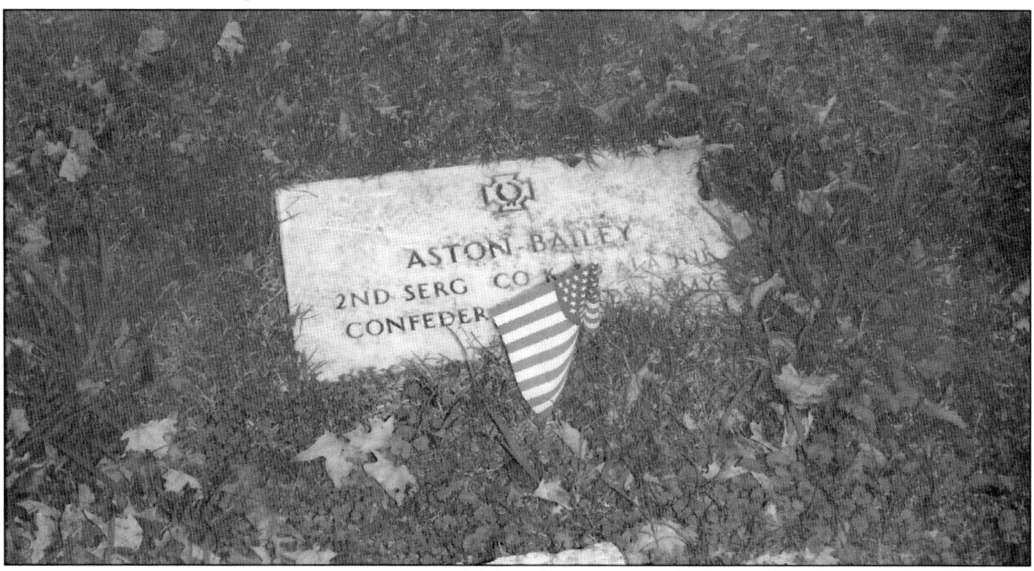

Aston Bailey's gravesite represents the town's strong sense of loyalty to states' rights, yet patriotic duty to country. The US flag is placed at his burial stone. Gen. Robert E. Lee publicly asked his soldiers to return home as American citizens and take up their lives with honorable professions. Shiloh Cemetery has many epitaphs and embellishments that indicate Leeds's Confederate veterans followed Lee's advice.

Andrew Jackson Hamilton of Leeds, grandson of Revolutionary War soldier Hezekiah Bayless, refused to sign Alabama's declaration of secession, warning that the cotton economy would ruin the South. He left for Texas, where he served as its first provisionary governor and became a congressman. Hamilton left a body of literature in the Library of Congress that advocated a non-slave economy and more humane treatment for the defeated Confederacy.

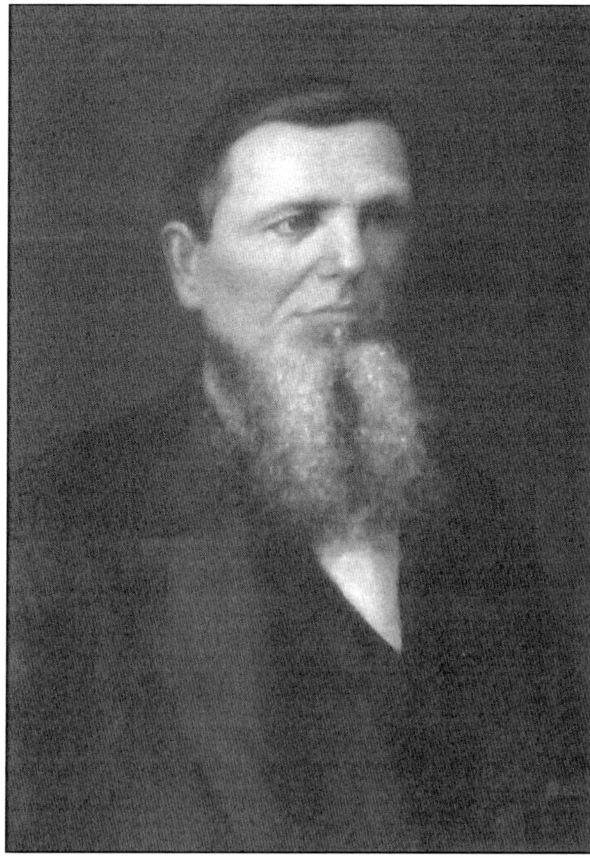

Thomas Rowan of Rowan Oaks Historical Home (pictured), a loyalist, was justice of the peace at Leeds during the Civil War. When Croxton's Union soldiers pushed eastward and burned the University of Alabama, the Cahaba Trail home guard cut trees to block the passage to Rowan's home. Although Leeds was spared, Union soldiers camped in Rowan's pasture. Rowan petitioned for replacements for cattle the soldiers took, saying he was a Loyalist. His request was denied.

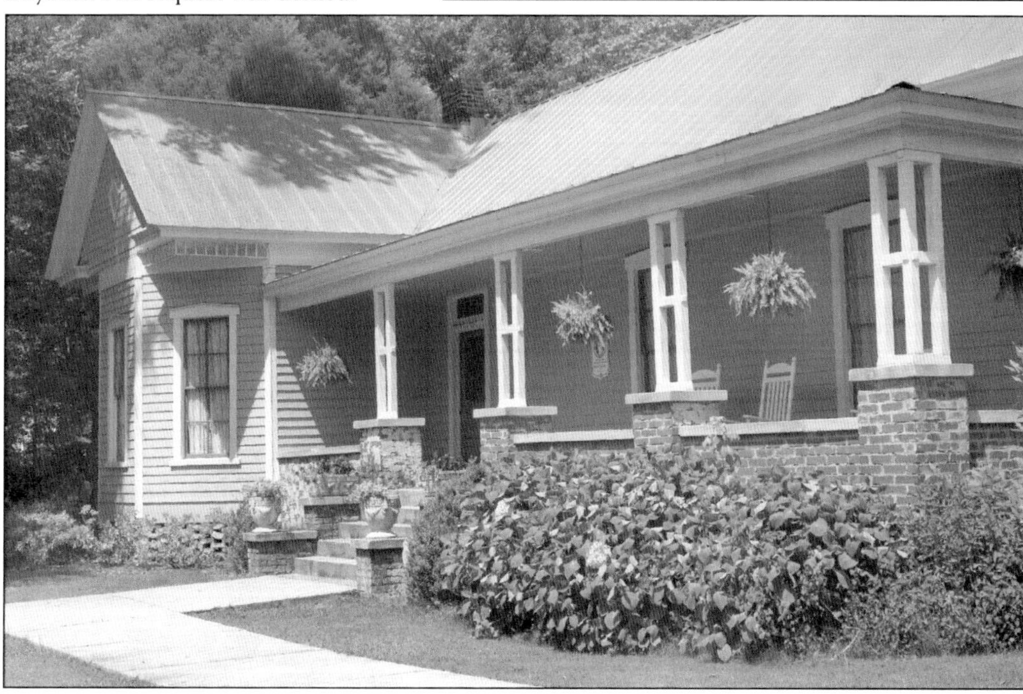

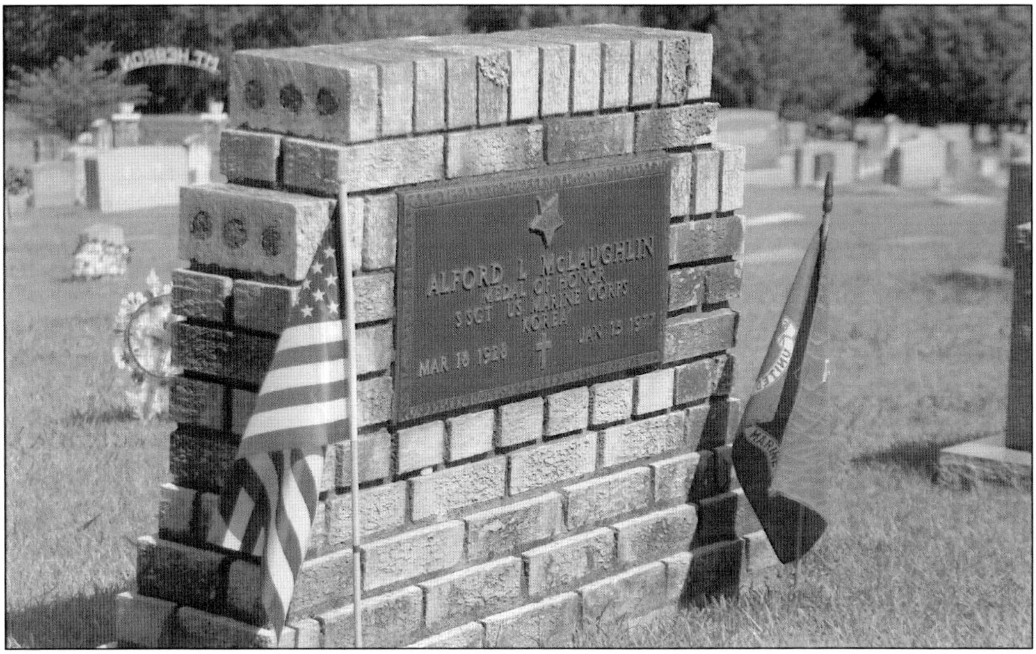

Mount Hebron Cemetery is the burial site of Leeds native Alford McLaughlin, recipient of the Congressional Medal of Honor during the Korean War. Mount Hebron Baptist Church is famous for embracing by 1829 the doctrine that African American people had souls. The church offered them membership and baptism.

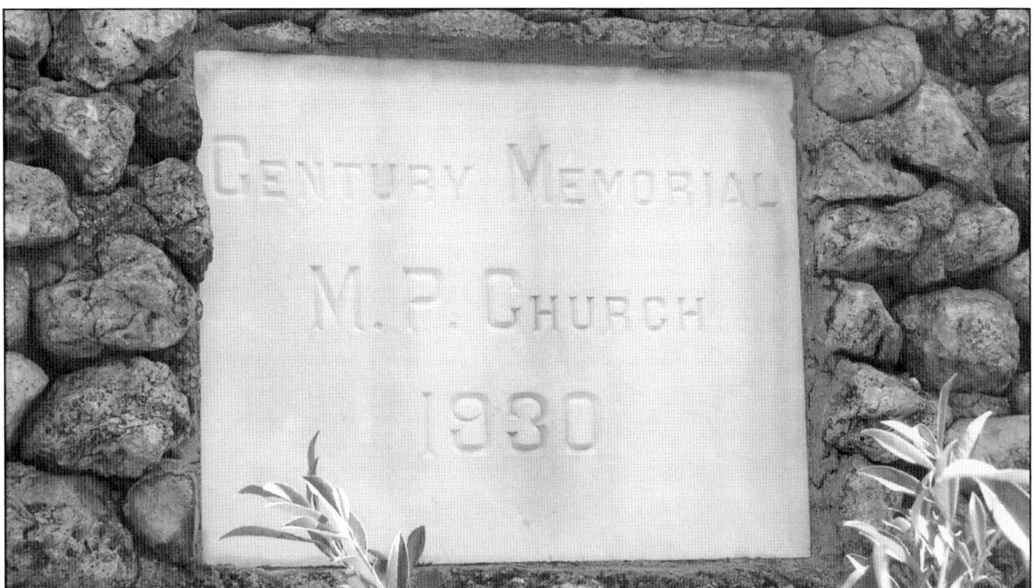

Dave Stewart was the son of Confederate hero Jeremiah Stewart, and both were prominent Cherokee residents from Stewart's Crossroads near Leeds. In 1928, Dave Stewart preached a revival that resulted in a congregation that built the Little Rock Methodist Church the same year on Leeds Scenic Byway. The Stewarts left some Leeds residents with legitimate claims to Cherokee royalty.

Four

Railroad Heroes of a New Economy

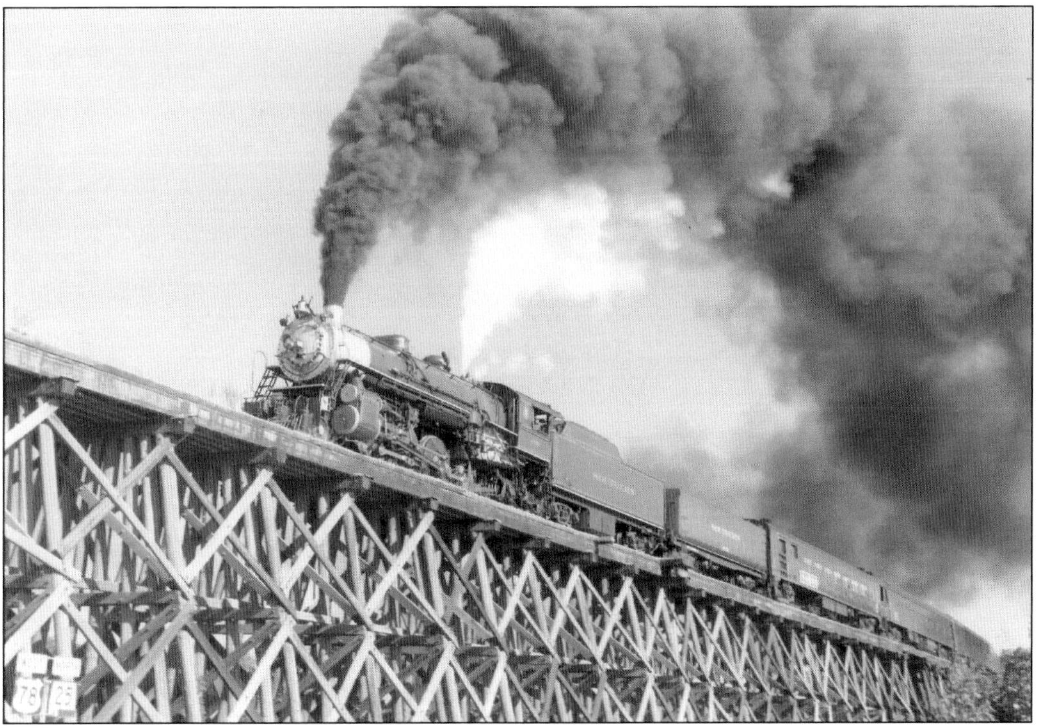

By 1870, the Southern Railway Company had moved Leeds into America's Industrial Revolution. This railroad became the focal point of building and development that forever changed the town without completely taking away an agrarian temperament in a culture that adheres to the tenet that character is a sign of a person's true worth. (LL.)

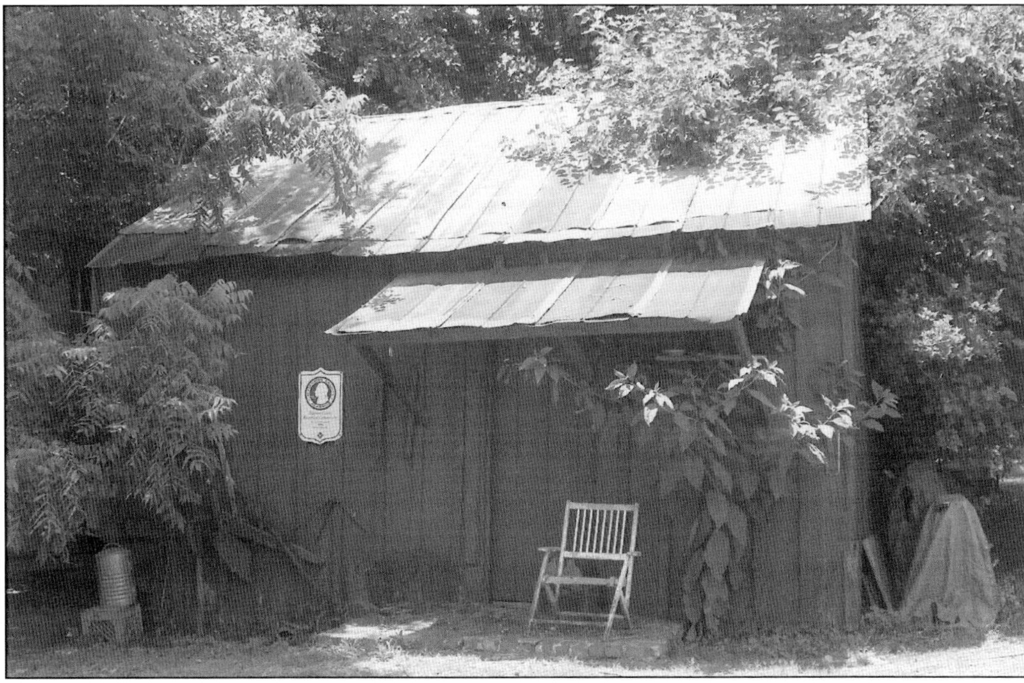

The Davis House Museum is a railroad worker's cabin that houses artifacts used by early Alabama slaves and tenant farmers. Ciscero Davis was a prominent railroad pioneer who came in the 1880s with other African American railroad workers. The Davises, along with the Marburys, Williamses, Polks, Jeralds, Harrises, and Beasons, helped build an industrial economy in the city.

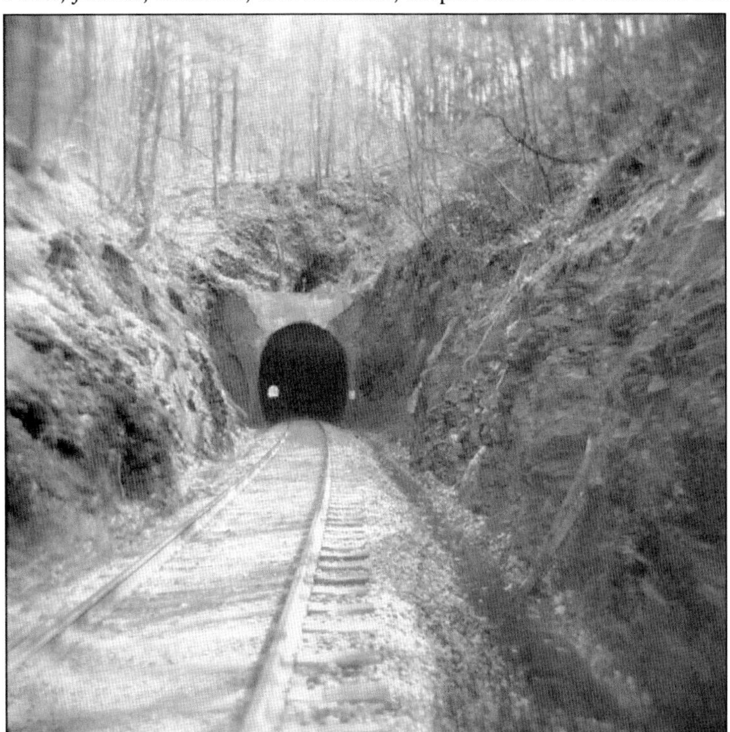

Symposium guests visited Oak Mountain Tunnel during Leeds's 2007 folklore symposium organized by Leeds native Dr. Carl H. Marbury and other Leeds citizens. Named John Henry in Leeds—the Celebration of a Local Legend, the event featured John Garst, professor emeritus at the University of Georgia, whose empirical research lends credibility to Leeds's John Henry legend.

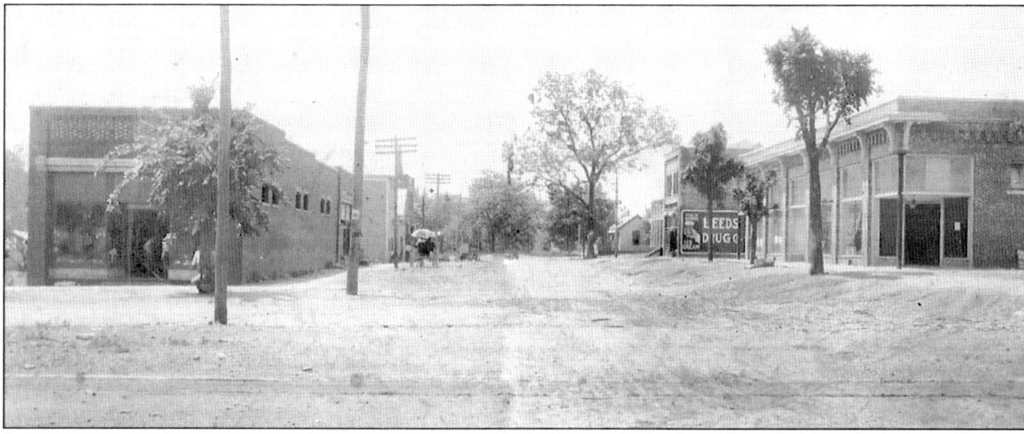

An early 1900s view of historic Ninth Street from the Southern Railway shows the Abercrombie/ Walker building on the right. J.H. Abercrombie was the first postmaster of incorporated Leeds. Harry W. "The Hat" Walker, an Alabama Sports Hall of Fame member, was one of baseball's finest hitters. A resident of Leeds, Walker married a Moor-Moore family descendant and lived in Leeds until his death in 1972. (LL.)

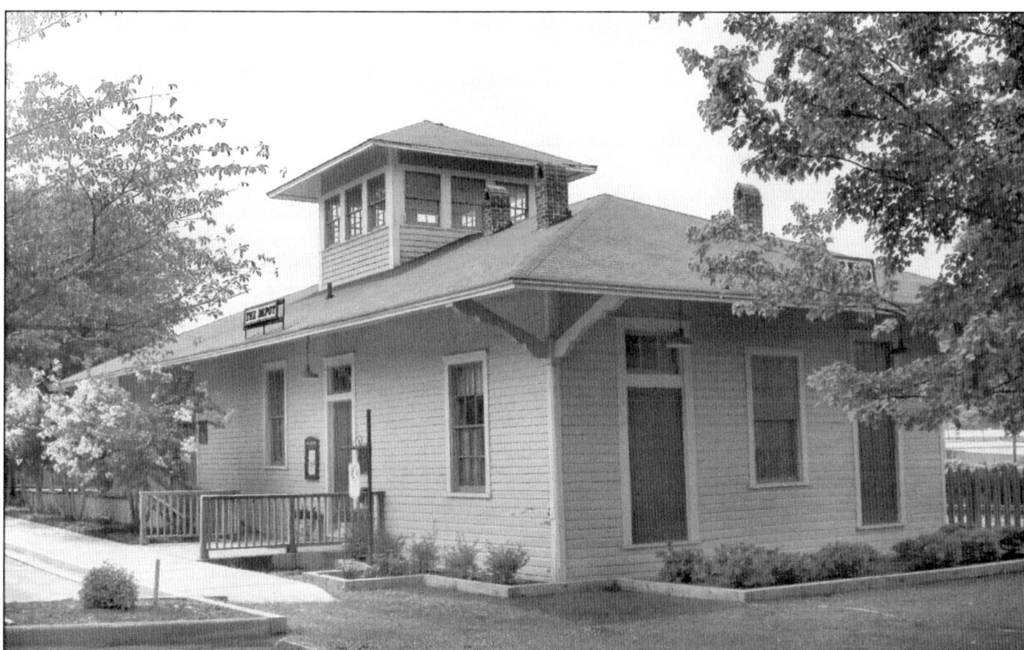

The Southern Railway Depot was restored in 1976 and remains a popular venue for meetings and events in Leeds. The city of Leeds owns the depot, and the Leeds Historical Society leases and cares for it. The Railway and Locomotive Historical Society, Mid-South chapter, maintains artifacts of railroad history there. The building is open to the public by appointment. Amtrak trains pass regularly as various groups meet in the baggage room.

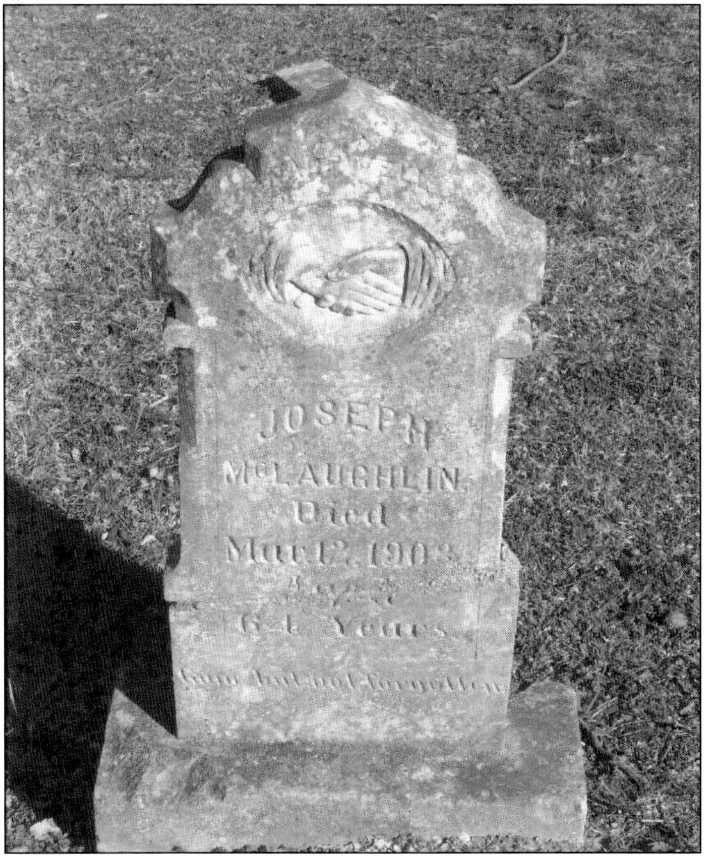

Joseph McLaughlin was buried in Shiloh Cemetery in 1908. His father and brothers served Gen. Andrew Jackson during the War of 1812, fell in love with the Cahaba Valley, and returned, setting stakes on land granted to them by the government as compensation for their service. Many of the grants were simply options to buy the land. Leeds's first settlers often dated land grant deeds with the year that they paid for the land.

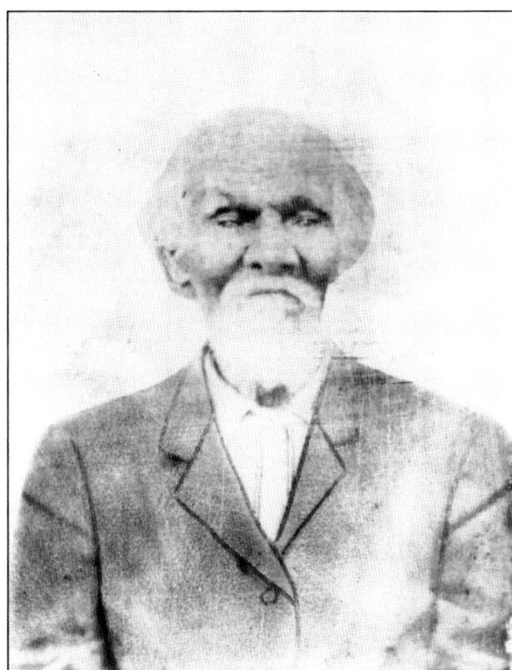

Born in 1820 in Virginia, Free Bob came to the Leeds area with the railroad. His mother was Caucasian and his father was mulatto. Bob was born Robert Hood, a free man, because Virginia law did not allow children of Caucasian women to be enslaved, according to Carl Marbury, a Leeds resident. Bob lived in Vandiver, Alabama, south of Leeds, and later moved to Leeds, where he lived at the home of Ciscero and Melissa Hood Davis. He died in 1910.

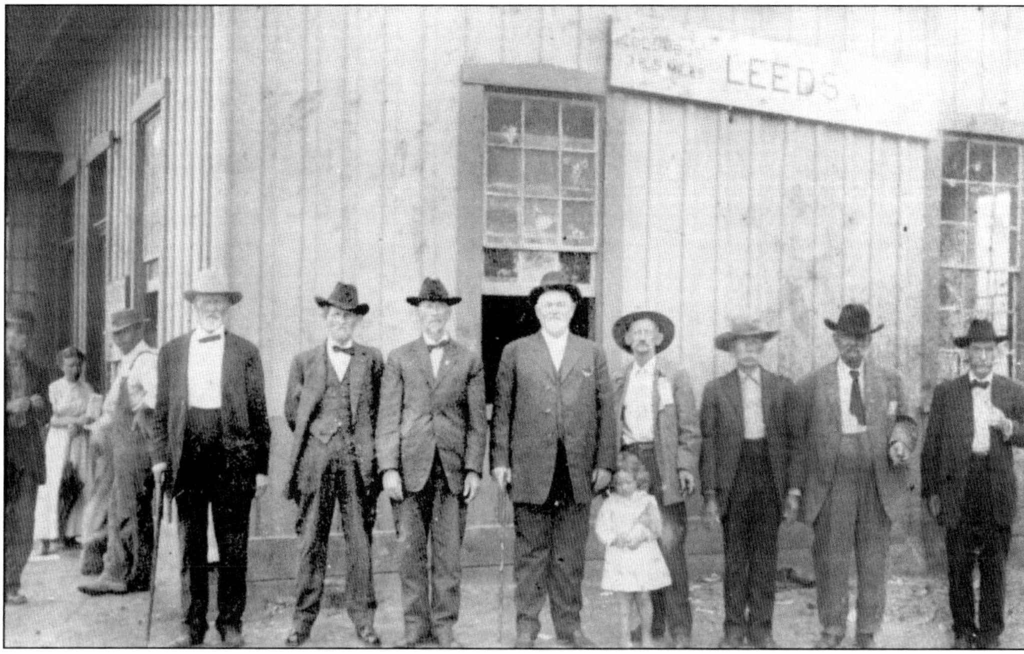

Confederate soldiers wait at the Central of Georgia Depot in Leeds for a train to take them to Columbus, Georgia, for a reunion. In the 1880s, the Central of Georgia Railroad and the Georgia Pacific Railroad (now Southern Pacific) built lines from Columbus and Atlanta respectively, routed through Leeds on the way to Birmingham. The railroads brought economic progress to Leeds by opening the city to people from other regions. (LL.)

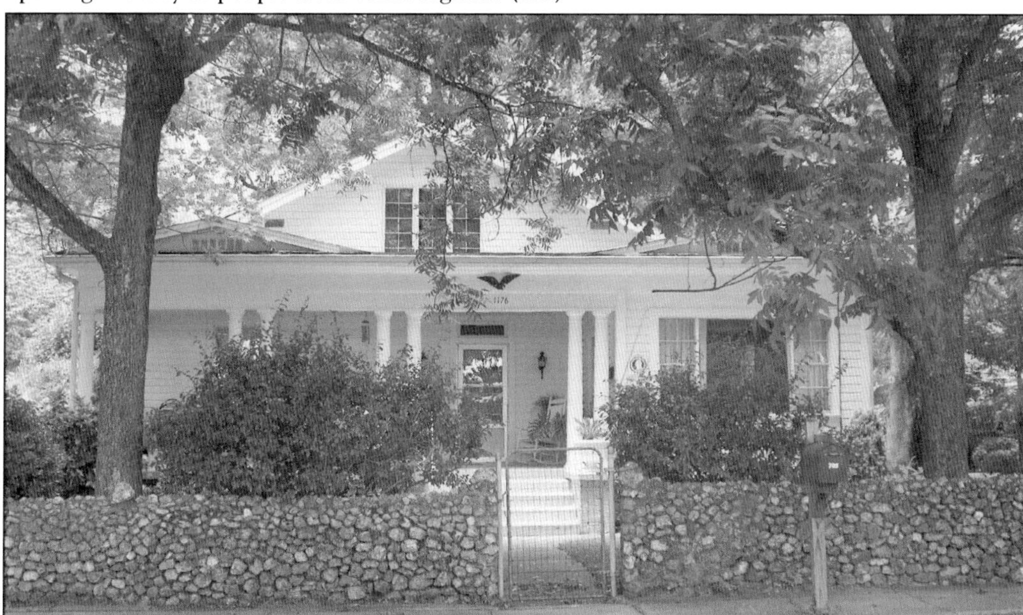

The original lumber of Leeds Academy, an early private school in Leeds, was used to build the Sharpe-Marsicano House on Ashville Road (US Highway 411), shown here as it looked in 1939. Professor Barnard, Leeds High School's first principal, built the house prior to 1923. For almost nine decades, members of the M.J. Sharp family owned and lived in the house.

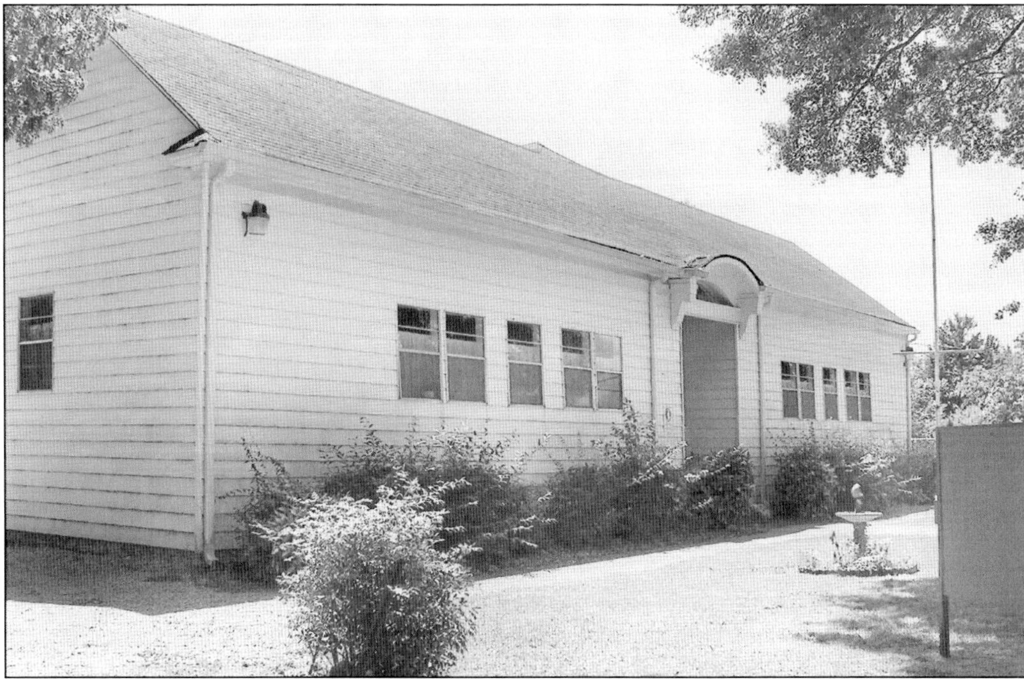

The building that housed Leeds Primary School was constructed in 1921 by Jefferson County as the first public school building for black students. It remains the oldest public school building in Leeds. The Industrial Revolution brought African Americans to Leeds to work on the railroads, and they facilitated the building of schools for their children.

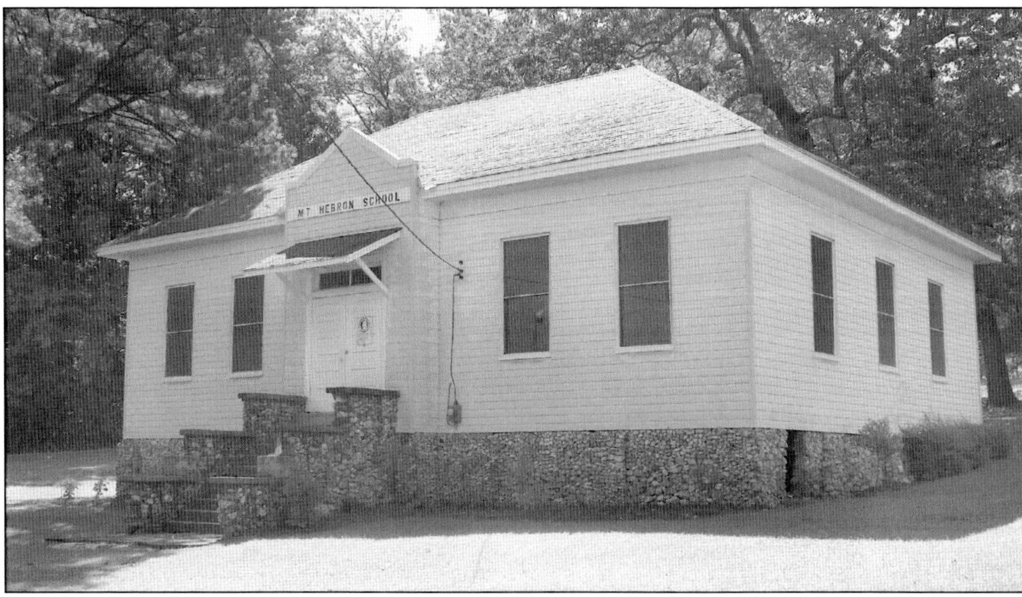

Listed in the Alabama Register of Landmarks and Heritage on April 1, 2010, Mount Hebron School was built by 1916. A one-room, Queen Anne–style structure, it served the southern end of Leeds's Cahaba Trail as a school until 1942. Early Jefferson County schools at Leeds were placed to accommodate the Little Cahaba River that sometimes served as a barrier from one end of town to the other.

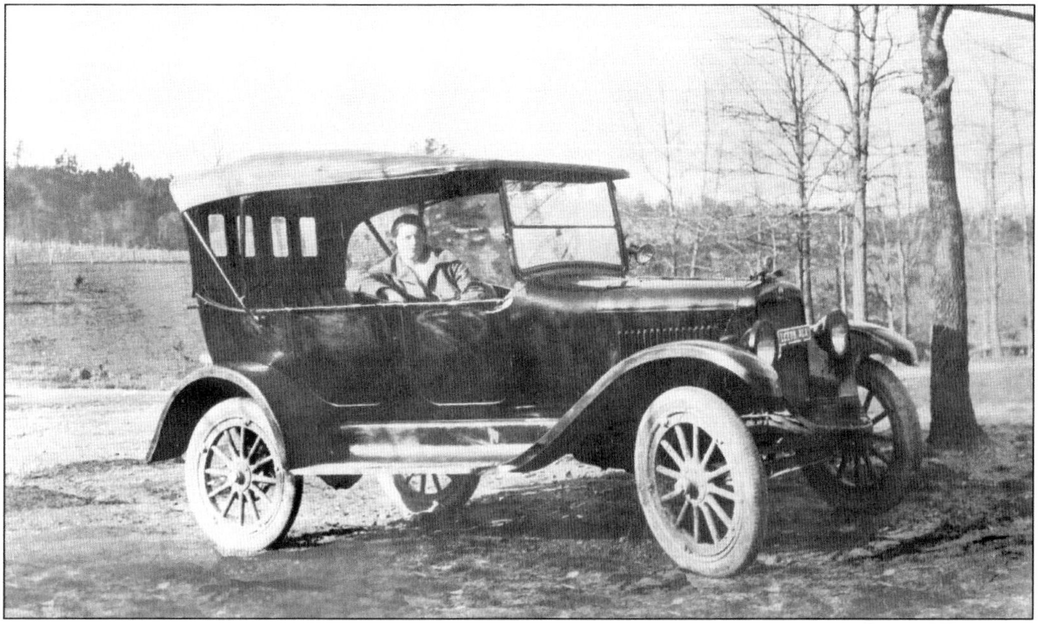

A Dort automobile in Leeds seems to be parked near Rex Lake Road in the very area where the Barber Vintage Motorsports Museum is now located. Dorts were produced from 1915 to 1924 in Flint, Michigan. Both Dort and Ford automobiles were sold at the H.G. Nelems dealership in Leeds as early as 1924. (BM.)

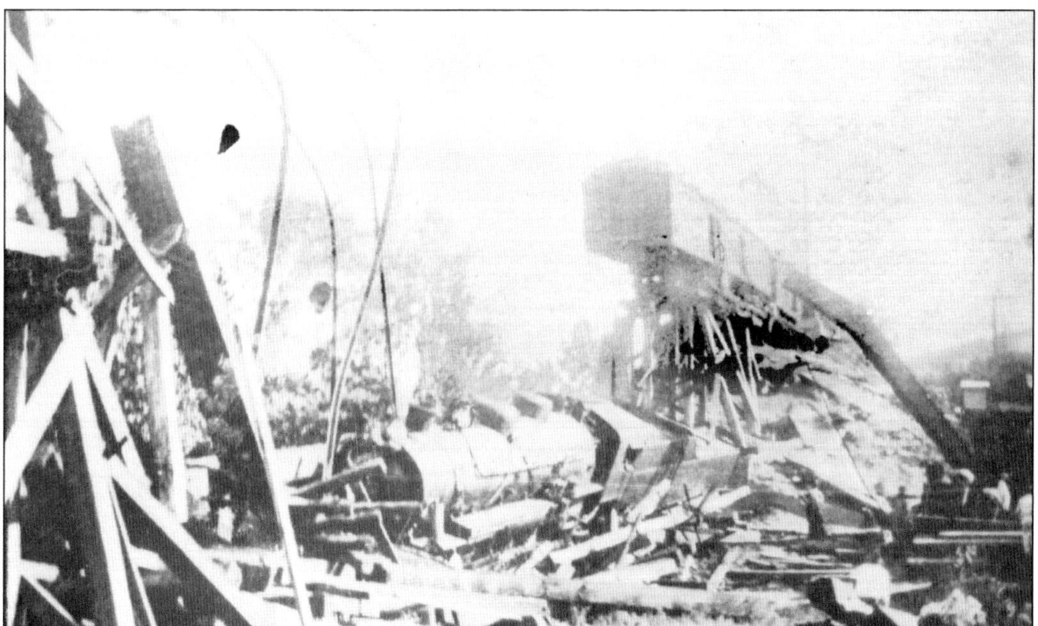

This 1918 photograph shows Leeds's only great train wreck. Many locals know that a passenger train wrecked and only one person was killed. Some realize that the date of the wreck coincides with World War I. During that war, members of the Alabama National Guard watched strategic parts of the tunnels near Leeds as trains entered the rich industrial areas of what is now Greater Birmingham. (BM.)

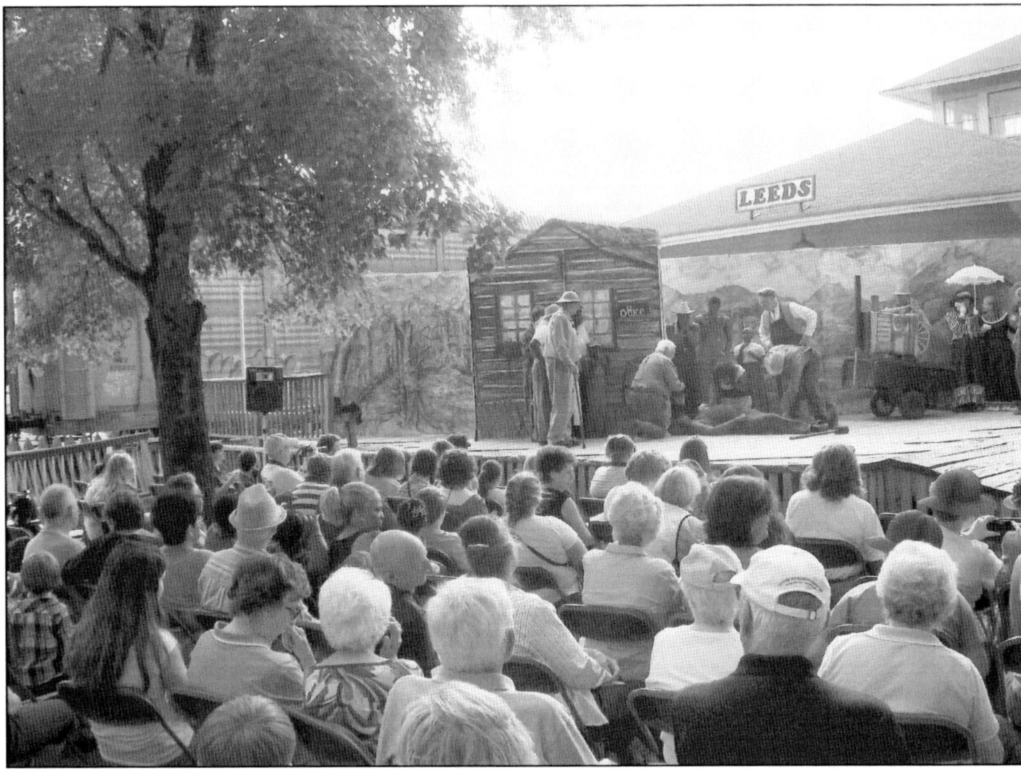

Leeds players reenact the story of John Henry. He was a railroad man in Leeds, according to witnesses who said he won an all-day contest, driving more spikes with his hammer than the steam drill he vowed to beat. According to a state historical marker in Leeds, versions of the blues song "The Ballad of John Henry" relate how the powerful man won the contest but died from exhaustion, hammer in hand.

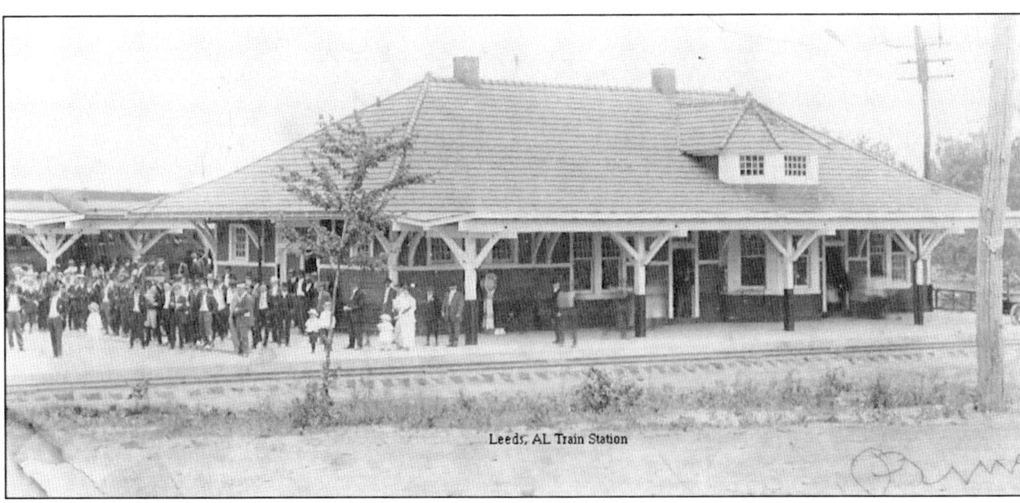

Pictured is the Central of Georgia Depot, Leeds's earliest train station. It was an active train stop that hosted travelers and citizens who found a way to live in a small town yet socialize and go to colleges, museums, libraries, entertainment, and shopping in Birmingham.

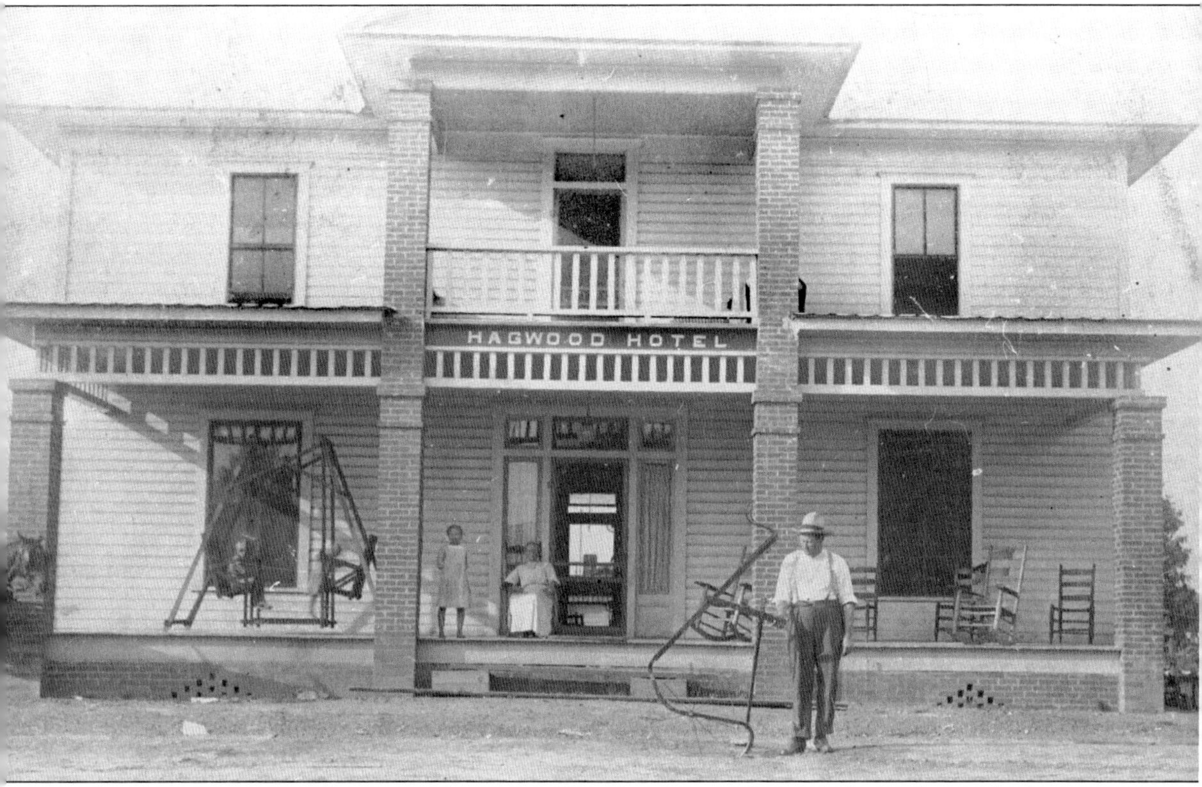

Railroad operators rented rooms and took meals at the Hagwood Hotel, shown here, which was built in 1910 across from Leeds's historic Southern Railway Depot. The hotel has remained in the Hagwood family for more than 100 years. Recently, it has served as the residence of a remaining Hagwood family member. Local tales reminisce about the men who stayed at the hotel. They worked on the railroad all day and came to the hotel to sleep at night. Stories say that after all their shoes were off, the stench in the house from dirty feet made sleeping almost impossible for the hotelkeepers. Leeds's town well was located less than a block from the hotel in the middle of Ninth Street near the railroad track. While Leeds water is known for its mountain artesian fresh taste, none of the workers seemed to be interested in bathing with it. The old livery, with its water troughs, was located next to the hotel.

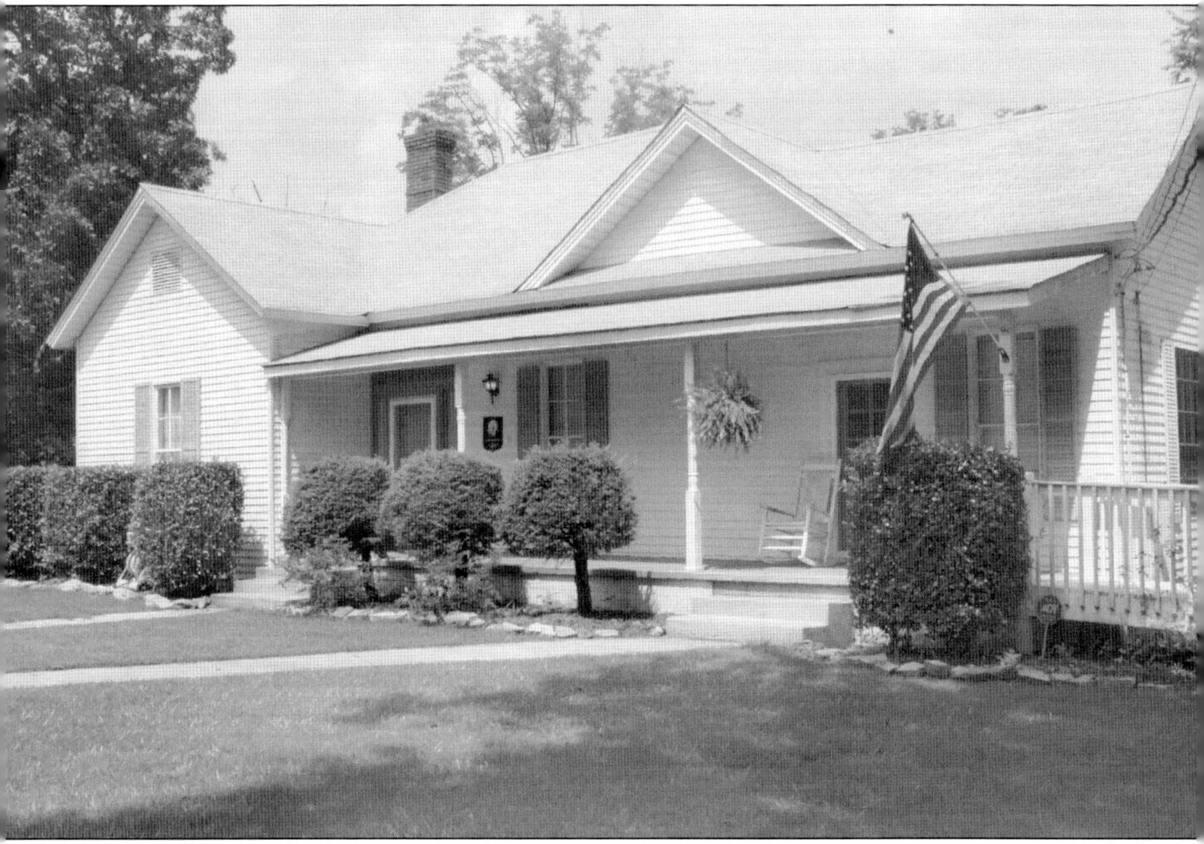

The historically marked Arthur Mason Spruiell (also spelled Spruill) House was built in 1903 and is named for its builder. Nancy Carmichael Spruiell, Arthur Mason Spruiell's grandmother, died the year the house was built. She was known to tell stories of her grandfather, John Bell, who fought under the command of Francis Marion, the "Swamp Fox," during the American Revolution. Bell arrived in South Carolina from Northern Ireland on board a ship of Irish Protestants in 1770. Nancy was born in South Carolina, where she married John Simpson Spruiell. She and her husband moved to Alabama in the 1850s. After she was widowed in 1879, she moved to Moody Crossroads, north of Leeds.

Five

The Home Front during the War to End All Wars

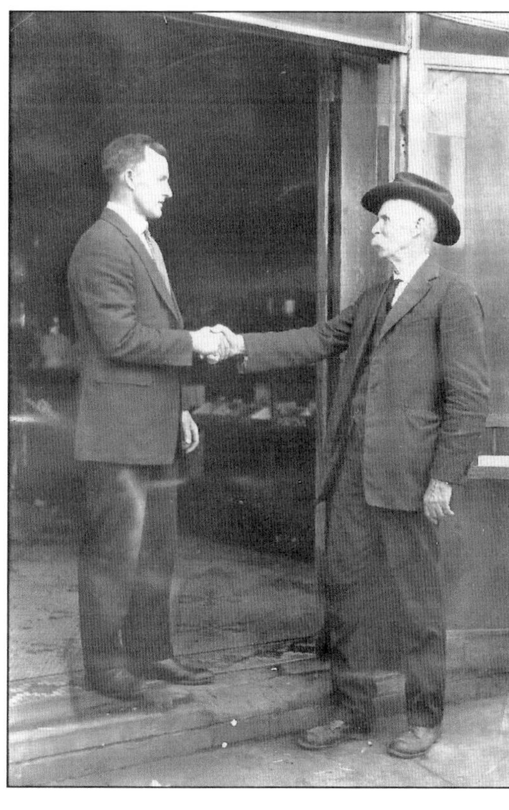

Melvin Spruiell shakes hands with James B. Elliott, known as the Duke of Leeds, at Leeds Drug Company. This building now looks the same as it did when Cpl. Joe Becker came to Leeds with the 4th Alabama Infantry Regiment of the National Guard. Troop H guarded the railroad tunnel south of Leeds. Becker's company joined the Rainbow Division, which fought during World War I. (LL.)

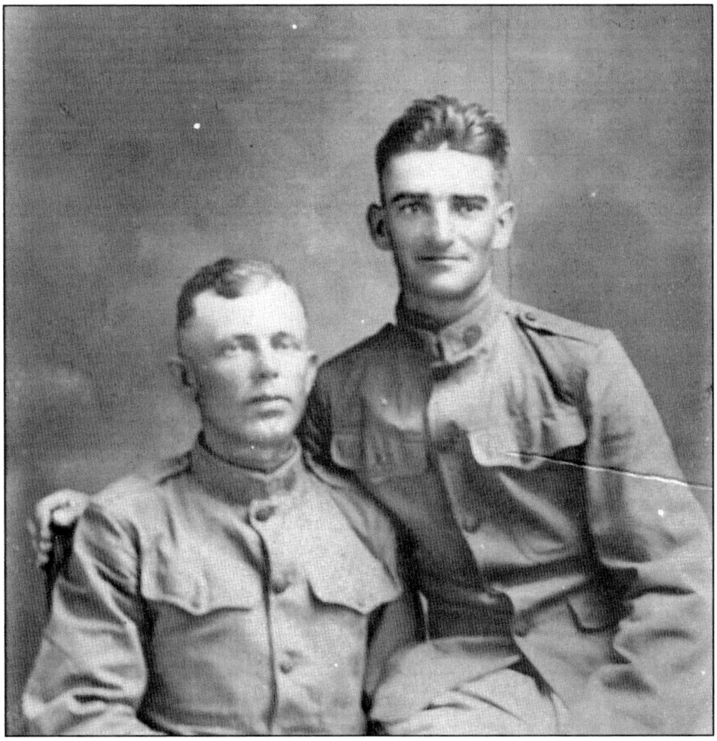

Rex McLaughlin (right) became a World War I doughboy along with Leeds descendants of the Ingram, Farley, Moor-Moore, Holley, DeShazo, Smith, Byars-Byers, Harris, Marbury, and Spruiell-Spruill families. Without enough food, these soldiers faced fire from enemy machine guns and marched into a war famed for nerve gas and trenches. They won battles and lost lives in an effort to make the world safe for democracy. (LL.)

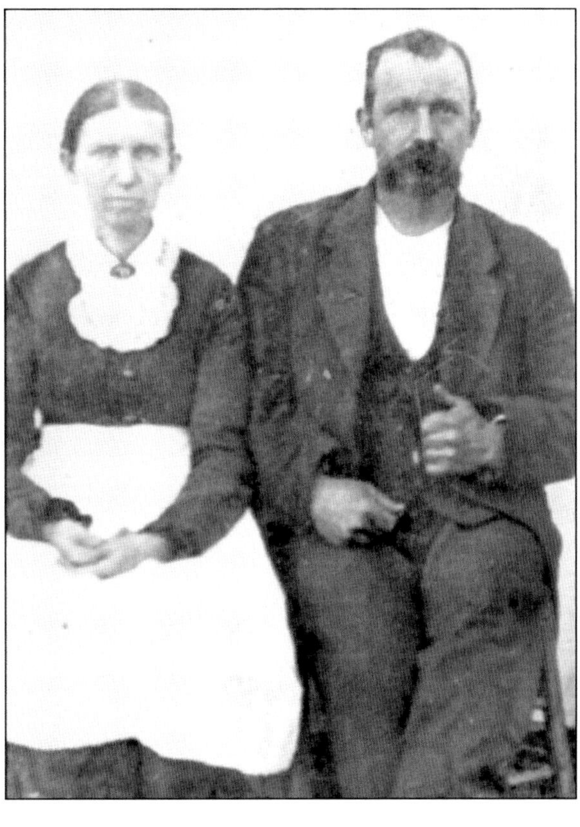

This photograph of Judge Samuel Walker Spruiell and his wife, Susan Winchester Spruiell, illustrates clothing worn in the 1880s. In 1887, about 225 people called Leeds home. Long skirts were still in style in 1919 when the World War I doughboys returned home. More than 900 people lived in the incorporated city limits at that time.

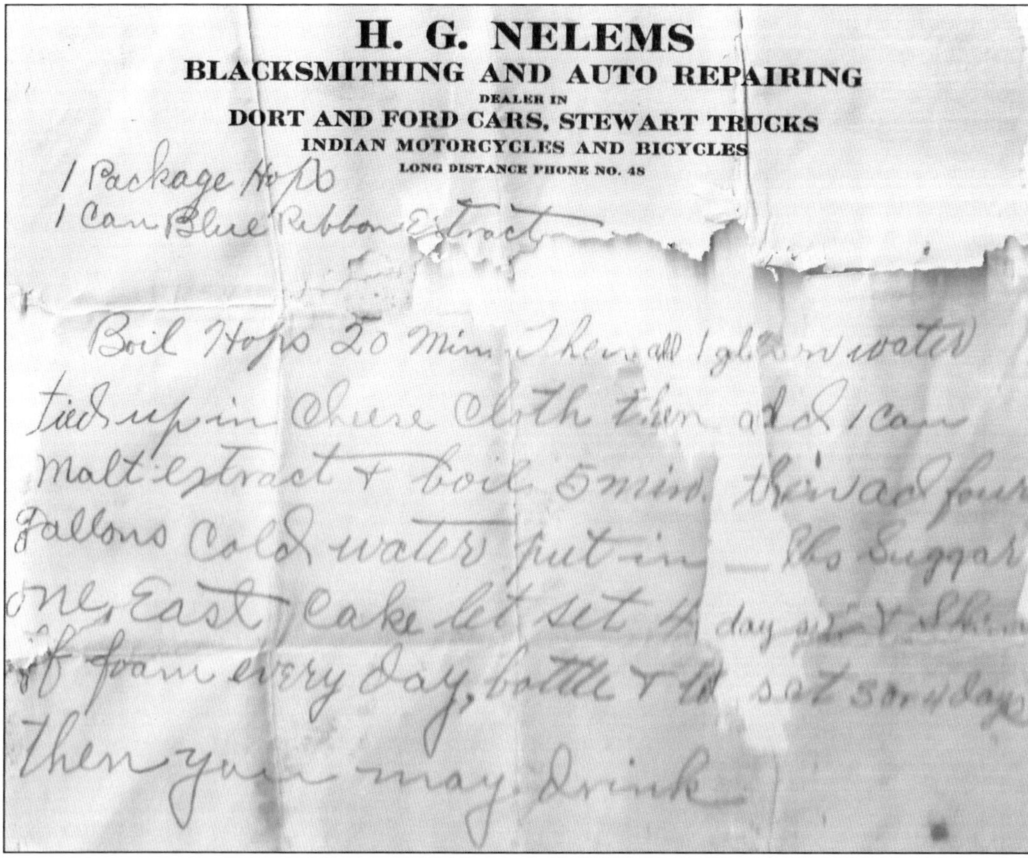
H. G. NELEMS
BLACKSMITHING AND AUTO REPAIRING
DEALER IN
DORT AND FORD CARS, STEWART TRUCKS
INDIAN MOTORCYCLES AND BICYCLES
LONG DISTANCE PHONE NO. 48

1 Package Hops
1 Can Blue Ribbon Estract

Boil Hops 20 Min. Then add 1 gl. water tied up in cheese cloth then add 1 can malt estract + boil 5 min. then add four gallons cold water put in ... lbs suggar one east cake let set ... day ... + skim off foam every day, bottle + let set ... days Then you may drink

An abundance of Ford automobiles were driven down Ninth Street in the early 1920s—quite a sight for doughboys coming home. Local liveries offered both blacksmithing and auto repair. Herman G. Nelems operated his business downtown at the corner of Parkway Drive and Eighth Street. Nelems and his partner Bill Poe brought unassembled chassis of Model A Fords from railroad cars to their dealership, where they assembled and sold them.

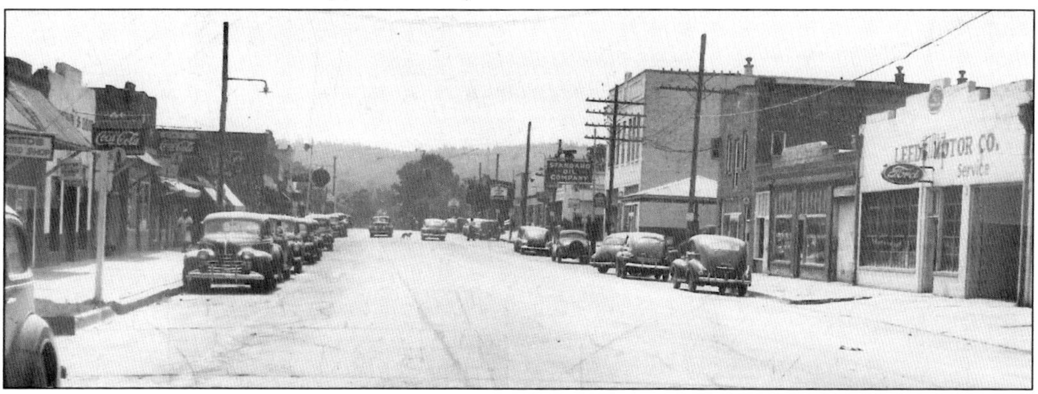

According to St. Clair County newspapers, buildings in Leeds had blood on them in the late 1920s. The Henry DeBardeleben family operated coal mines at nearby Acmar and Margaret, which furnished a large payroll that miners spent in Leeds. In 1929, the mines tightened procedures and watched over workers with a socialistic protection when economic problems began closing Leeds's businesses. Armed guards were posted as workers resisted attempts to unionize. (BL.)

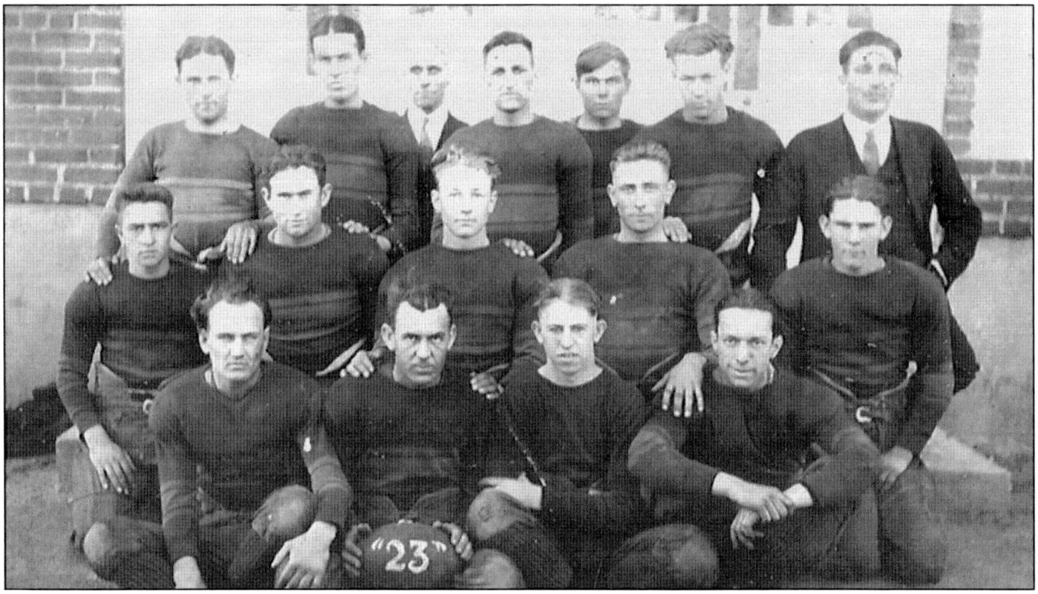

Leeds High School had its first football team in 1923, and team members distinguished themselves by winning six of the seven games they played that season. Throughout Alabama, people took notice that Leeds was a growing city. Athletics were added to the high school curriculum by 1914, led by a basketball program. Student athletes came from families that founded the town and included McLaughlins, DeShazos, Joneses, Lawleys, Whitmires, and Moor-Moores.

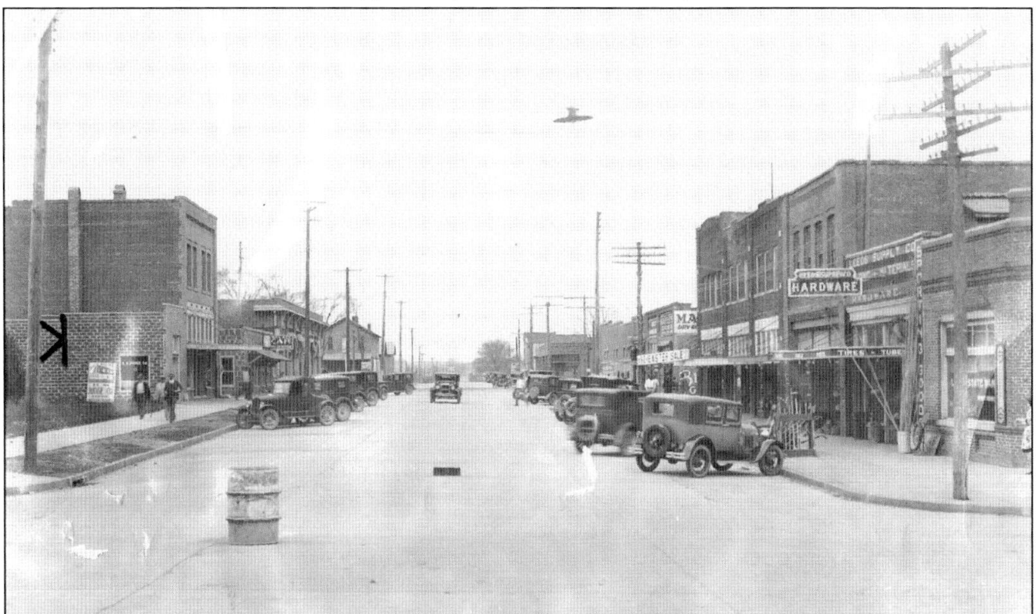

By 1915, Leeds had electric street lights, its first movie theater, wealthy planters, and its first telephone company. The names Lee, Posey, and Lacey became prominent in town. By 1916, the Standard Portland Cement Company was producing about 3,000 barrels of cement daily. Leeds State Bank, established locally in 1910, operated with assets of $250,000 in the same time period. (BM.)

High school students performed plays while lifelong neighbors started businesses on Parkway Drive, the name of the expansion around the corner from Ninth Street. Lee, Whitmire, Sharp, and Powers would dominate the marquees of stores for decades. Actors in high school plays came from the pool of names of long-time citizens, including Bailey, DeShazo, Dorough-Dorrough, Pool-Poole, Lawley, and Asman. (BL.)

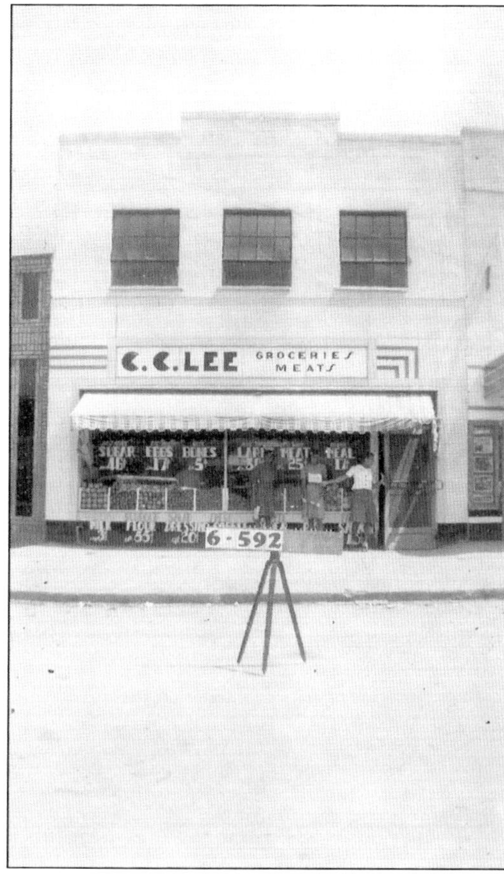

In the 1930s, cars jammed the downtown streets. C.C. Lee was operating a grocery store on Parkway Drive by 1937. Businesses supported the schools by buying advertisements in annuals and programs. In 1929, class officers included Hogan, Murphy, Nelms-Nelems, Kincaid, Bass, Elliott, Bagby, and graduates Whitmire and Hurst. (LL.)

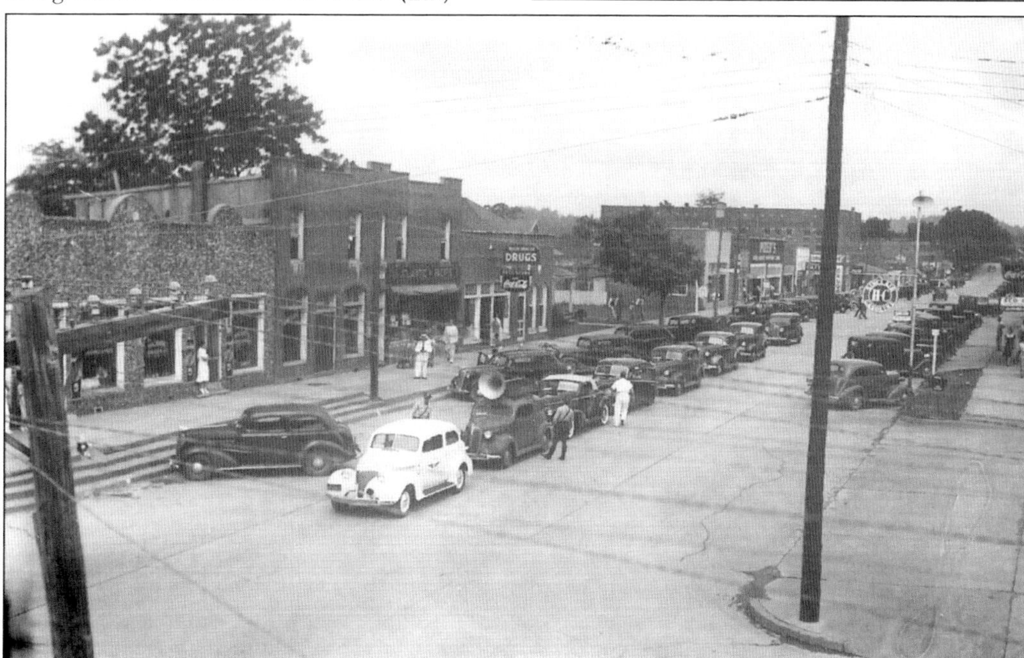

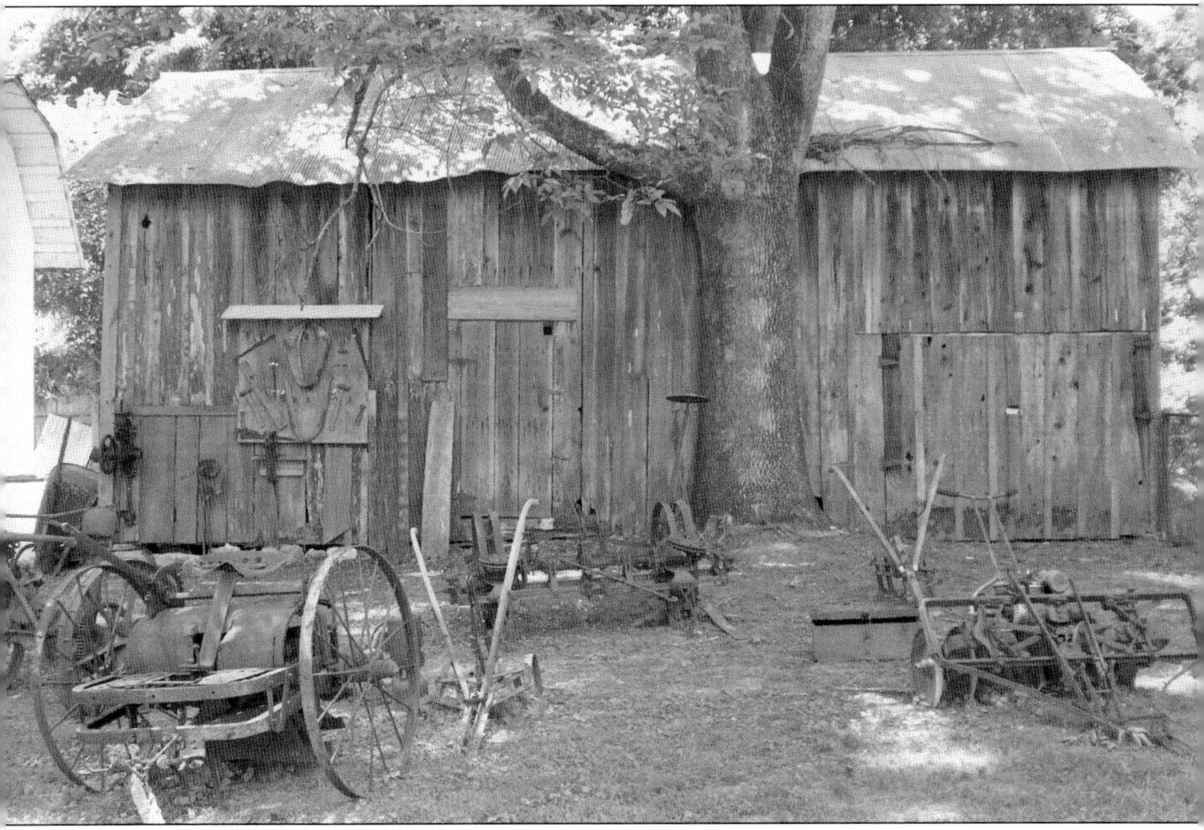

Modern farm tools replaced farm implements on prosperous farms, and some of those farmers became banking families in Leeds as the first economic boom pushed an agrarian culture into industrialism. Members of the Spruiell-Spruill, Lewis, Hurst, Parnell, Courson, and Dorough-Dorrough families managed business and banking in Leeds by the 1930s. The name Parnell is still associated with banking in Leeds. Today, farms have become cattle and horse farms that serve as venues for entertainment and recreation and also for specialized programs such as Apple's Kids at Lachlan Farms in Leeds. Apple is a blind horse, and the program strives to use the horse's story to inspire at-risk children to care for animals. Riding and grooming lessons are offered in conjunction with a sponsorship that makes scholarships available. Lessons are given on a weekly basis, and the program strives to address the unique needs of each student.

Six

WPA: SOLDIERS OF THE GREAT DEPRESSION

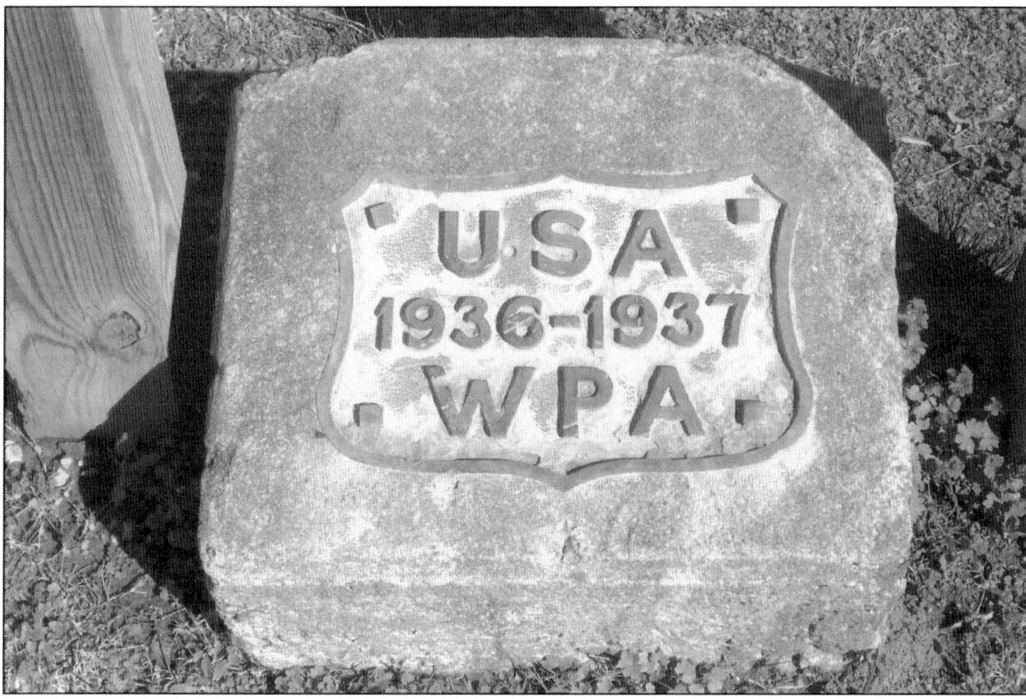

This Works Progress Administration (WPA) cornerstone marks a river and bridge project during which Leeds's first city park was built. A national public works program, WPA provided jobs for unemployed people during the Great Depression in cooperation with state and local governments, which provided 10 to 30 percent of the costs. In addition to the park, WPA projects in Leeds included cataloging real estate and building sidewalks.

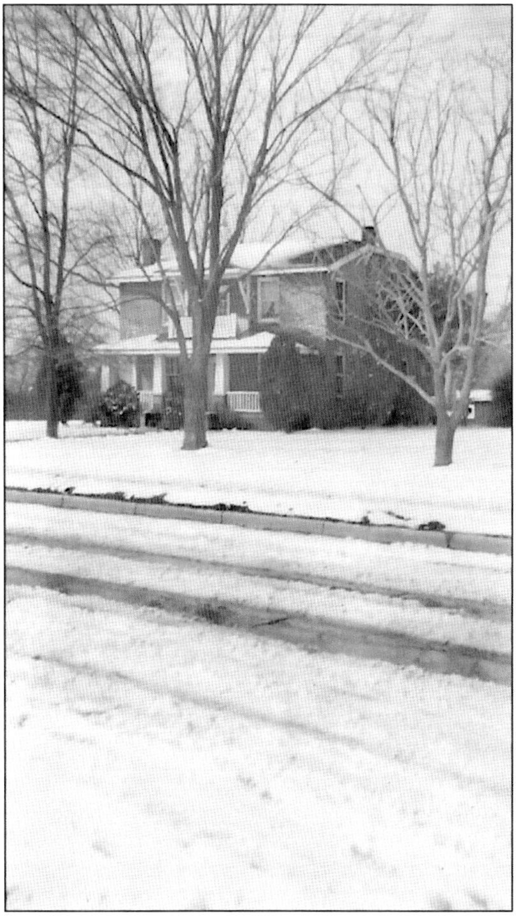

Shown here is the Farley-Blair House, acquired by Dwight Blair Sr. during the Great Depression. His daughter, Carolyn Blair, reminisced about remodeling the house and talked of street-watering trucks that were a delight to local children. "In spite of the Great Depression, life in the new home was good," she said.

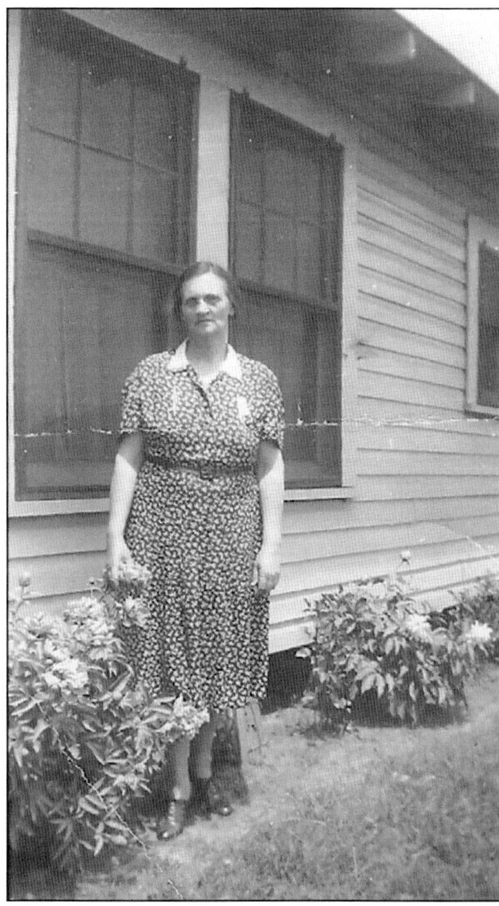

During the Great Depression, Dwight Blair Sr. prepared to live in his home by applying Kemtone paint to freshen and brighten the rooms. Across town, Hattie Nelms (pictured here), who was descended from Leeds's first mayor Josiah Hawkins and Revolutionary War soldier Hezekiah Bayless, kept her dignity. Her Scots-Irish roots required this grandmother to dress up before posing for a photograph with her prize peony.

Boy Scouts were the pride of Leeds. Early Eagle Scouts included Ray Little (pictured), Bryant Whitmire, and Malcolm Nelms. These Eagle Scouts were teenagers in the years leading to the Great Depression. According to family notes, later in life they maintained the knowledge and many skills they mastered in scouting.

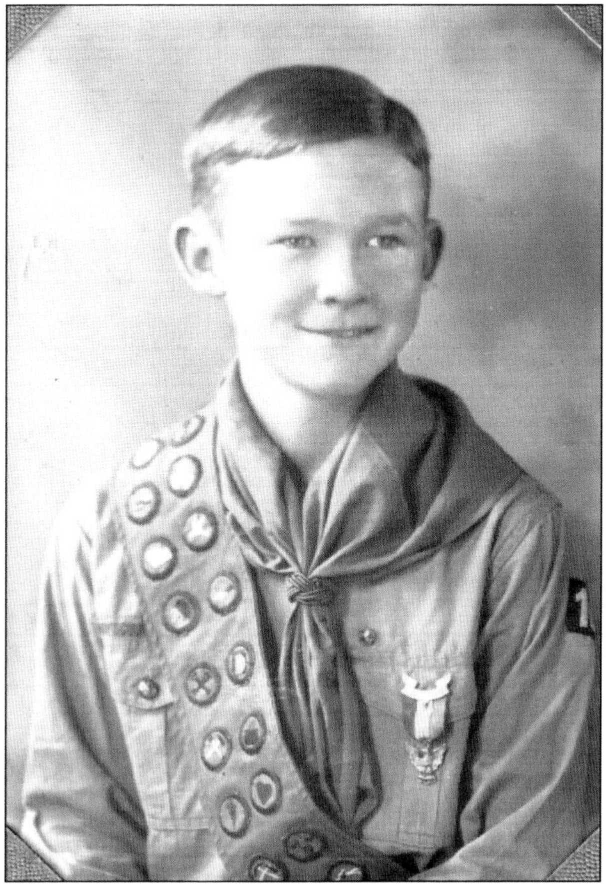

The building pictured here in 1934 at one time housed Leeds's first municipal offices. The building was in downtown Leeds adjacent to the Idaburg residential development. Designed in 1913 by James B. Elliott, an economic developer from Birmingham, Idaburg was named for Elliott's wife, Ida. (BM.)

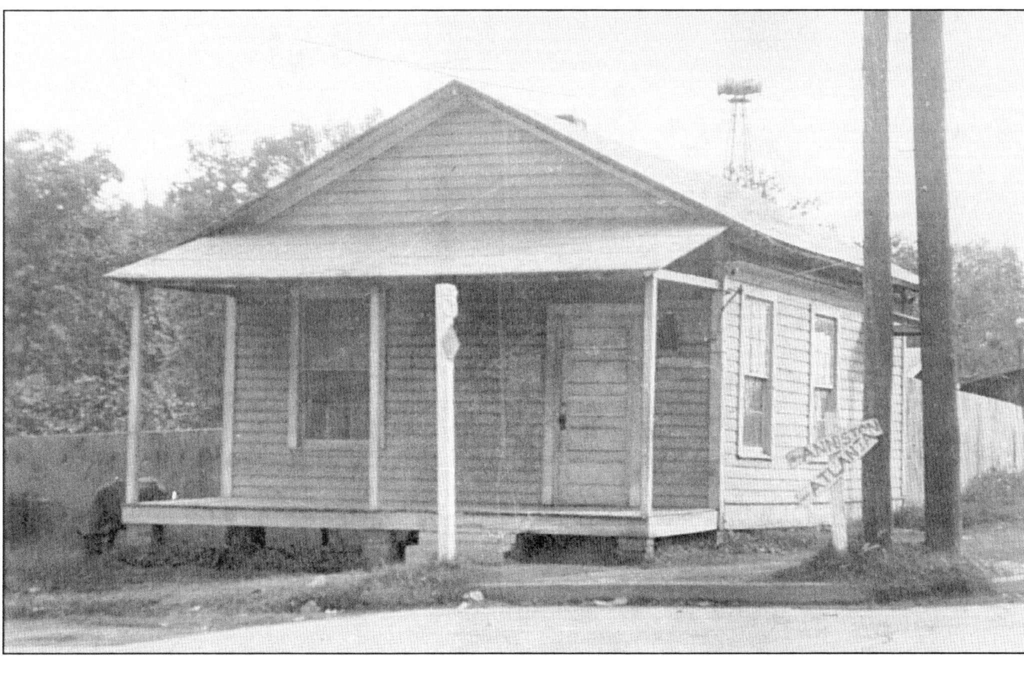

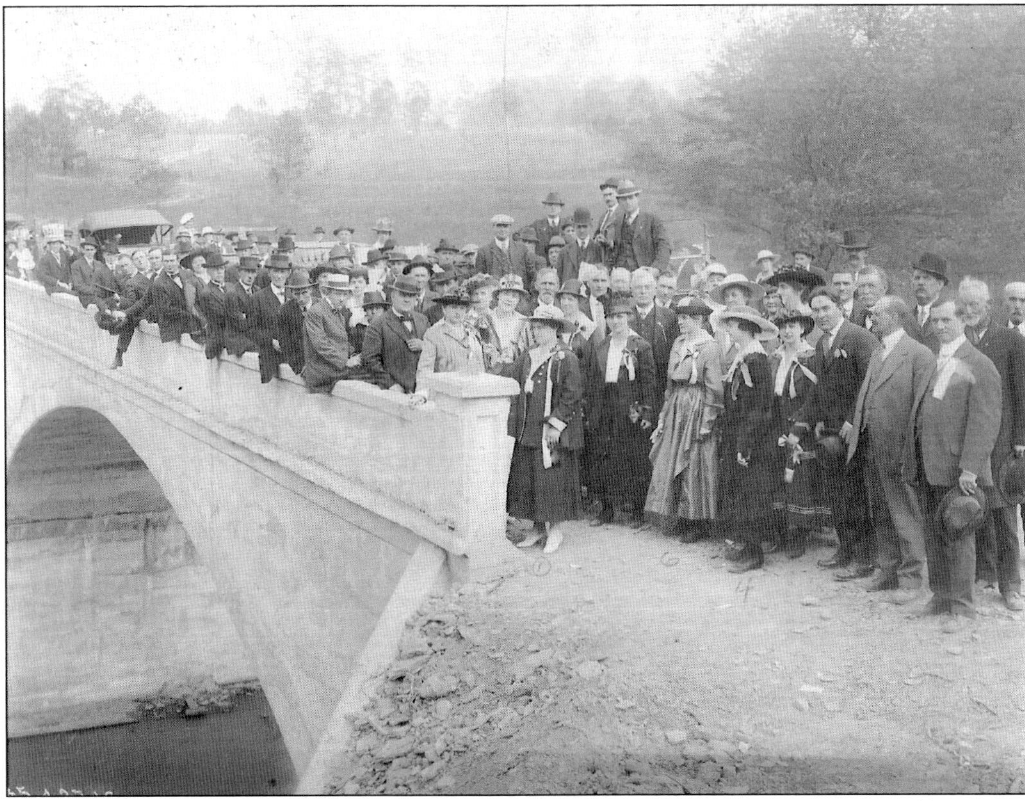

Although the Cahaba River often appears to be a small stream, it becomes a raging river that covers neighborhoods with water during flash flooding. In this photograph, citizens of Leeds and Birmingham turn out for the opening of a bridge that spanned the river and connected Leeds to Birmingham. Family members from Leeds pictured here include Lee and Elliott. (LL.)

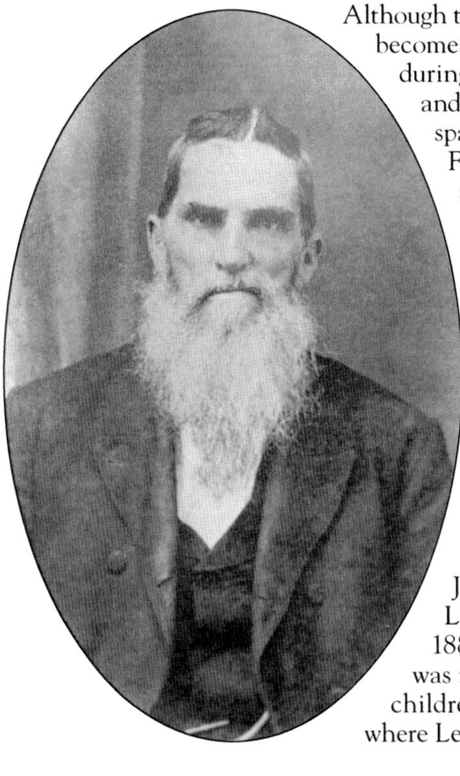

Josiah Hawkins, pictured here, was the first mayor of Leeds when the town was incorporated on April 27, 1887. He came to Leeds from Birmingham. Hawkins was married to Louise Lawley Hawkins, and they had six children. In his younger days, he farmed on the property where Leeds Elementary School now stands. (BM.)

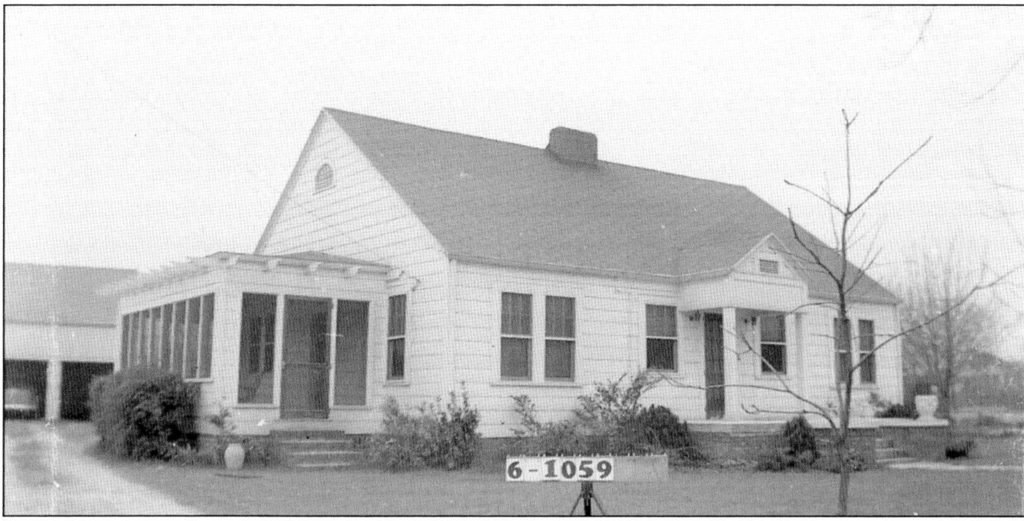

The Board of Equalization used WPA workers to photograph buildings and homes for permanent real estate records. One of the recently marked historic homes for which these records were provided is the Acuff-Funderburg House, shown here, which was built in 1924 and altered in the 1960s. This house on US Highway 411 retains its basic shape, roofline, windows, and siding. It housed families with teenagers from the 1950s until the early 1980s. (BL.)

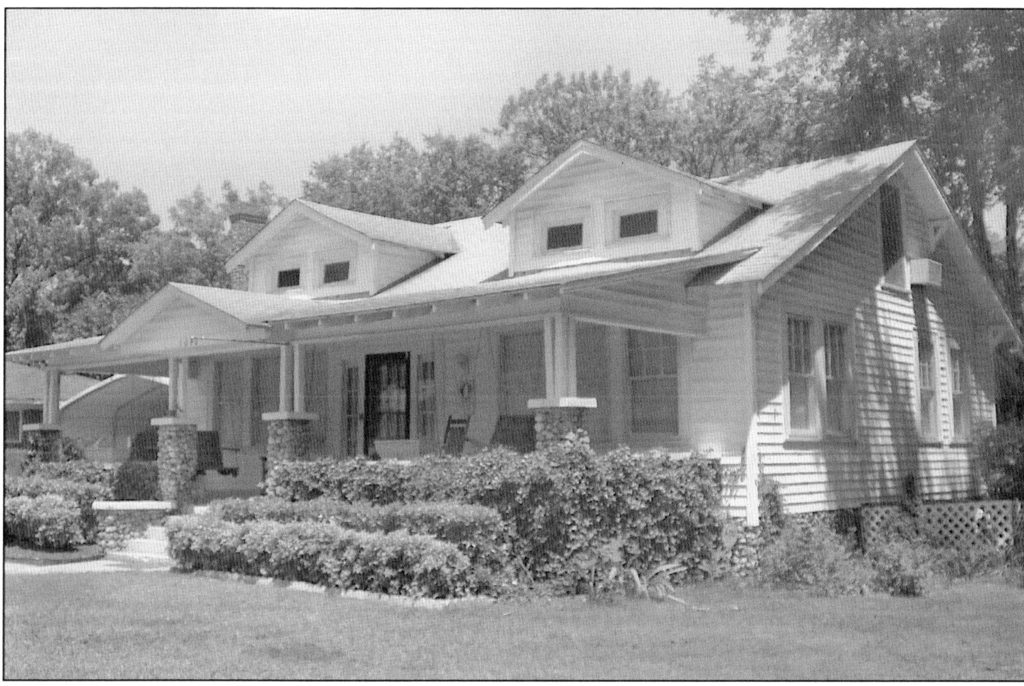

A WPA worker archived the Elliott-Spruiell house. This four-bedroom house was built in 1910 by Shelby and Myrtle Elliott, who had nine children. The five daughters slept upstairs in two bedrooms; the four sons shared one downstairs bedroom, and their parents slept in the other downstairs bedroom. Myrtle gave haircuts to neighbors. In 1929, they sold the home to William and Willie Mae Spruiell. Willie Mae lived there until 1985.

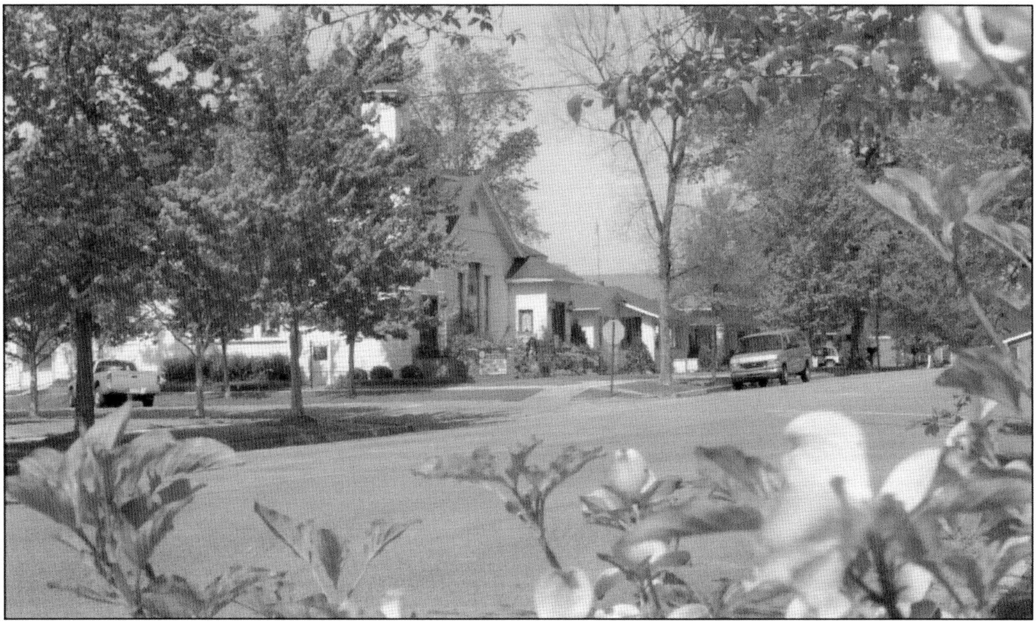

First Avenue forms a part of an older Leeds neighborhood that was centered on the schools and Leeds Presbyterian Church. The area looked much the same during the Great Depression as it does today. The church was founded in the Oak Ridge community in 1820 and moved to its current site in 1913. It remains the oldest church building in the downtown area.

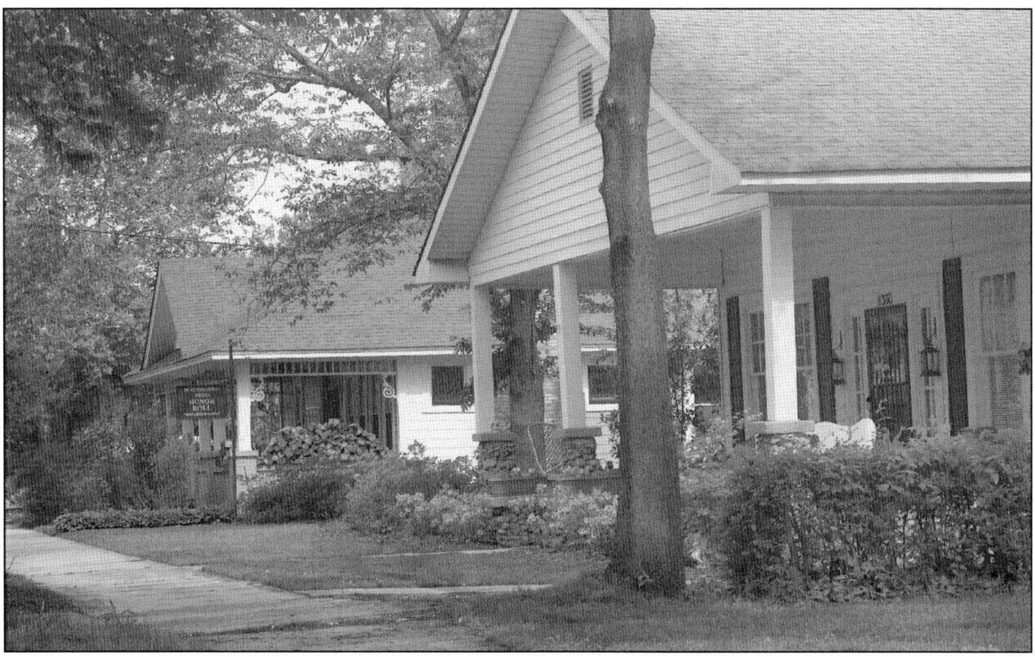

The Spruiell subdivision contains the oldest houses in a subdivision in Leeds. It was originally known as Oak Ridge Settlement, the oldest settlement in the town. The oldest remaining servants' quarters in Leeds are in the Spruiell subdivision on the property surrounding the Sharp-Marciano house. By 1903, Mason Spruiell and his progeny had established both permanent residence and influence in the development of Leeds.

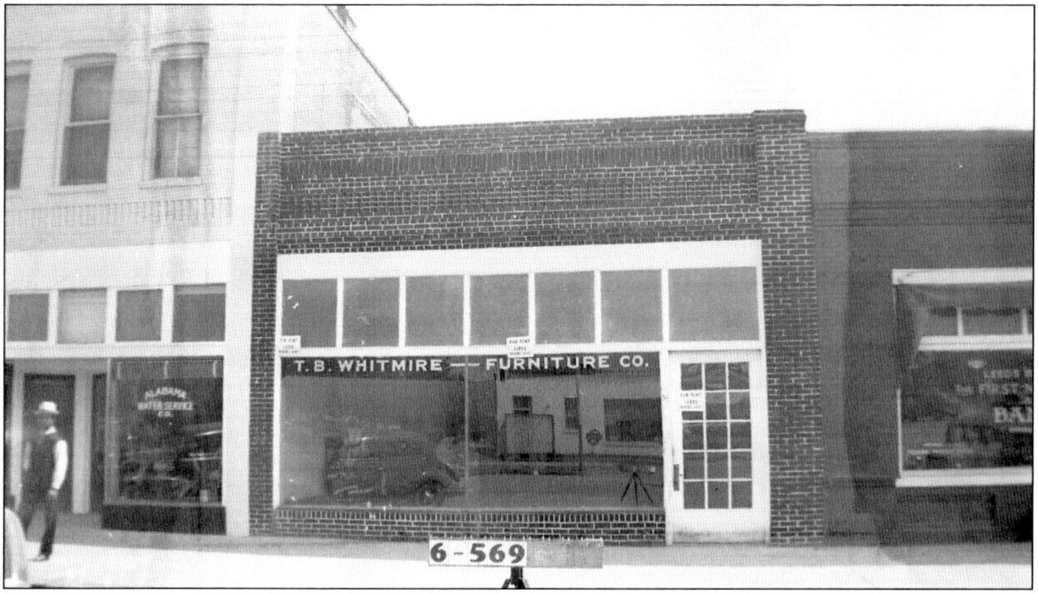

The WPA project employed qualified engineers and surveyors who were out of work. Those who worked for the WPA in Leeds documented buildings with precision for the Jefferson County Board of Equalization records. Photographs like the one above are archived at the Birmingham Library Department of Archives and Manuscripts. Today, these archives help preservationists find documentation and are a source of information for realtors who research property titles. (BL.)

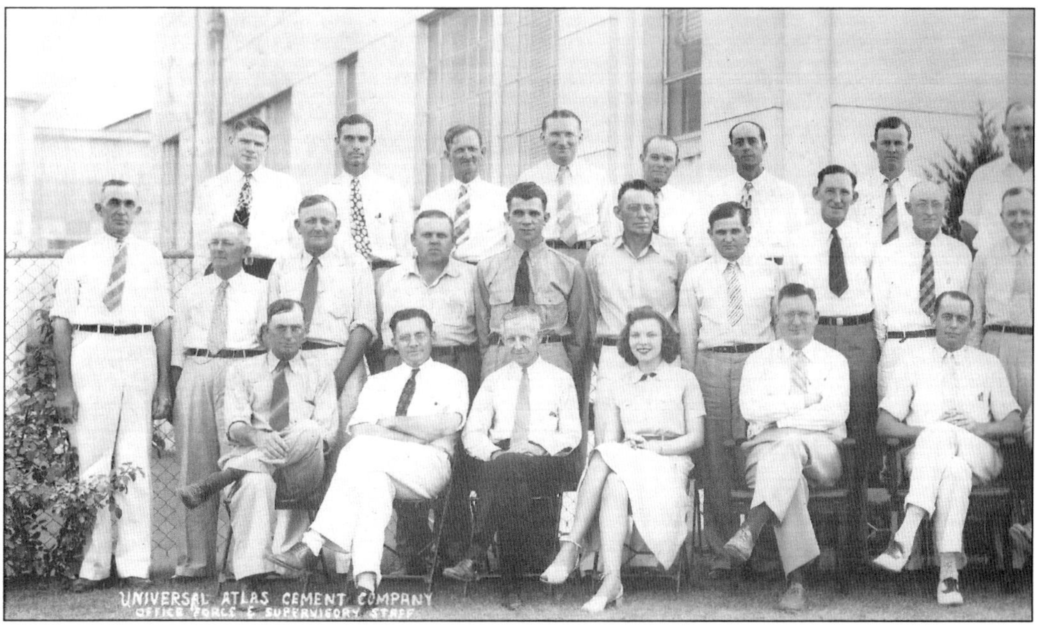

Leeds's 1939 members of the cement plant staff are pictured outside the plant's office building. A Portland cement structure designed by famous Art Deco architects Warren, Knight, and Davis, the office was built during the Great Depression as part of a 1930s expansion of plant operations. The plant remains the largest employer in Leeds after more than 100 years. Leeds's Lehigh is the only producer of green Portland cement in the world. (LHS.)

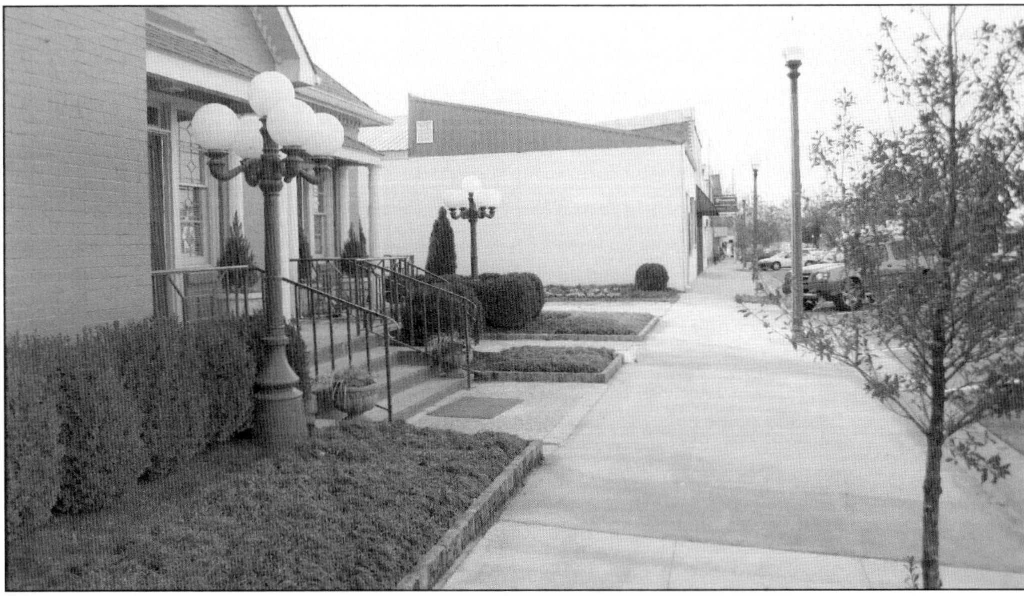

This photograph shows Parkway Drive between Eighth and Ninth Streets where Dr. E.C. Clayton's medical clinic was located. Doctor Clayton started his practice in the Falletta house earlier in that decade. Dr. Harold Fendley opened a dental practice elsewhere in 1949 and moved it to the old Clayton clinic, which he renamed the Fendley Dental Building. The restored building houses Dr. Scott Koplon's dental practice.

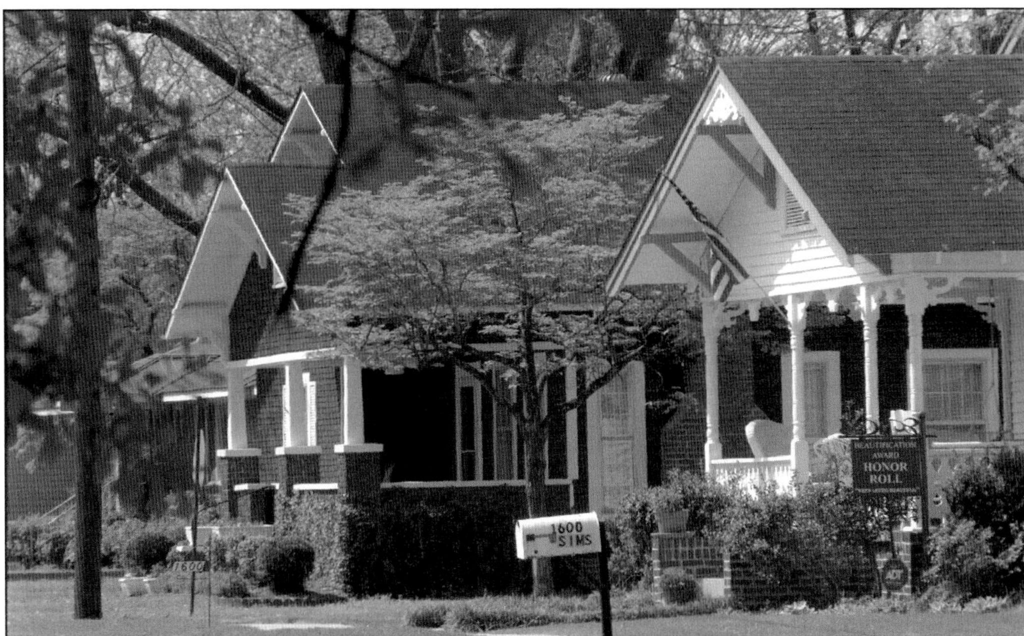

During the Great Depression, people left quaint, tree-shaded homes to work in shipyards in Mobile. Some members of the Harding family managed to save their property in Leeds and make a living in Mobile. People who went to Mobile in search of jobs sometimes took shifts sleeping in the public library there, because the city could not house the large number of workers who came.

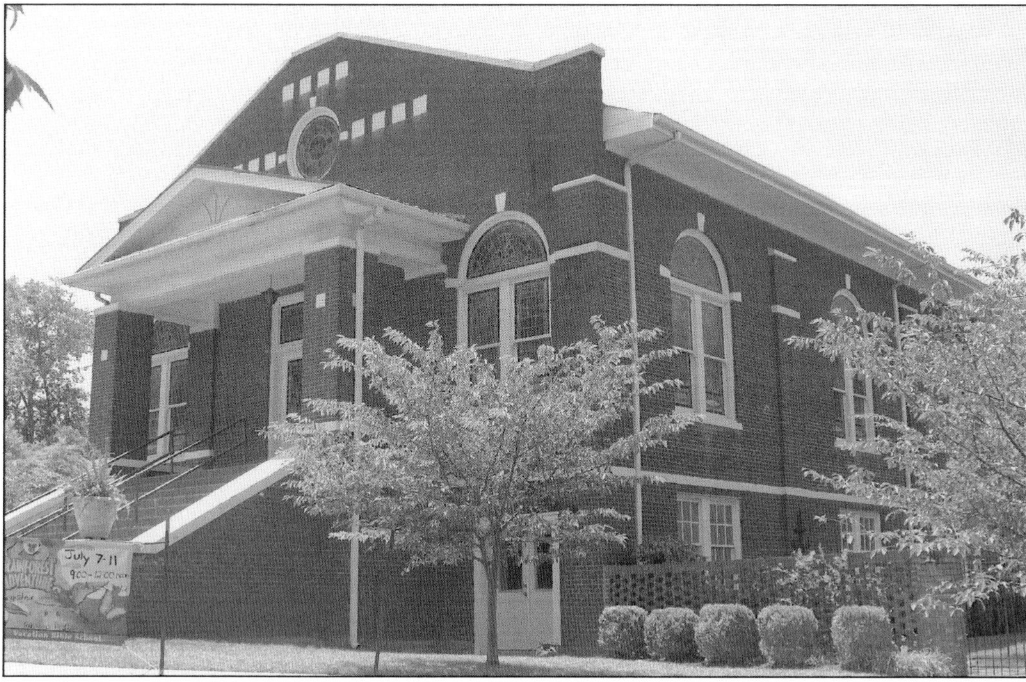

The descendants of the founders of First United Methodist Church saved quarters during the Great Depression to send to their family members to help them continue college courses at Alabama Polytechnic Institute (API). Bob Harding graduated from API during these difficult economic times and came back to the area as an educator.

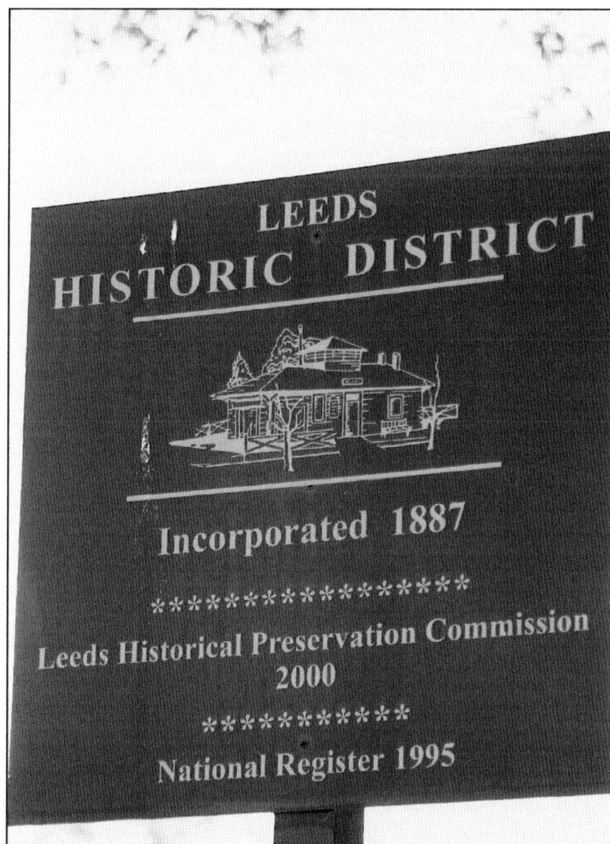

The Leeds Historic District sign marks the spot from where Lawrence Nelms left to ride the rails during the Great Depression. He returned home, but the adventurer left again to fight in World War II. One of Leeds's decorated World War II veterans, Nelms was awarded three Distinguished Flying Crosses for flying "the Hump," a supply route over the Himalayan Mountains, with the US Army Air Force troops that replaced the Flying Tigers.

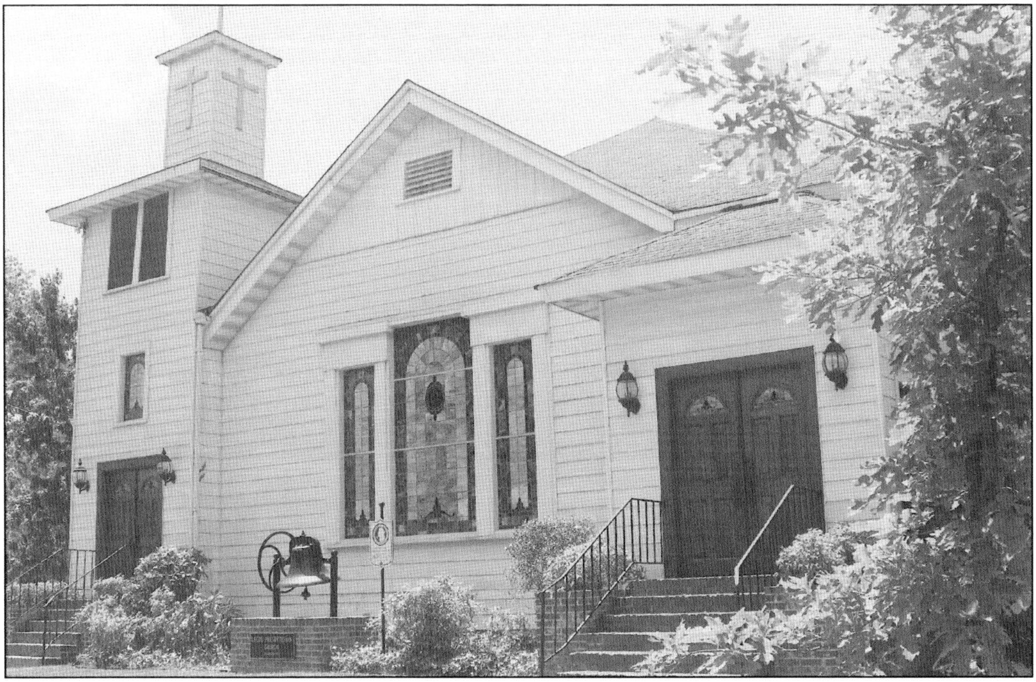

Like the Methodists, members of the Leeds Presbyterian Church supported, with one coin at a time, their family members who attended college during the Great Depression. Bill Dorrough graduated from Alabama Polytechnic Institute during that time. After college, he came home to his family and later became mayor of Leeds.

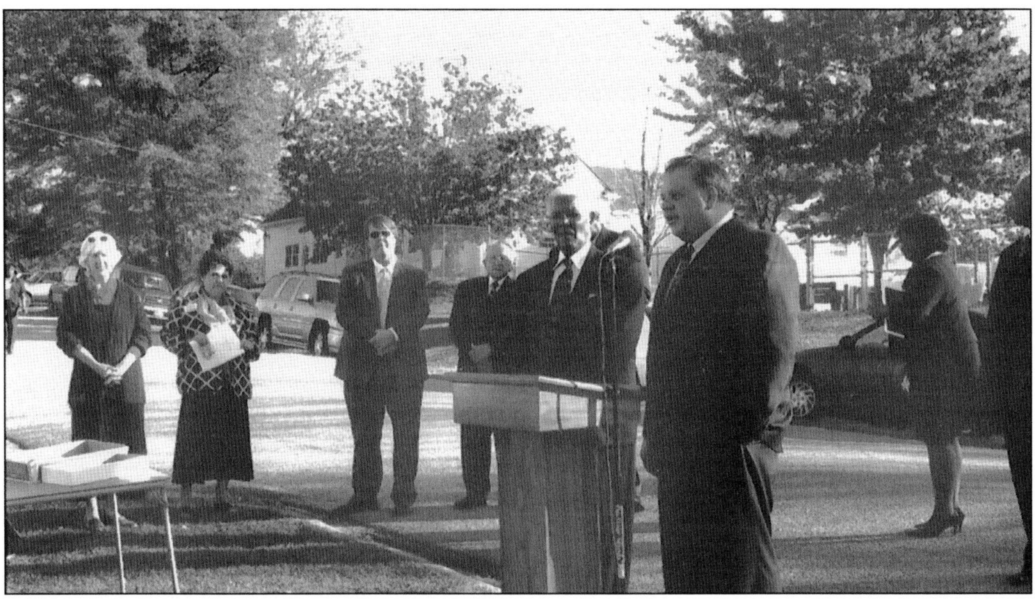

In this photograph, Leeds dignitaries, a mayor, a state representative, a local historical society president, a Jefferson County Historical Commission director, and preservationists dedicate a memorial to the district that built the first African American school. The school's first graduating class received diplomas on the eve of the Great Depression.

Seven

SIDEWALKS OF AN AMERICAN TOWN

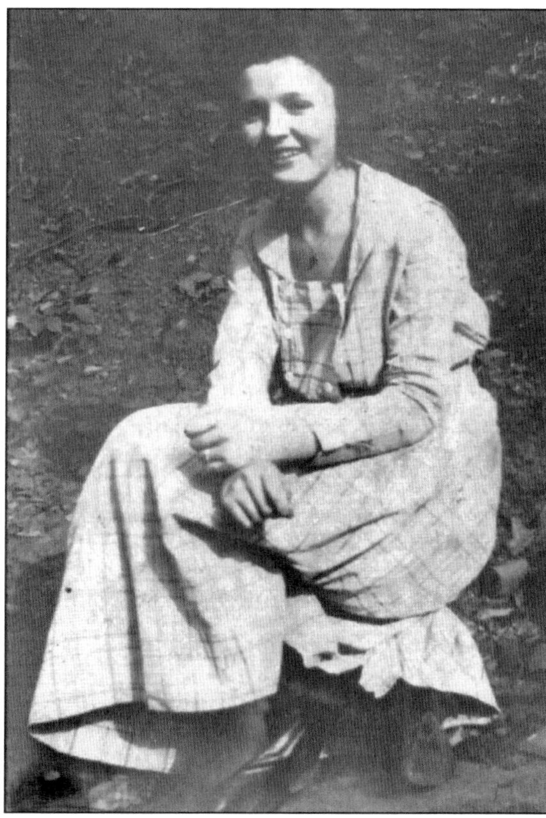

The Great Depression is the low point of an era that began during World War I and ended prior to the prosperity of the 1940s. When the era began, hemlines were modest, as exemplified by a descendent of Hezekiah Moor seen here. Hemlines were higher in the 1920s and 1930s. The rise and fall of economic conditions was a barometer for skirt lengths, even in a small Southern town. (LL.)

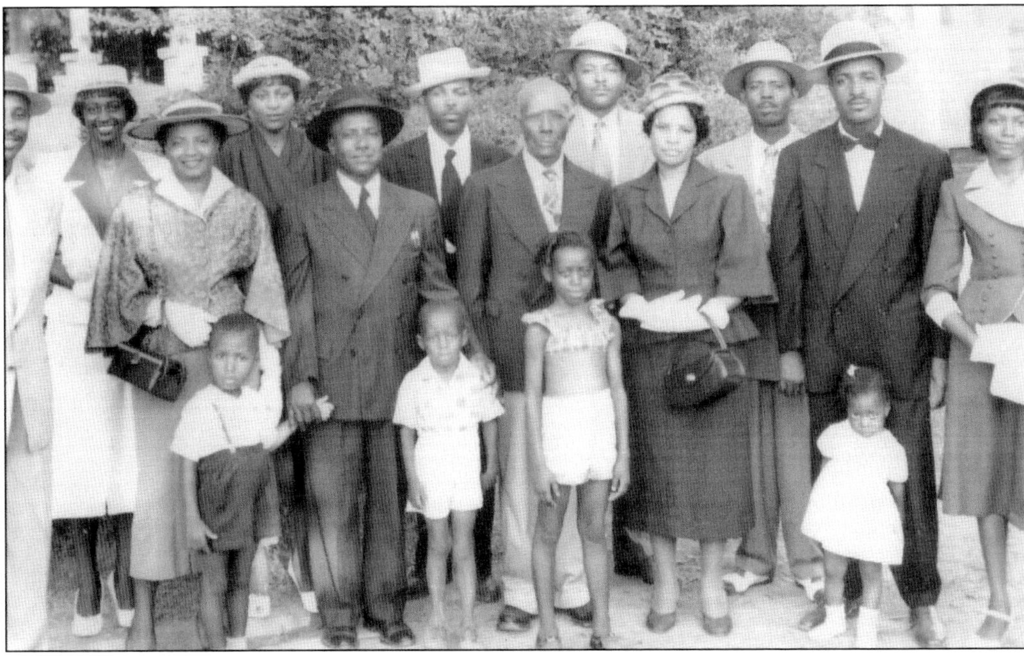

Hemlines would fall again, but the next two decades would see a proliferation of get-rich-quick schemes that led to reckless speculation. The speculation brought a long-running bull market to an end and closed Leeds State Bank before ladies wore their skirts the length that Moore family women wore in this photograph, taken at their family reunion. (Courtesy of Carl Marlbury.)

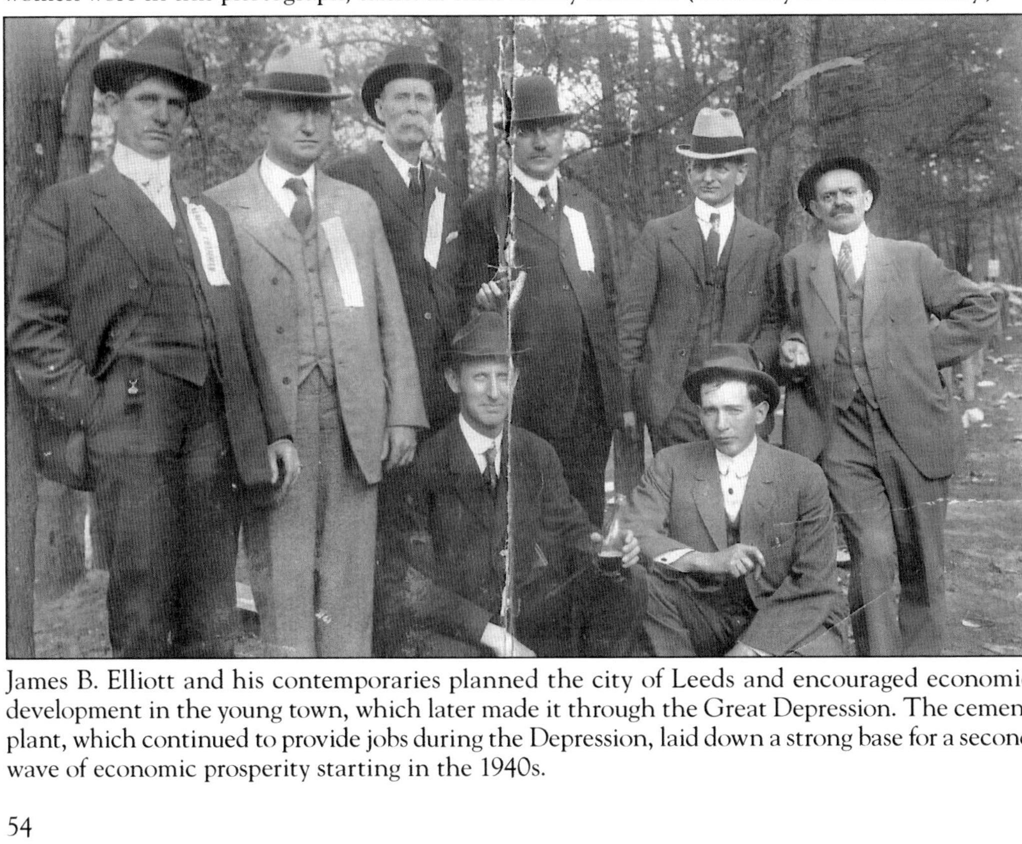

James B. Elliott and his contemporaries planned the city of Leeds and encouraged economic development in the young town, which later made it through the Great Depression. The cement plant, which continued to provide jobs during the Depression, laid down a strong base for a second wave of economic prosperity starting in the 1940s.

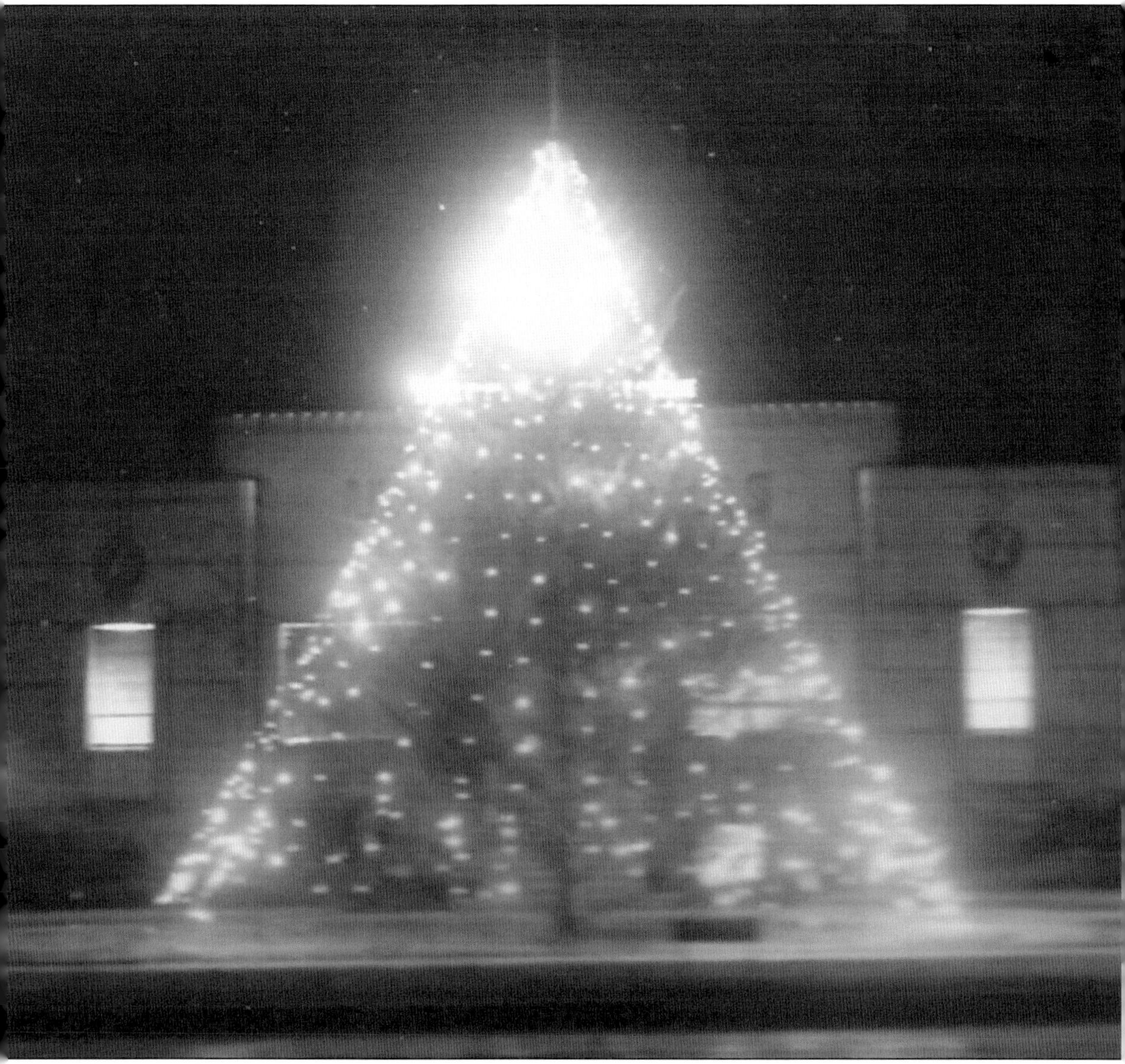

By the 1930s, the town's showpiece during the holiday season was a brightly lit Christmas tree that stood in front of the main office at the cement plant. Homes in the nearby Idaburg subdivision keep the look of the period, even today. When homeowners decorate for the holidays, their decorations seem to complement the candlelight services at nearby churches. The sidewalk's route in Leeds has remained almost the same for more than five decades, largely because the Leeds Tree Commission continues to plant shade trees and keep them growing. Through the years, schoolchildren have walked along the sidewalk to Leeds Presbyterian Church, where they dropped in to play ping-pong; to the First Methodist Church, where they examined the latest Chrismons (Christmas symbols or ornaments); and to the downtown area, where they attended Miss Gilda's Dancing School. After dancing class, they walked down another sidewalk to the Green Spot café for soft drinks and potato chips. (LHS.)

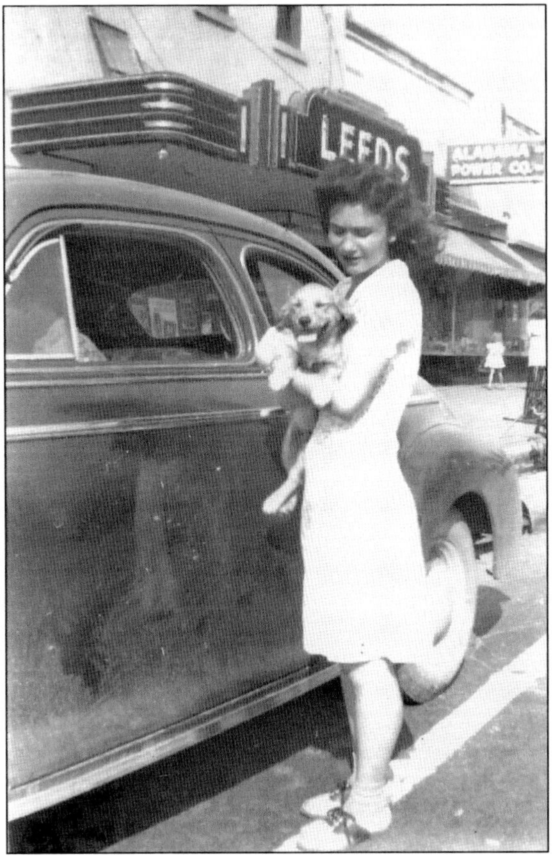

For young women in Leeds, hemlines were slightly above the knee as World War II beckoned soldiers to its three theaters of war: Europe, Africa, and the Pacific. Men and women in Leeds answered the call and joined the Army, Air Corps, Navy, Marines, and Coast Guard. A theater in downtown Leeds showed daily news reels about American troops abroad, and mothers and children attended regularly. (BM.)

The Leeds branch of the First National Bank of Birmingham was the bank's first branch when it opened in 1935. The earliest bank in Leeds was Leeds State Bank, which was established in 1910. Since 1954, local banks have been founded, including the Citizens Bank of Leeds and the more recent Covenant Bank. (BL.)

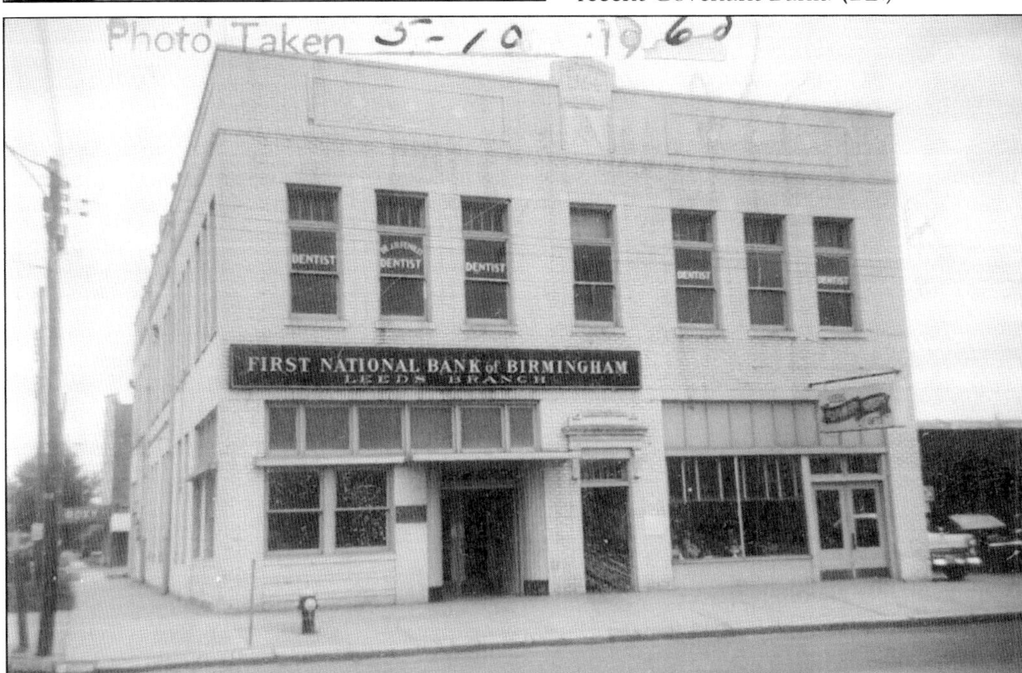

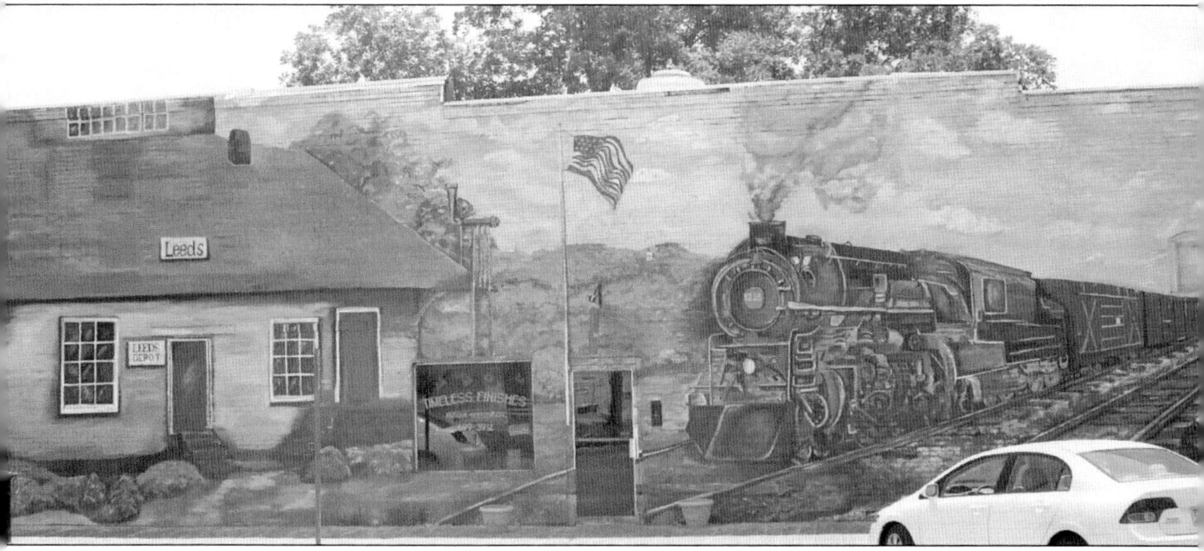

The train mural on historic Ninth Street is the largest mural of its kind in the southeastern United States. It was restored in 2008 as a symbol of a community that still enjoys stories of the railroad. It was the site of the Green Spot, a gathering place for Leeds's young people. Experienced local artist Peggy Smith drew the mural freehand, with no stenciling or projections involved. She followed the same train dimensions, but the mural's overall proportions covered the whole side of the building. Her expertise allowed her to paint her ideas directly onto the brick surface with no restrictions of scale or design. To assist Peggy, Judy Isbell worked with the Leeds Scenic Byway to acquire paint from a regional dealer. The safety ladder equipment was provided by Leeds local Tri Counties Heating and Air. The painting took about a month to complete. Onlookers helped hold paint buckets, and passing joggers stopped to help.

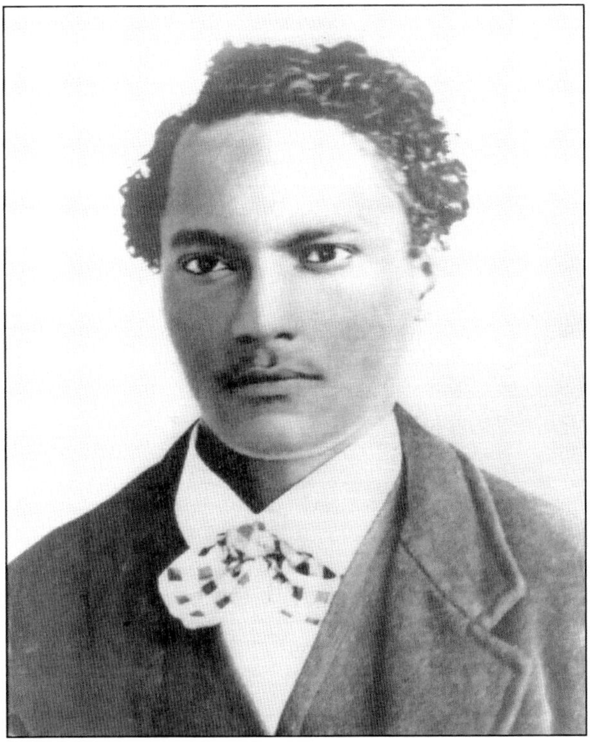

Shown here in a famous portrait, Ciscero Davis settled in Leeds in the 1880s with his wife, Melissa Hood Davis. Both had Cherokee Indian heritage, and he worked on the Georgia Pacific and Southern Railways. Ciscero's progeny includes the families of Davis, Marbury, Williams, Polk, Jerald, Harris, and Beason. Many of their descendants, shown below at a family reunion, still reside in the Leeds area, including doctors, teachers, military officers, police officers, and ministers. Exemplifying the high quality of these accomplishments, their sons fought in the Ardennes during World War II, attended Harvard University, and became state troopers. Davis also left a legacy that has become a local museum of early farm implements. (Both courtesy of Carl Marbury.)

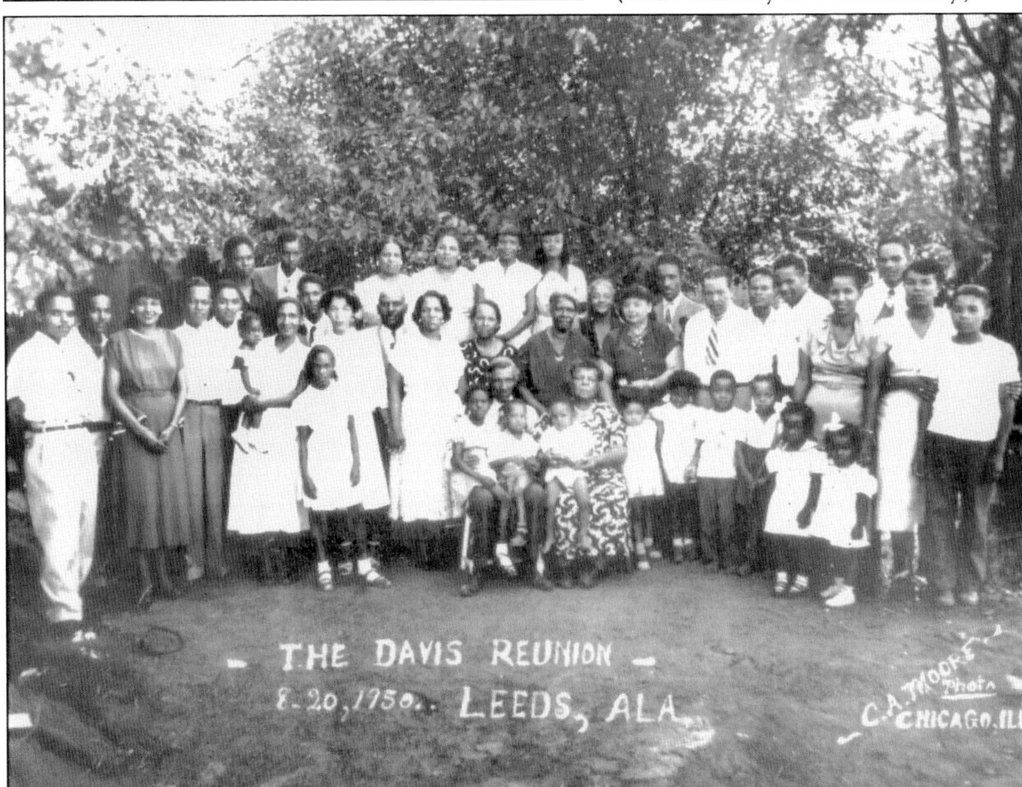

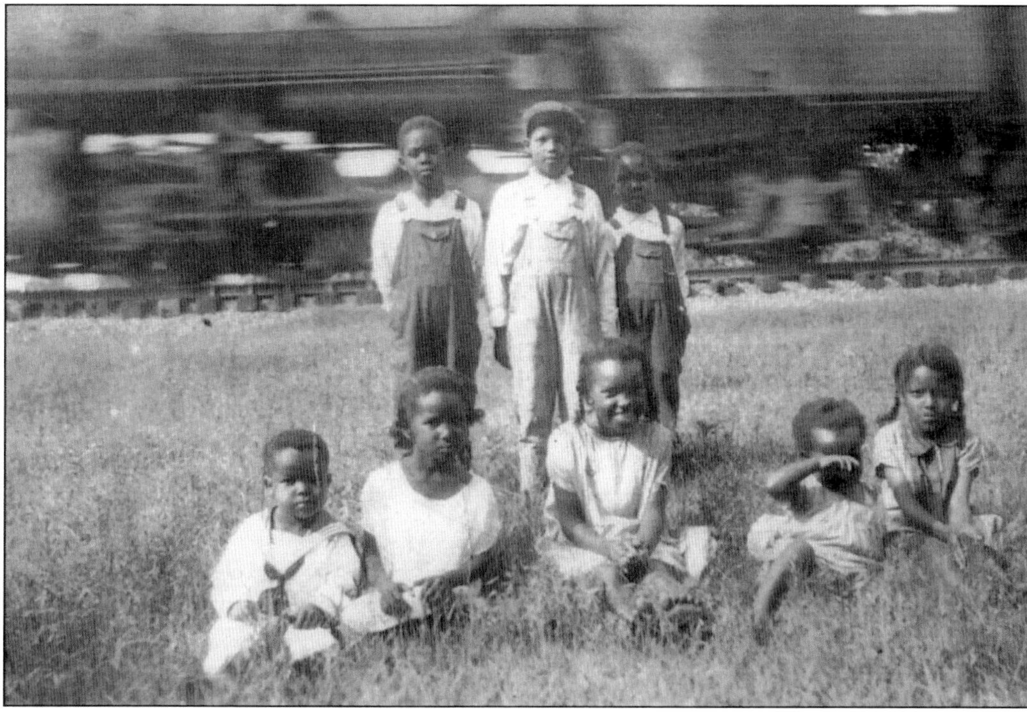

The Marbury children pose for their parents as the Southern Railway freight train passes by. Grandfather Ciscero lived downtown, where sidewalks connected his house to the railroad tracks. Davis's grandchildren played hopscotch on the sidewalks near the house. (Courtesy of Carl Marbury.)

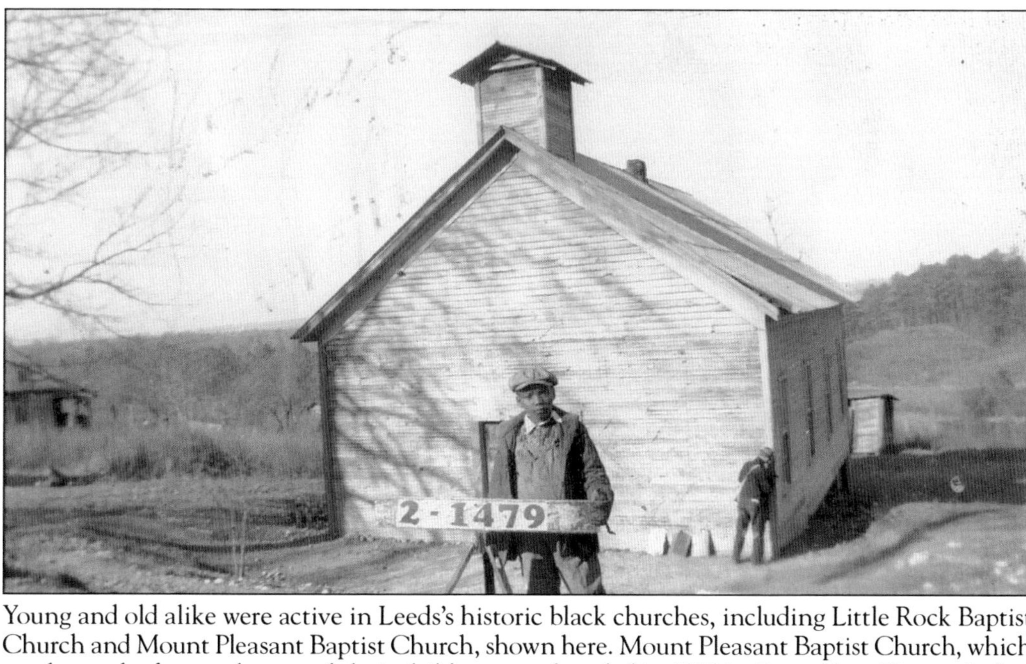

Young and old alike were active in Leeds's historic black churches, including Little Rock Baptist Church and Mount Pleasant Baptist Church, shown here. Mount Pleasant Baptist Church, which was begun by former slaves and their children, was founded in 1874 in Scott City, 13 years before Leeds was incorporated. (BL.)

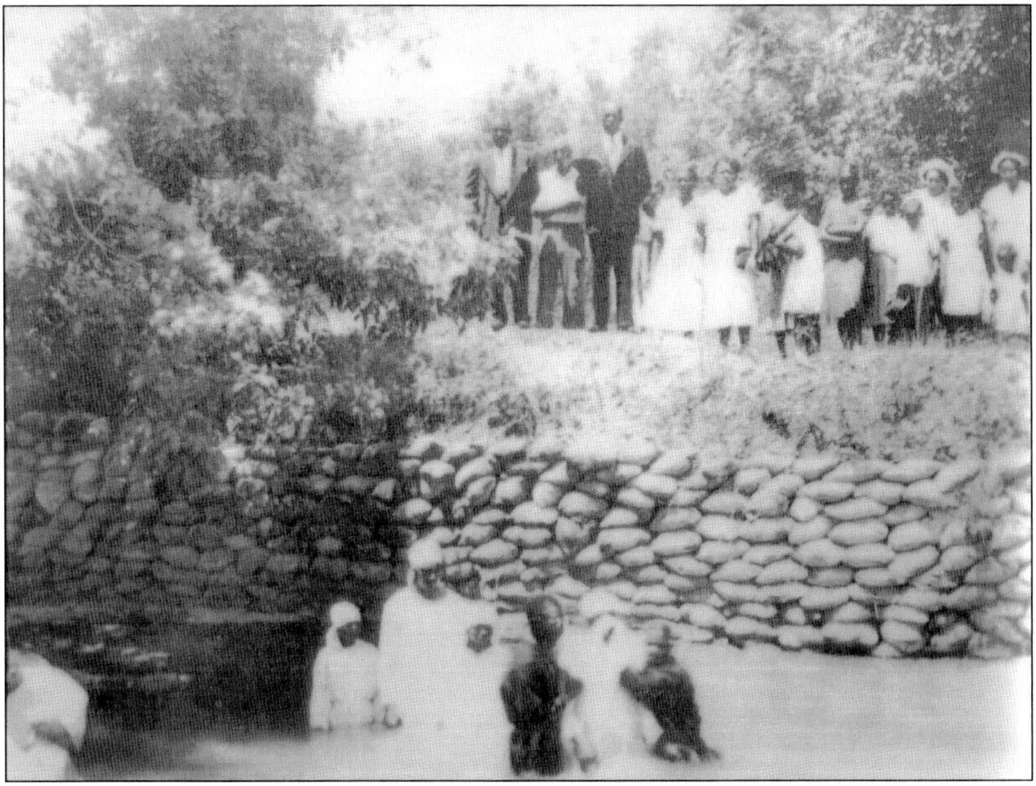

A bend in the Little Cahaba River served as an outdoor baptismal area in this picturesque scene. Leeds's African American worshippers would gather at their historic churches, cross US Highway 78, and walk through a field to get to the river, where they sang hymns and rejoiced over the baptism of children and adults. (BM.)

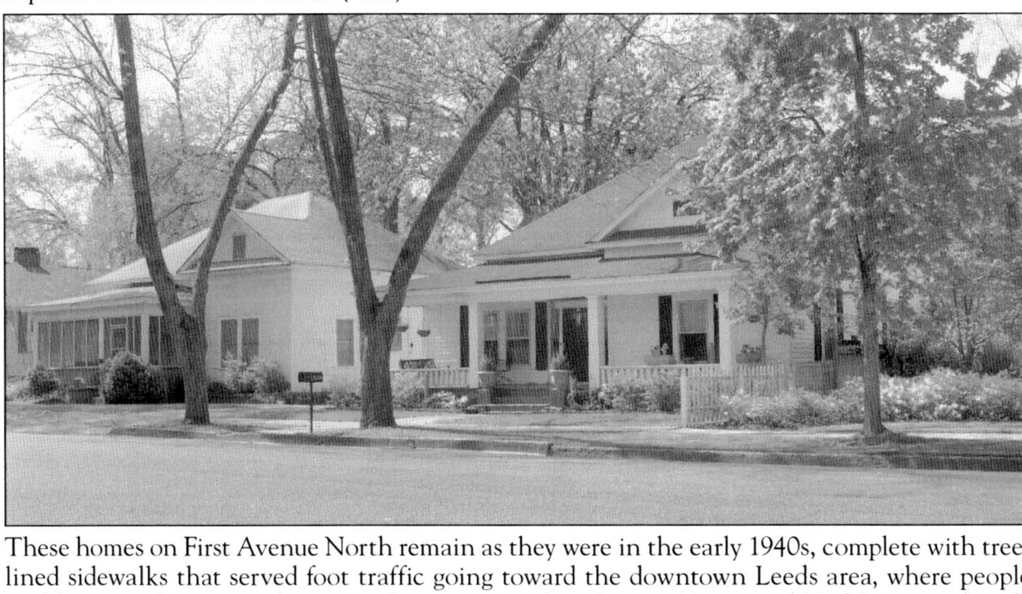

These homes on First Avenue North remain as they were in the early 1940s, complete with tree-lined sidewalks that served foot traffic going toward the downtown Leeds area, where people could wait on buses, watch movies, buy groceries from Jimmy Moore and Ned Jones, and trade at Lindley Spruiell's drugstore.

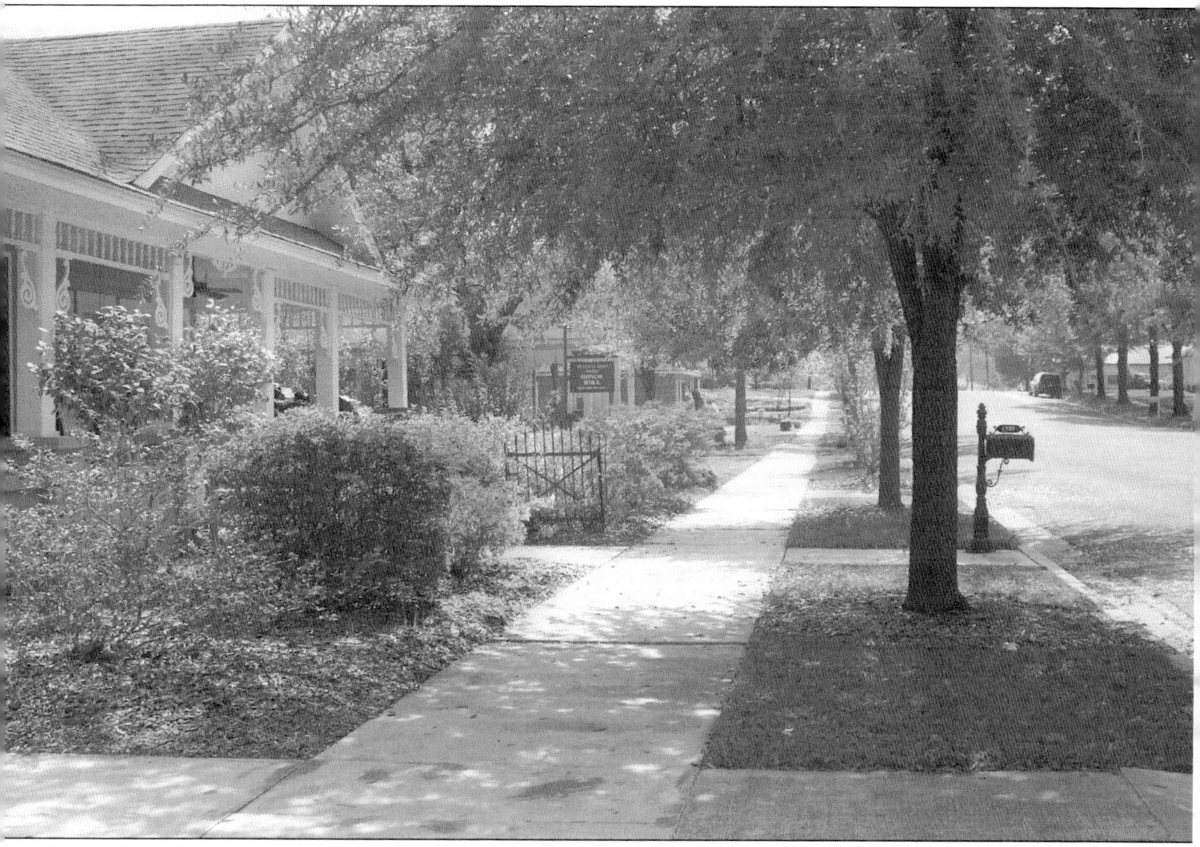

The sidewalk in this photograph led to an empty lot at the corner of First Avenue North and Seventh Street in downtown Leeds. Tent events, including dog shows, carnivals, and open-air revivals were held on this lot in the 1930s and 1940s. Dave Stewart, a descendent of Cherokee patriarch John Ingram Paschal Stewart, preached a revival here that so impressed groups who came to hear him that they built a Methodist church, which is located on Montevallo Road (Alabama Highway 119) two blocks south of the current location of Leeds Elementary School. Because it was built with field rock, townspeople called it Little Rock Methodist Church. At that time, Reverend Stewart was living in the New Merkle area of Birmingham and representing the Methodist protestant conference. Members of the church included people in the Pool-Poole, Bearden, McLaughlin, and Minor families. The sidewalk created a social network and connected churches, schools, and the downtown area.

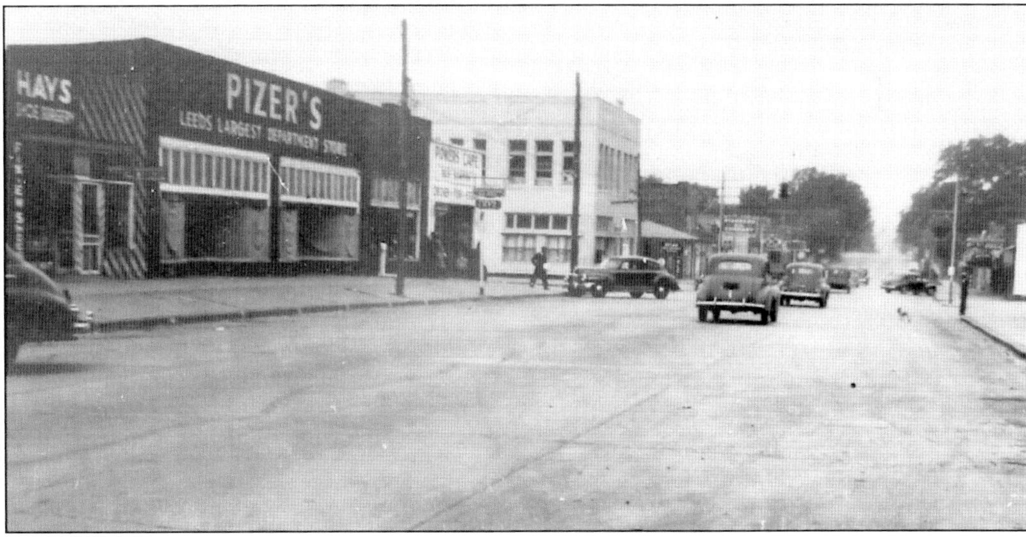

This sidewalk leads from the first building that housed Leeds Board of Education (far left) to the historic site of the Leeds branch of the First National Bank of Birmingham (two story white building). After a fire destroyed the bank building in 1941, the bank was housed briefly in the Masonic Building. The bank returned to the building pictured here, which was later modernized. It reopened in these new and expanded facilities in 1975. (BM.)

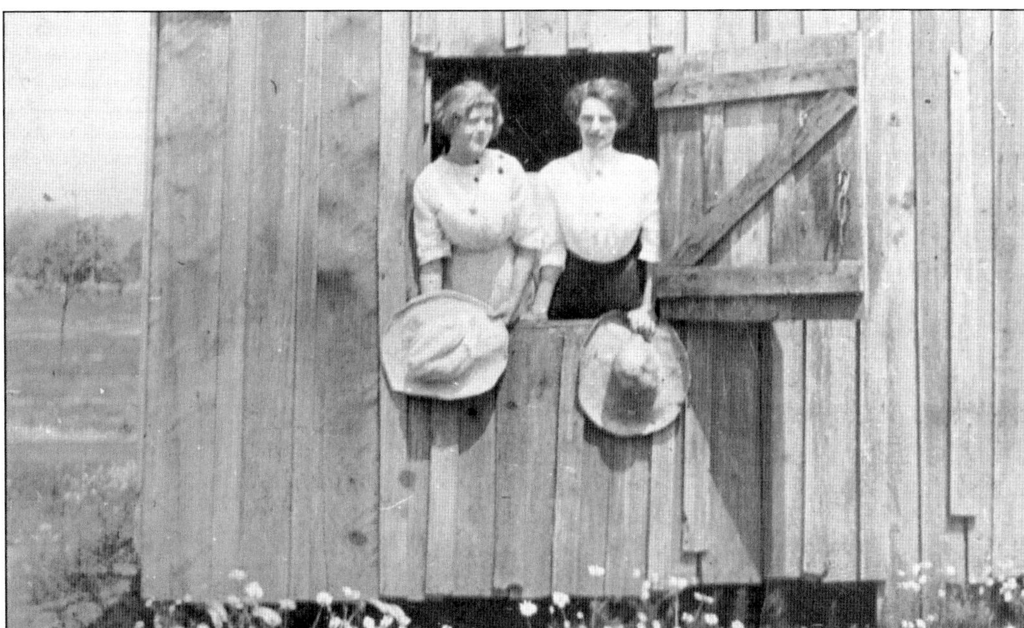

Era Jones Owen (left) and Erma Jones Owen, shown here in the 1920s, admired flowers, as did the youth of the 1940s and 1950s. Youngsters in Leeds stopped to smell the flowers at the Acuff-Funderberg house on their way to the swimming hole in the Little Cahaba River. The home was later owned by both old Leeds families and newcomers, including the Campbells, Hargons, and the Michael Nelms family. (LL.)

Eight

THREE MEDALS OF HONOR FROM 5,000 PEOPLE

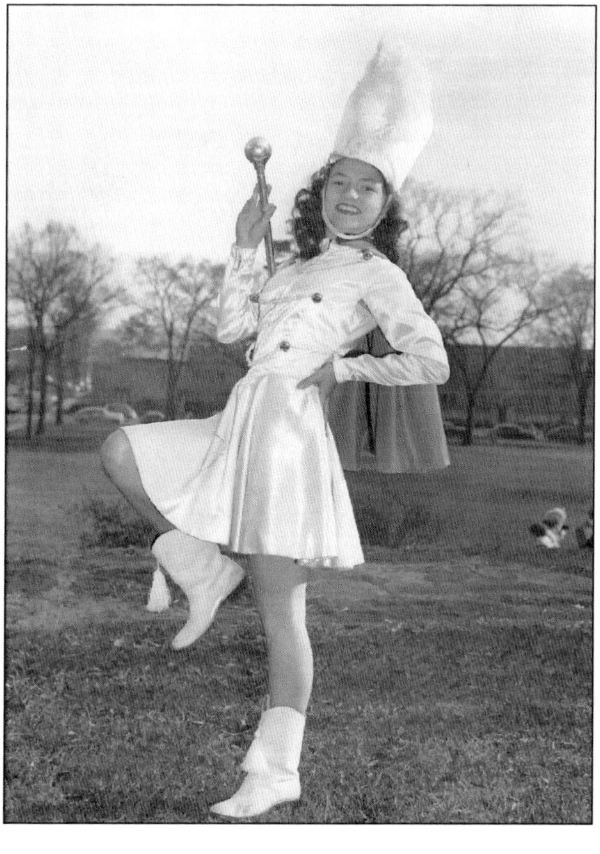

More than once, majorettes and honor guards led parades on Parkway Drive in downtown Leeds to honor the city heroes, soldiers, athletes, and more. The 1940s drum majorette in this photograph is a descendent of Col. Thomas Lee, who fought in the American Revolution. Lee's descendants settled in Shelby County in the 1800s and have remained in Leeds.

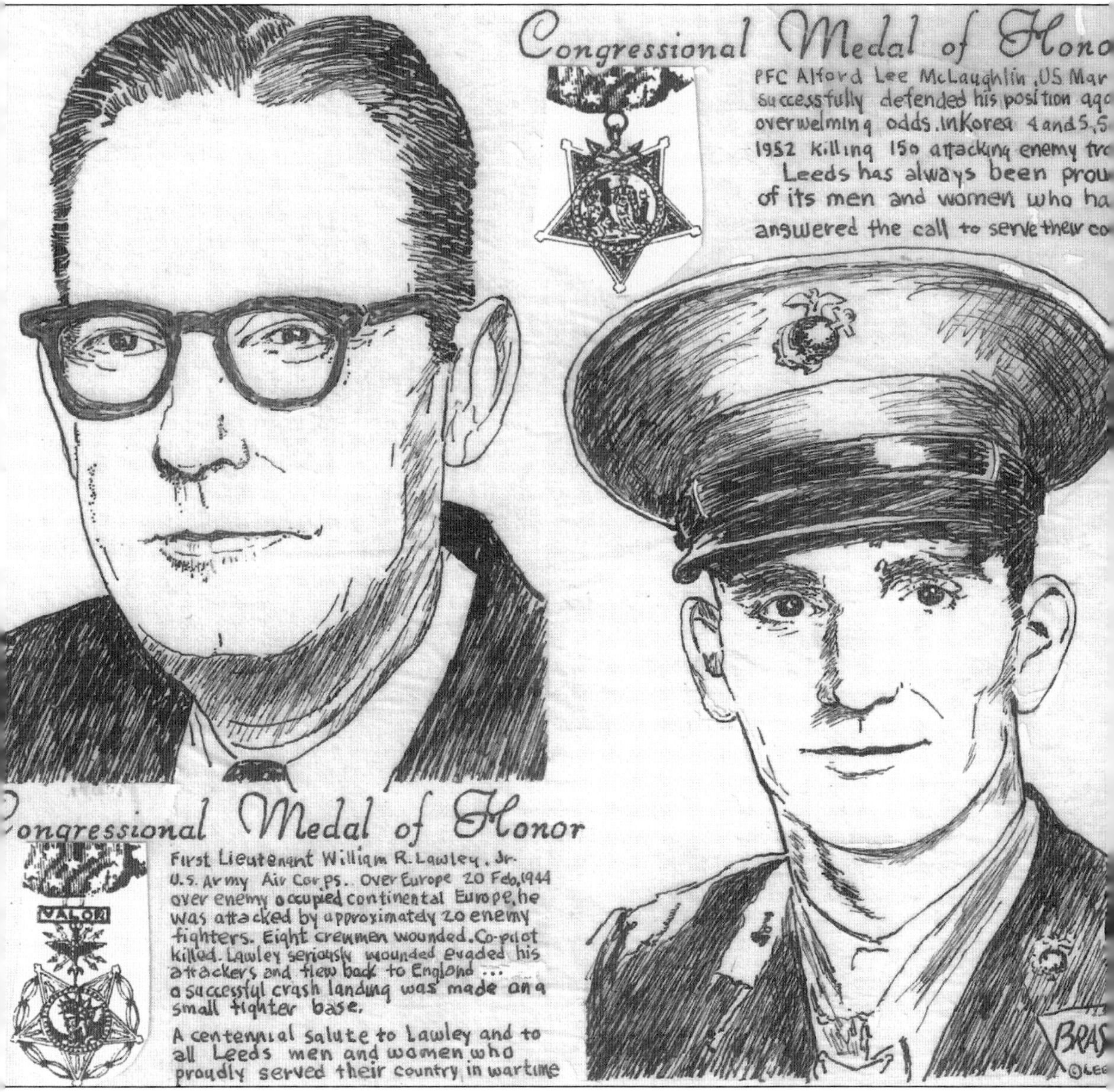

Leeds natives William R. Lawley Jr. (left) and Alfred Lee McLaughlin received Congressional Medals of Honor. Lieutenant Lawley was a crewmember in a B-17 airplane over Europe in World II, when the plane was attacked by enemy fighters. When the pilot and copilot were killed, Lawley landed the airplane that was crippled by engine fires, even though he was seriously wounded. When told that some crew members were too severely wounded to bail out, he remained on the plane and brought the crew to safety. McLaughlin served his country as a Marine during World War II and the Korean War. In Korea, he defended an outpost far in advance of the main line of resistance. During enemy attacks, although he was wounded, he maintained a constant flow of devastating fire using two machine guns, a carbine, and hand grenades, and accounted for an estimated 150 enemy dead and 50 enemy wounded and was instrumental in preventing the vital outpost from falling into enemy hands. (LL.)

Henry E. "Red" Erwin Jr., a US Army Air Force airman, received a Congressional Medal of Honor for valor in World War II. During a B-29 bombing mission in 1945 over Japan, he was wounded by a prematurely exploded bomb. As smoke filled the plane, Erwin picked up the device, carried it to the cockpit, and tossed it out a window. He suffered severe burns, but saved the plane and its crew. (BM.)

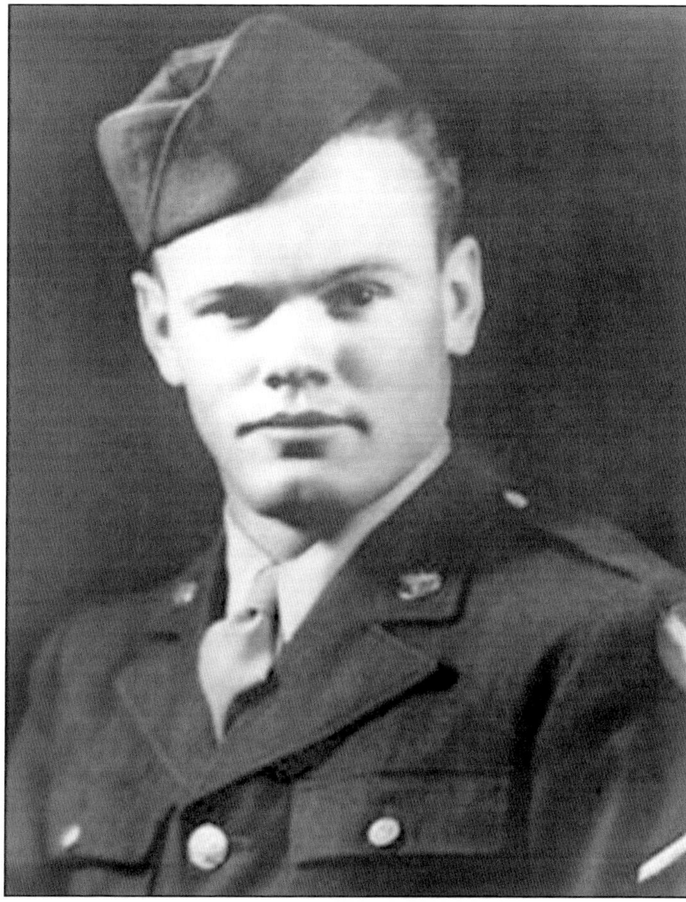

Leeds resident Kenneth L. Farmer, survivor of the infamous Bataan Death March, is shown here presenting an award to the Leeds Boy Scout troop after World War II. During the war, he was held as a prisoner of war when his unit was overrun by the Japanese in the Philippine Islands in 1942. Farmer was liberated by the Russians in Manchuria in 1945. (BM.)

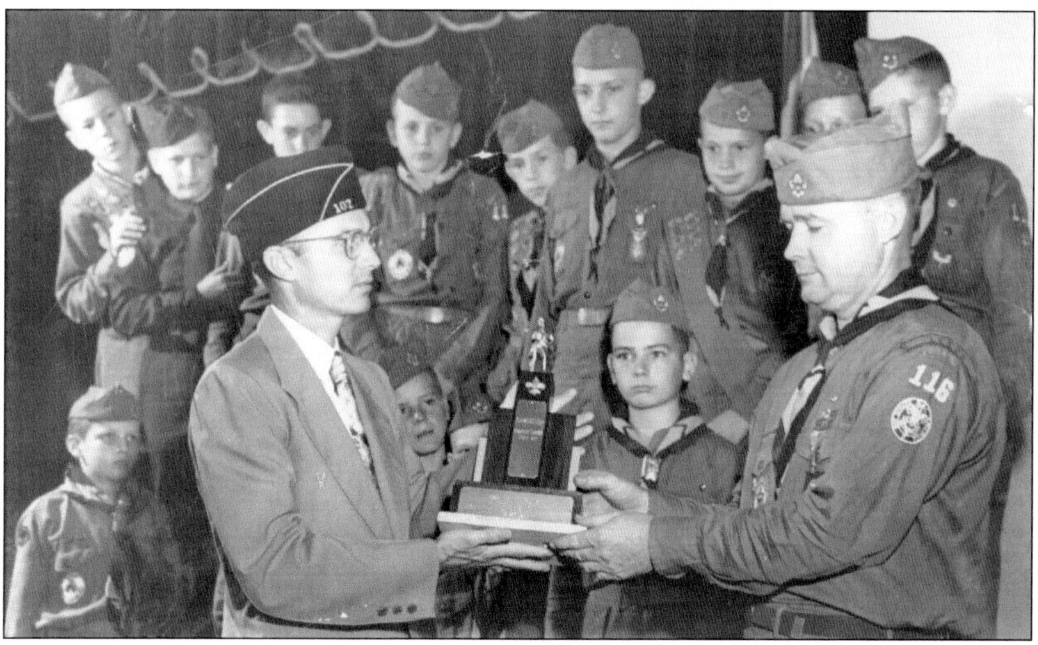

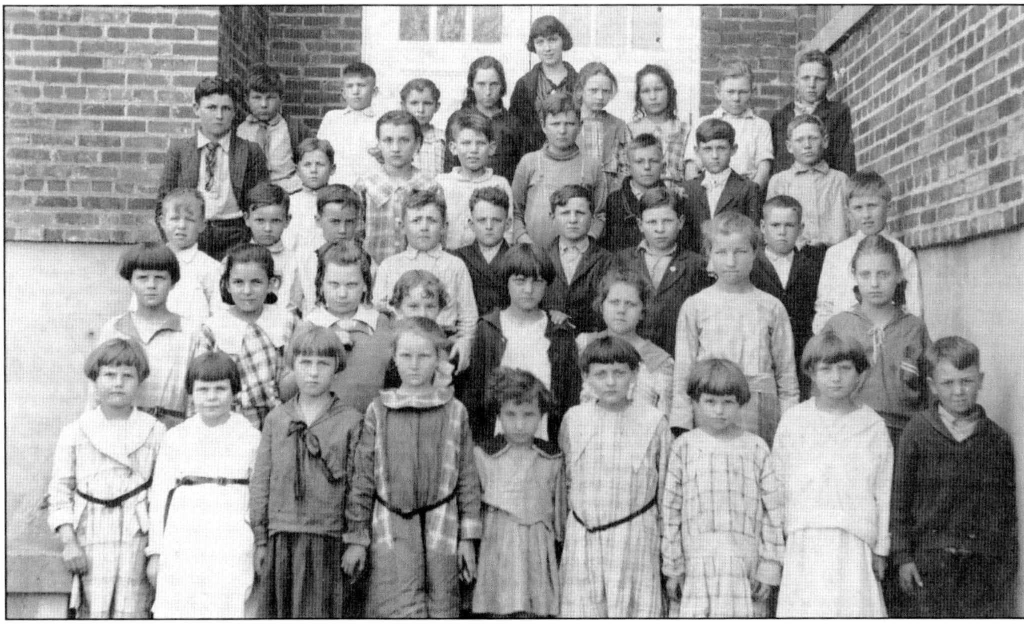

The 1918 fourth-grade class poses for a photograph at Leeds School when America was celebrating the homecoming of her World War I soldiers. Some of these students bore the names of the McLaughlin, Lawley, Spruiell-Spruill, and Nelms-Nelems families. Members of the same families would be in Leeds to celebrate VJ Day. The class would become a part of the World War II generation.

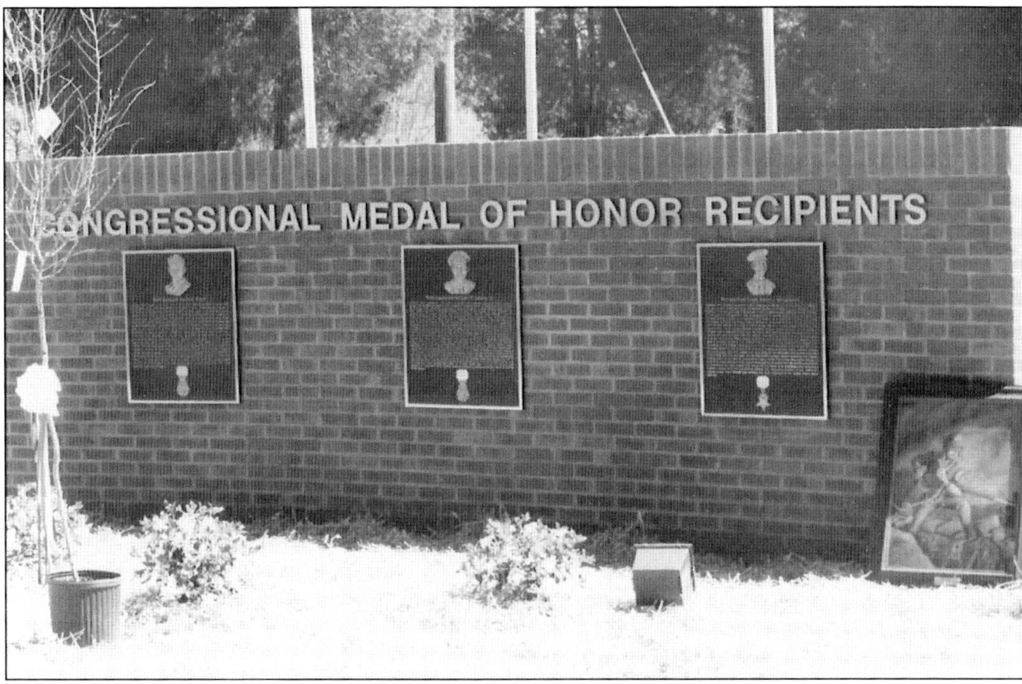

The heroic acts of Alfred L. McLaughlin, William R. Lawley, and Henry E. "Red" Erwin, Leeds's three Congressional Medal of Honor recipients, are recounted on brass markers on a brick monument in Leeds Historical Park. The monument features flags from the three branches of the military service in which the three men of valor served.

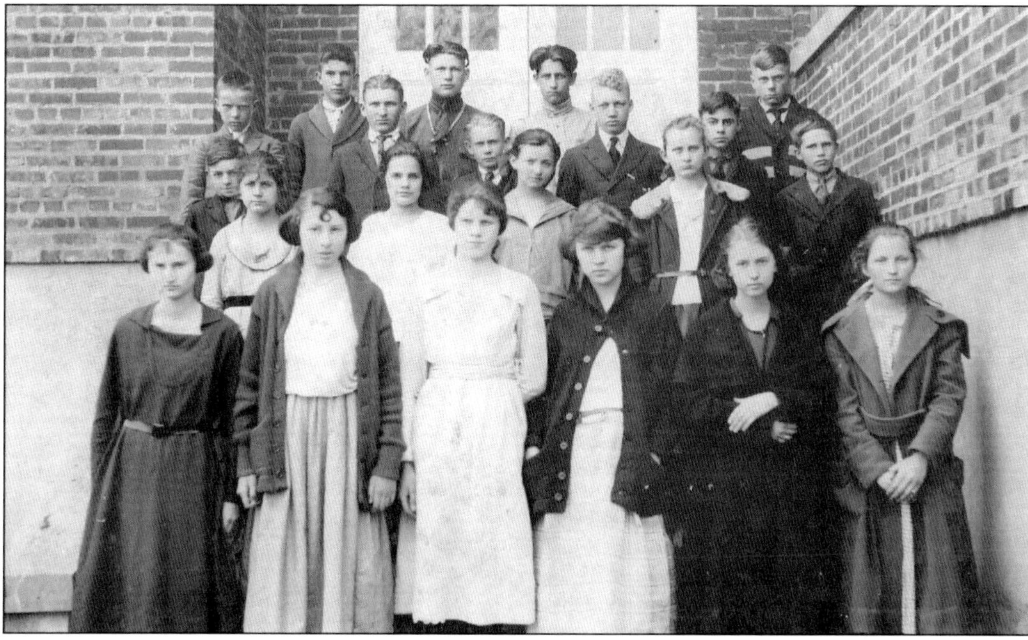

The students in this 1918 sophomore class at Leeds School bear some of the same family names as those on plaques and monuments commemorating Leeds residents who received Congressional Medals of Honor and other awards for distinguished military service. Their family names include Lovell, Jones, Farley, Lawley, Isbell, Whitmire, and Hartsfield.

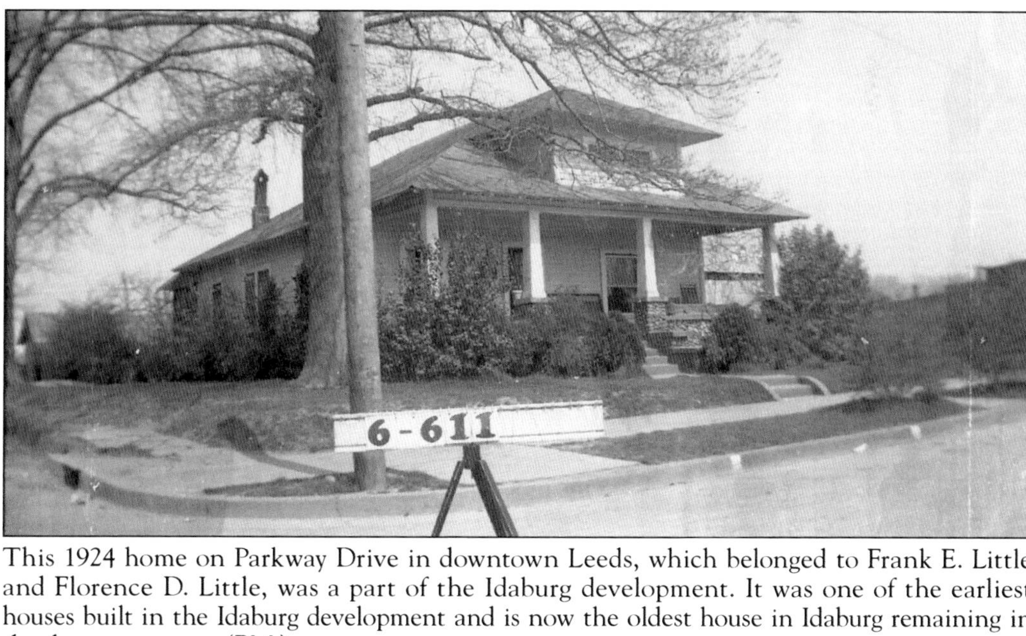

This 1924 home on Parkway Drive in downtown Leeds, which belonged to Frank E. Little and Florence D. Little, was a part of the Idaburg development. It was one of the earliest houses built in the Idaburg development and is now the oldest house in Idaburg remaining in the downtown area. (BM.)

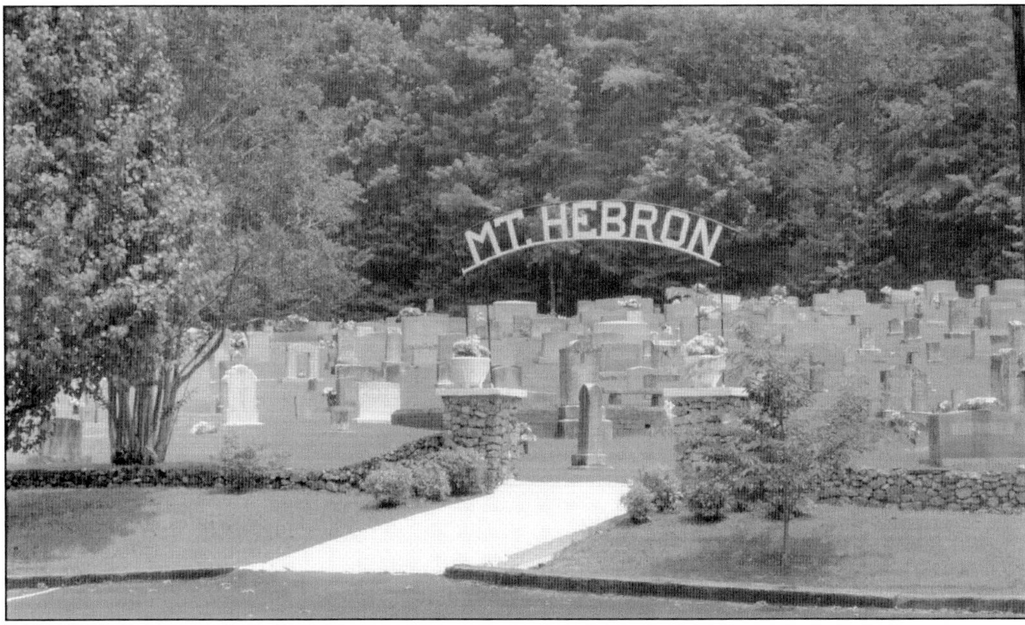

Congressional Medal of Honor recipient Alfred McLaughlin is buried in historical Mount Hebron Cemetery along with veterans from the Civil War to the Vietnam War. In 2003, the University of Alabama Office of Archaeological Research identified 861 graves in the cemetery. The oldest marked grave is for Hepsey Hering, who died October 6, 1848. Mount Hebron Cemetery was added to the Alabama Historic Cemetery Register on August 17, 2009.

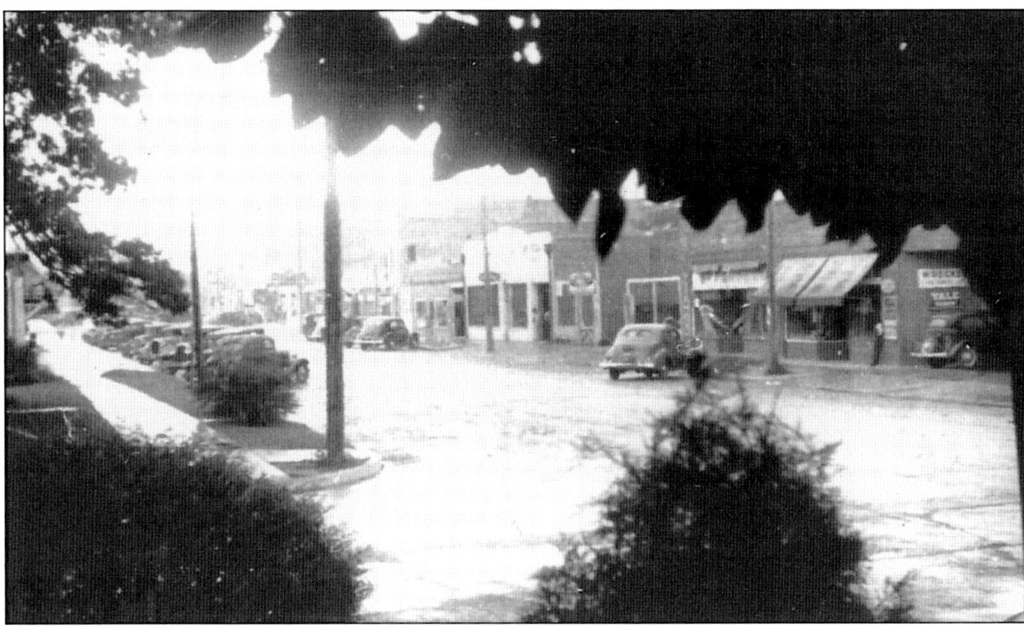

A bird's-eye view of Idaburg, through branches of trees that lined Leeds's streets, shows a bustling downtown area in the 1930s. People who lived nearby and those traveling between Birmingham and Atlanta frequented downtown Leeds, which was a regional commercial hub. By the 1930s, Parkway Drive between Seventh and Eighth Streets, shown here, had replaced Ninth Street as the center of downtown. (LL.)

Nine

Celebrating in a City of Valor

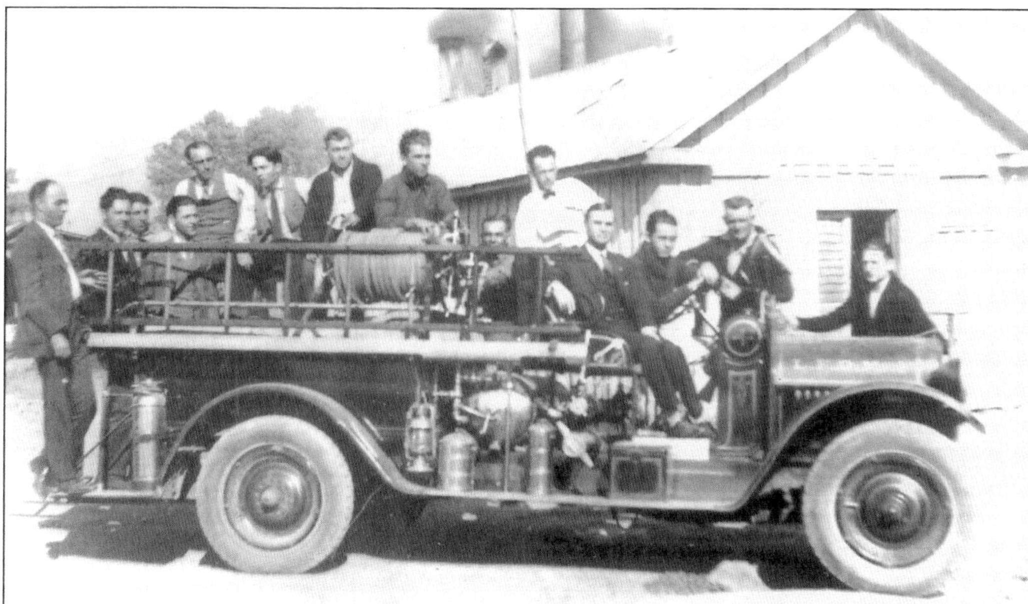

Parades in Leeds often honor military heroes and other famous citizens. Almost every parade in Leeds includes a fire truck. In the 1920s, the names of Leeds's first volunteer firemen included Carlisle, Postelle, Pool-Poole, Pledger, Stone, Parham, Lee, Hartsfield, Farley, Rew, Bicknell, Calloway, Funderberg, and Dorough-Dorrough. In 1946, police chief J.W. Isbell was appointed by the city council as chief of the fire department. Although the city bought its first fire truck in 1925, the Leeds Fire Department was staffed by volunteers until 1969. (LHS.)

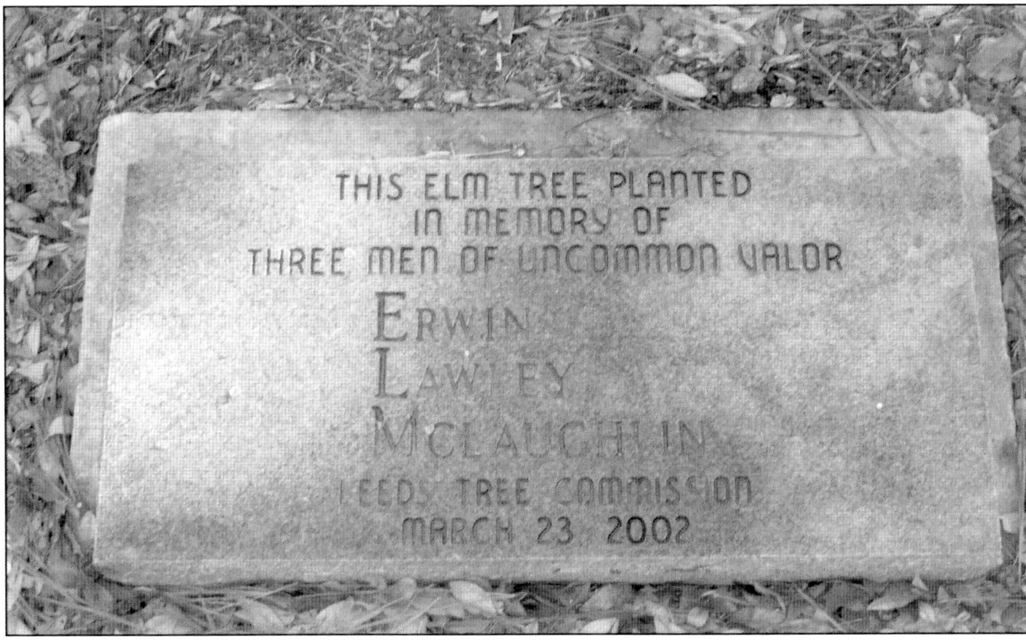

A marker at the base of an elm tree in Leeds Historical Park pays homage to the Leeds Congressional Medal of Honor recipients. The tree and the marker were presented to the city of Leeds by the Leeds Tree Commission. The commission plants trees on city property and works with the Leeds Street Department to maintain all trees on city property and within the city rights-of-way.

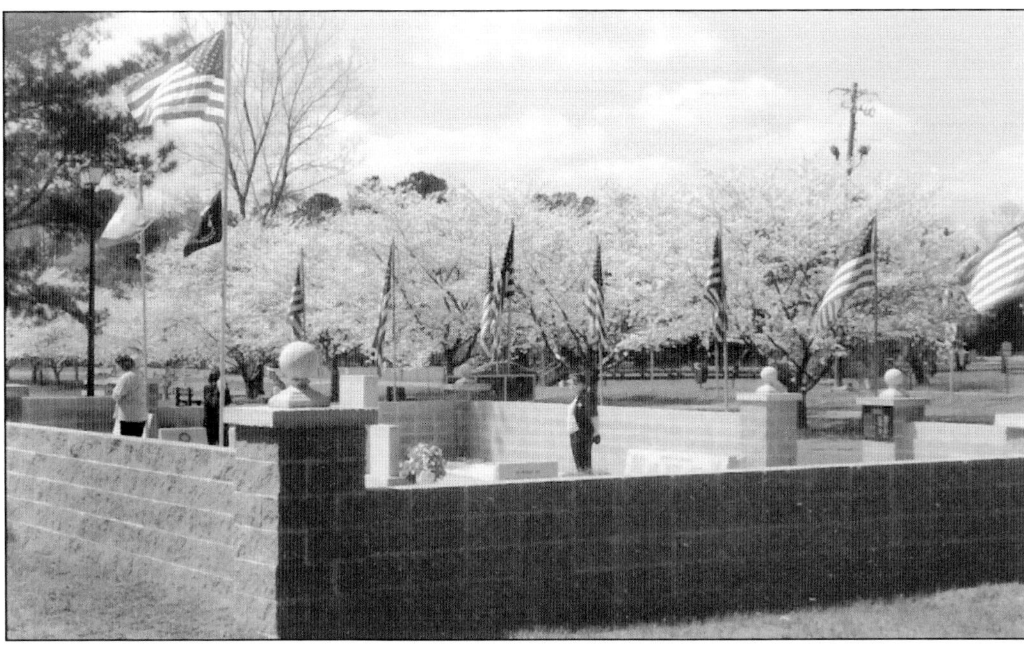

Leeds Memorial Park serves as a memorial to all veterans from the Leeds area, including those killed or missing in action. The park evolved from an Avenue of Flags salute to veterans in downtown Leeds. Following the development of the front part of the park, all the flags and markers were moved from Parkway Drive to the park.

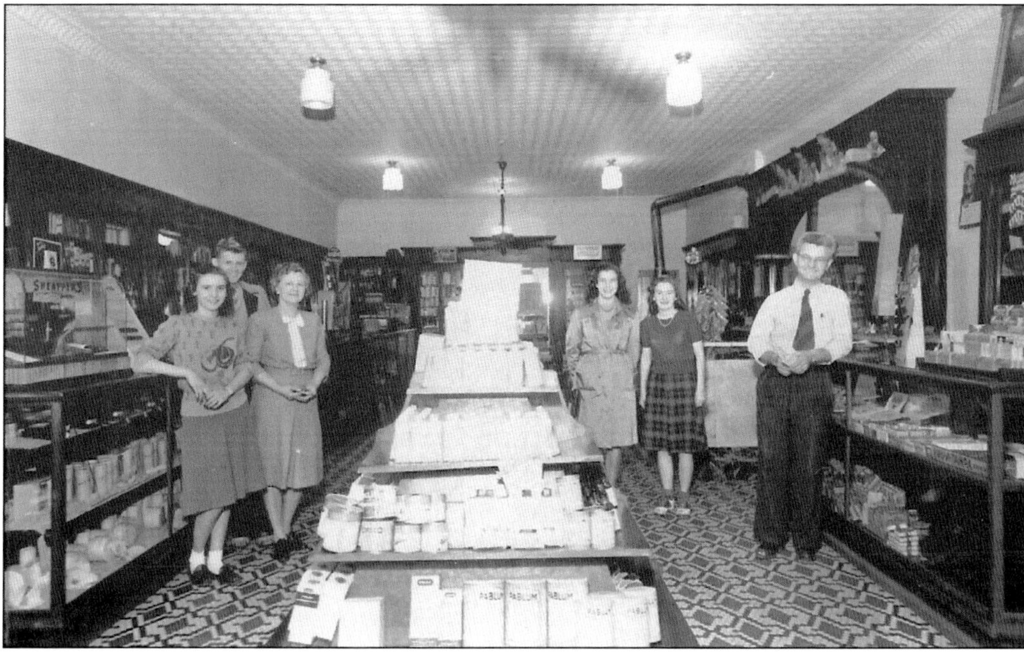

Spruiell Drugs was in its second location during the 1950s. Teenage girls in their bobby socks frequented the soda fountain after school for banana splits or cherry sodas. Occasionally, they might ask Lindley Spruiell for medicine for a sick puppy. Other requests from schoolgirls concerned cosmetics, and Bessie Morton Spruiell was the expert in that department. (LL.)

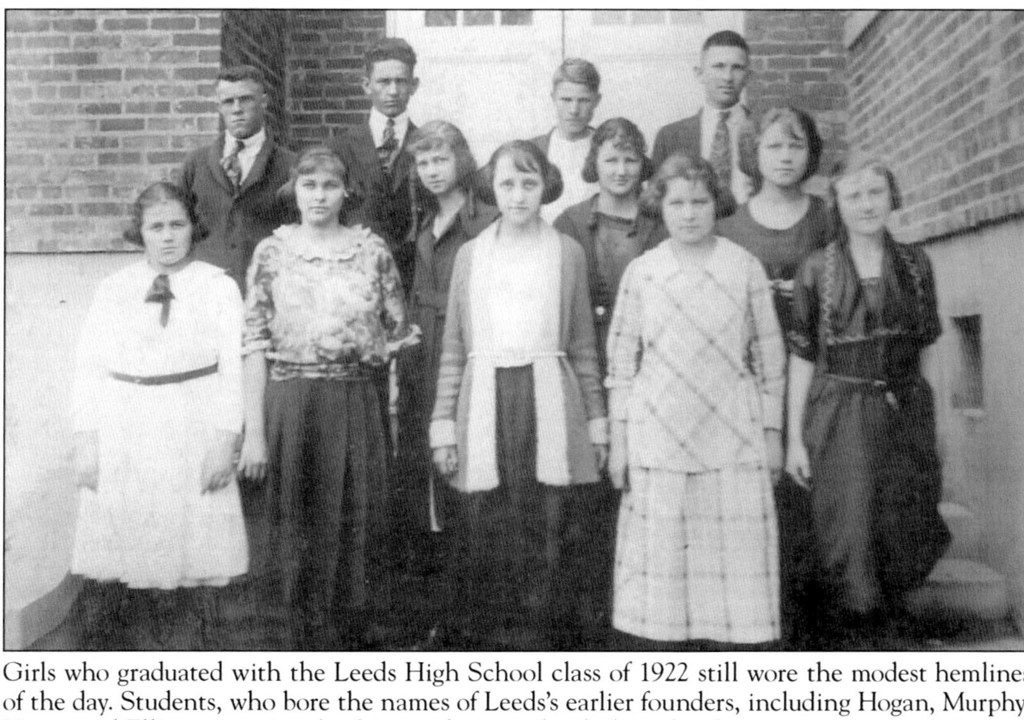

Girls who graduated with the Leeds High School class of 1922 still wore the modest hemlines of the day. Students, who bore the names of Leeds's earlier founders, including Hogan, Murphy, Hurst, and Elliott, were involved in producing school plays that became major entertainment in Leeds. (LL.)

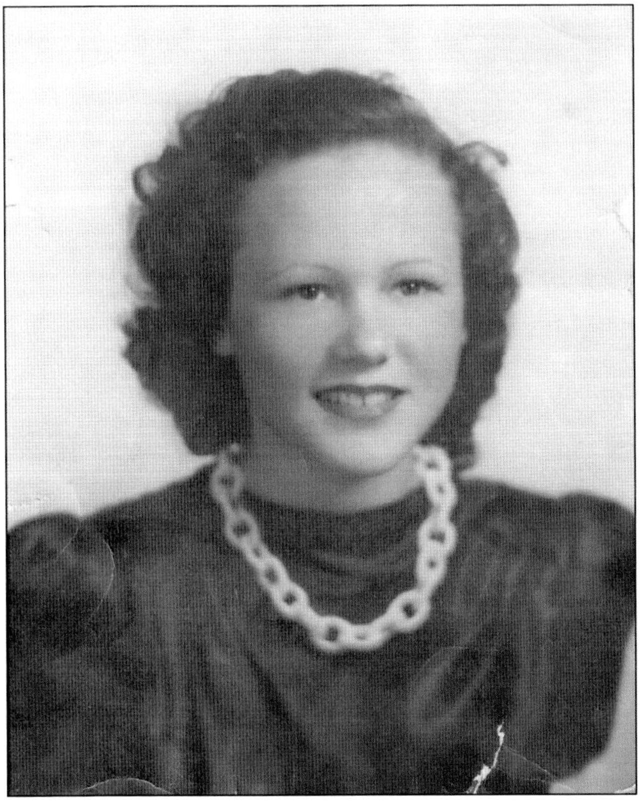

Mildred Nelms, a 1940s housewife, spent time raising her children, serving as PTA president, and shopping. Her ice, groceries, *Birmingham News*, and Spruiell's Dairy milk were delivered to her house. She shopped in downtown Leeds. On Saturdays, she and her daughter boarded a Greyhound Bus at Power's Café and went to Birmingham, where they shopped at Loveman's department store.

On the eve of the Great Depression, the first class of Leeds Primary School graduated. Prof. J.J. Harrison held ceremonies for students from families with names that included Hill, Moore, and Thomas. Although the students graduated into a world where jobs were scarce, they found positions in a variety of occupations, including nursing. (LL.)

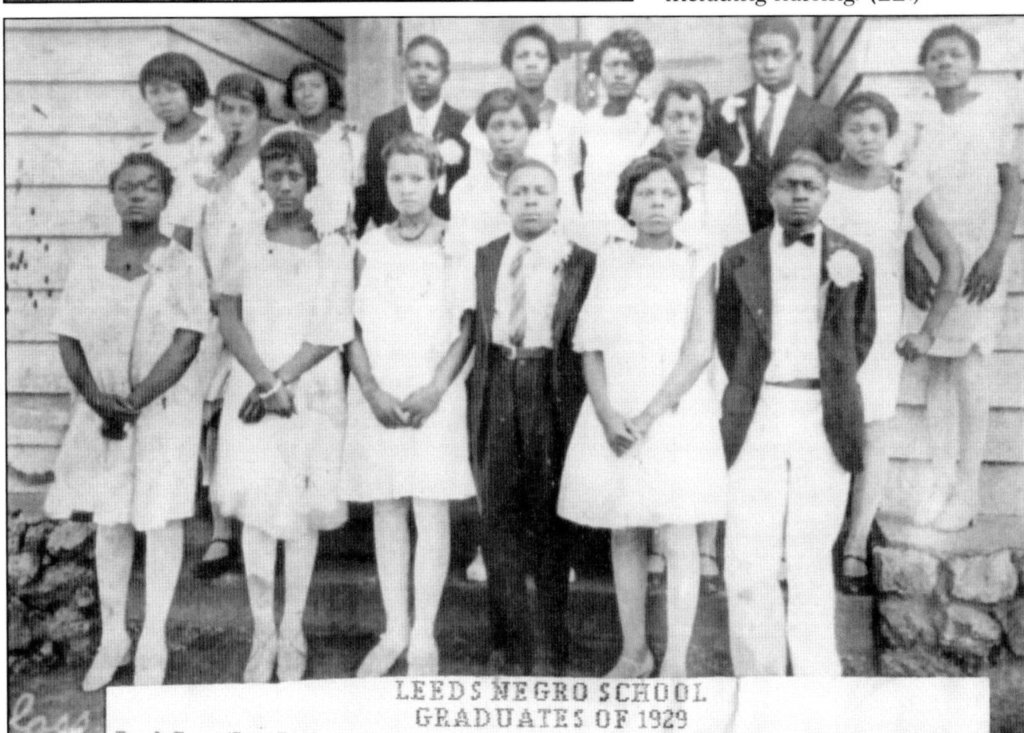

In the 1940s, satin reigned over America's fashion, while cotton fabric served as everyday apparel for young women. Billie Joyce Lee, whose ancestors included Needham Lee, wore a prom dress made of satin in this photograph. She posed with Jimmy Weidenbach, the young man she would marry. Within the next year, he left for the Korean War.

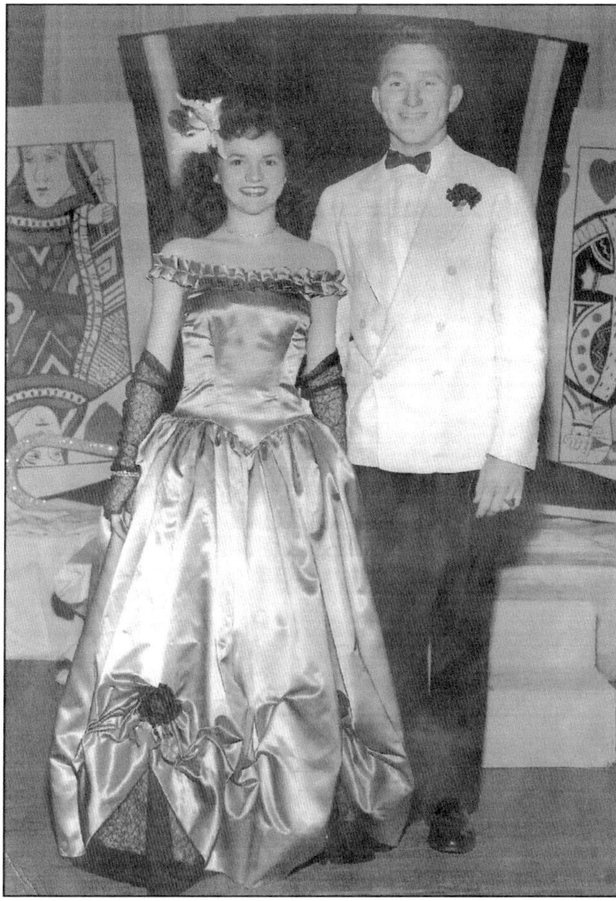

The last livery in Leeds belonged to the Hagwood family. In earlier days, this traditional livery provided horseshoeing. But shortly before it closed in the 1960s, the building included a small machine shop that repaired irons and other household appliances. The livery was the last remaining business in Leeds that harkened back to the days of horses and buggies. (BM.)

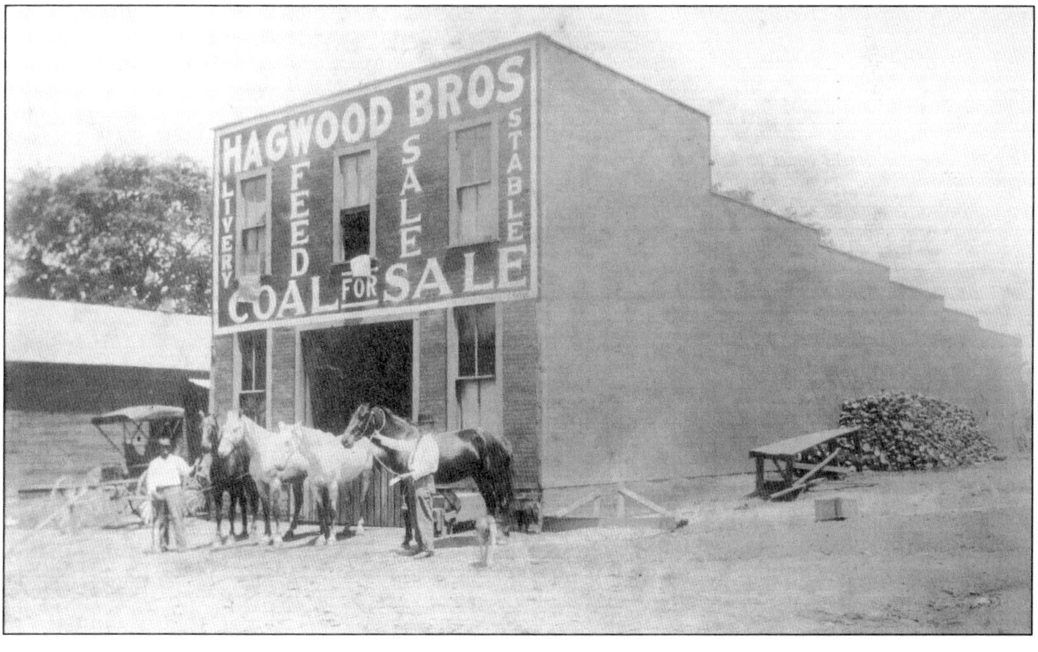

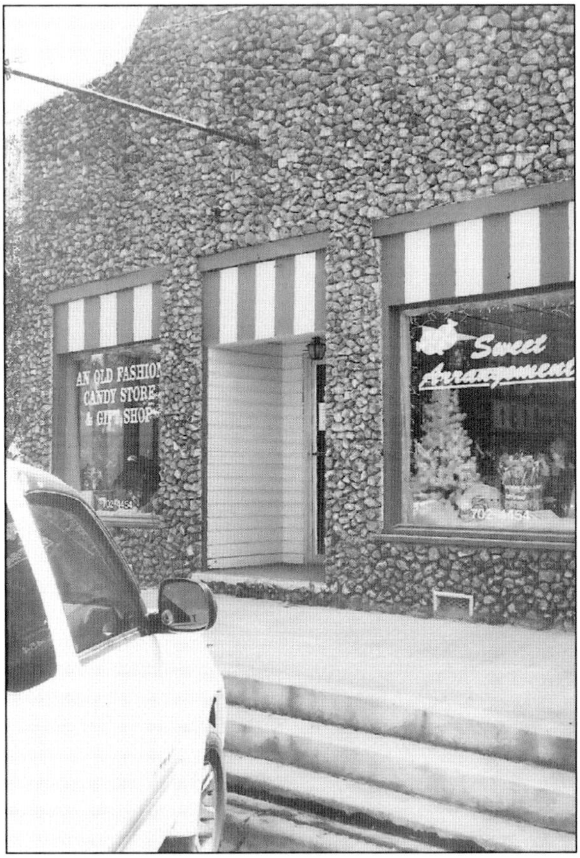

This field rock building is located on the corner of Parkway Drive and historic Ninth Street in downtown Leeds. It was previously owned by C.C. Coupland. More recently, it was a quaint, old-fashioned candy store that was the delight of club women, who frequented the store to buy candy to be served at club meetings.

The house pictured here served as the parsonage for Leeds's historic First Baptist Church. The parsonage was built in 1947. The house looks basically the way it did when it was built, except for changes to the roof. Many women in Leeds have memories of being married in the parlor of the parsonage or dressing in the parsonage to be married in the church across the street.

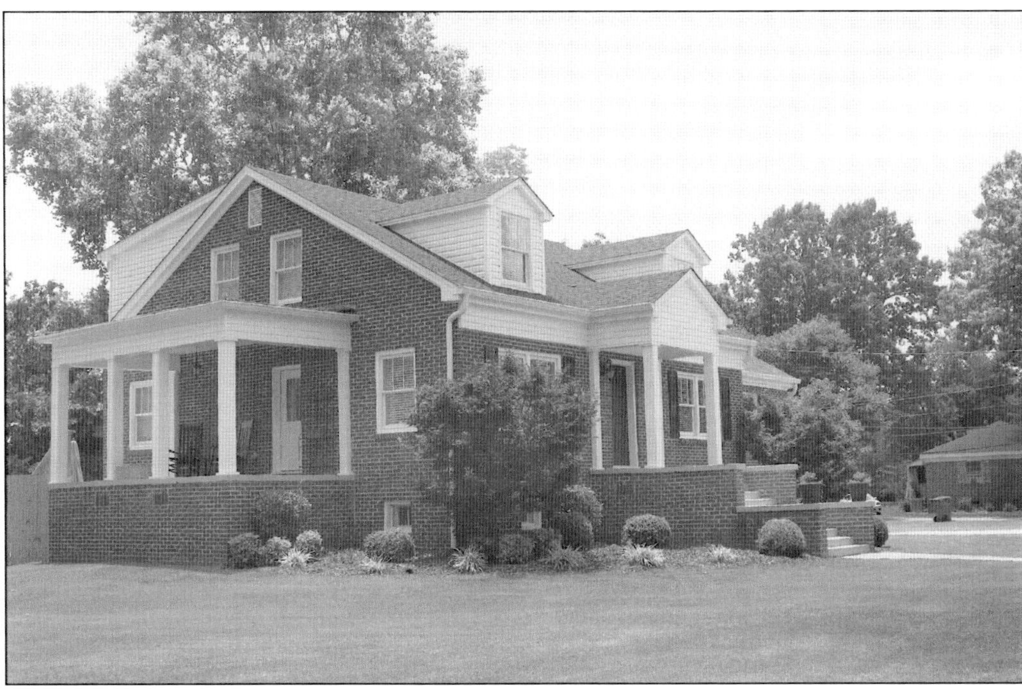

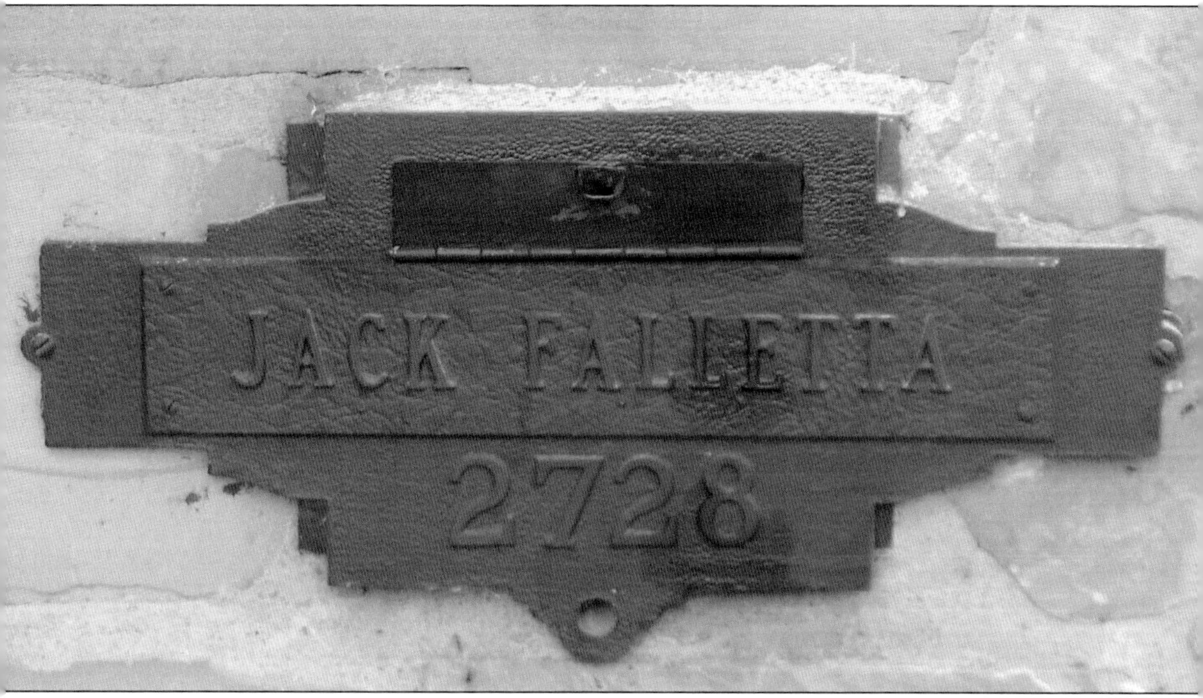

Jack and Imogene Wright Falletta used their house to welcome hundreds of guests through the years. In 1955, Imogene entertained one of her most famous guests, Elvis Presley. Her son-in-law, who was a disc jockey at the University of Alabama in Tuscaloosa, recognized Elvis at Power's Café, a local restaurant and bus stop in downtown Leeds. He asked Elvis for an interview for his radio show. Elvis agreed, and they went to Falletta's house, where he spent a large part of the evening interviewing. Leeds teenagers gathered at the house throughout the interview. Local young people continued to enjoy Imogene Falletta's hospitality for most of her life. In a fitting tribute to a gracious woman, the city of Leeds, in 2008, opened a visitor center in the old Falletta home that includes the office of the Leeds Area Chamber of Commerce. The home also serves as a formal mayor's office and meeting rooms until the newly proposed city hall is built.

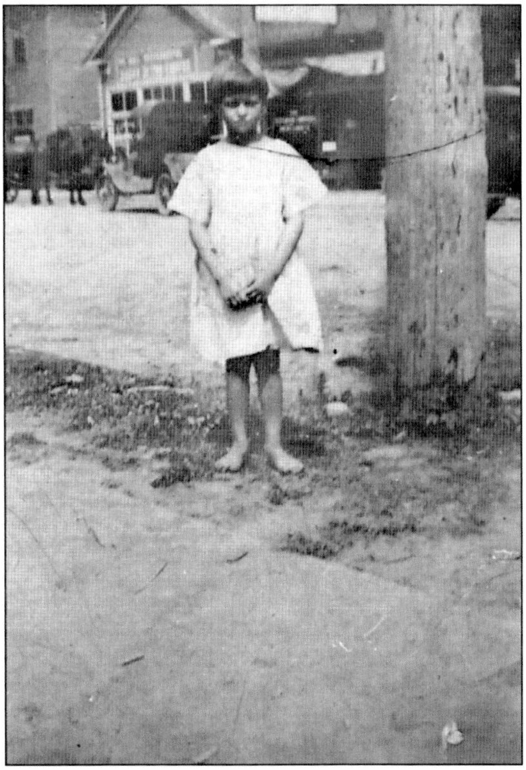

During World War I, the downtown streets of Leeds were still unpaved. This 1921 photograph shows a child playing in bare feet on a dirt street and mules pulling up beside early model Fords. By 1928, the first cement street paving was completed in downtown Leeds. By the 1930s, the downtown area was completely paved. (LL.)

Dirt trails on the Leeds Scenic Byway were frequented by boys who followed the trails to caves with walls covered with early Native American drawings and modern graffiti. Some featured streams of water trickling down the walls. Aquifers and fresh water springs gave even more delight, and arrowheads could be dug out of the dirt.

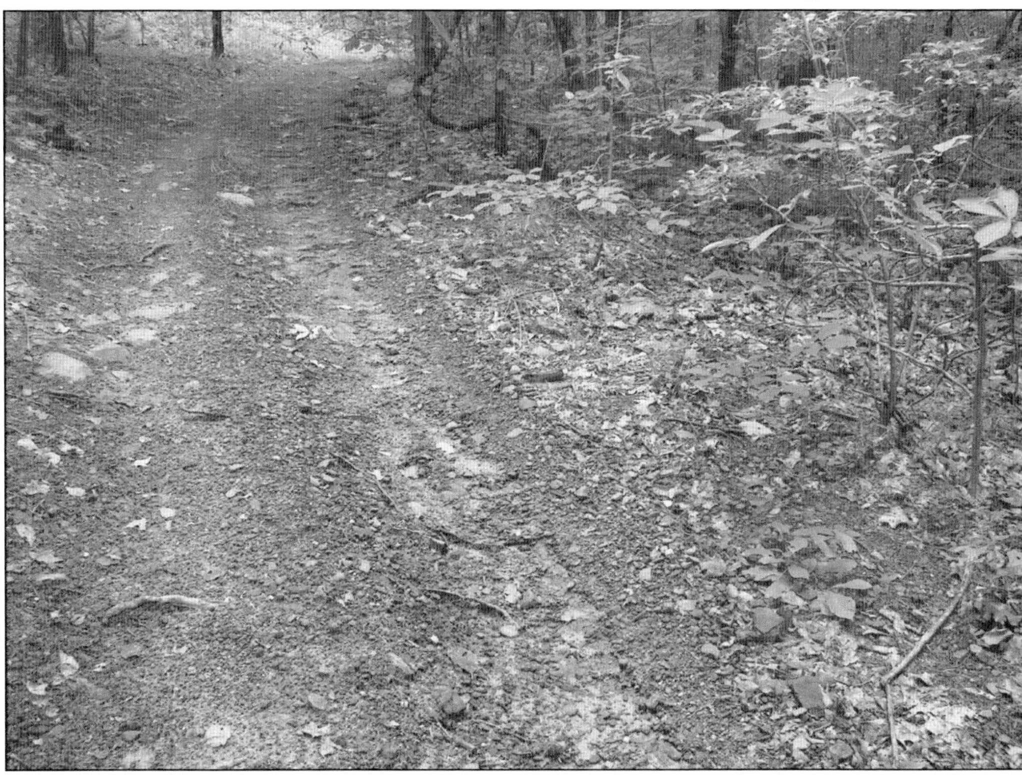

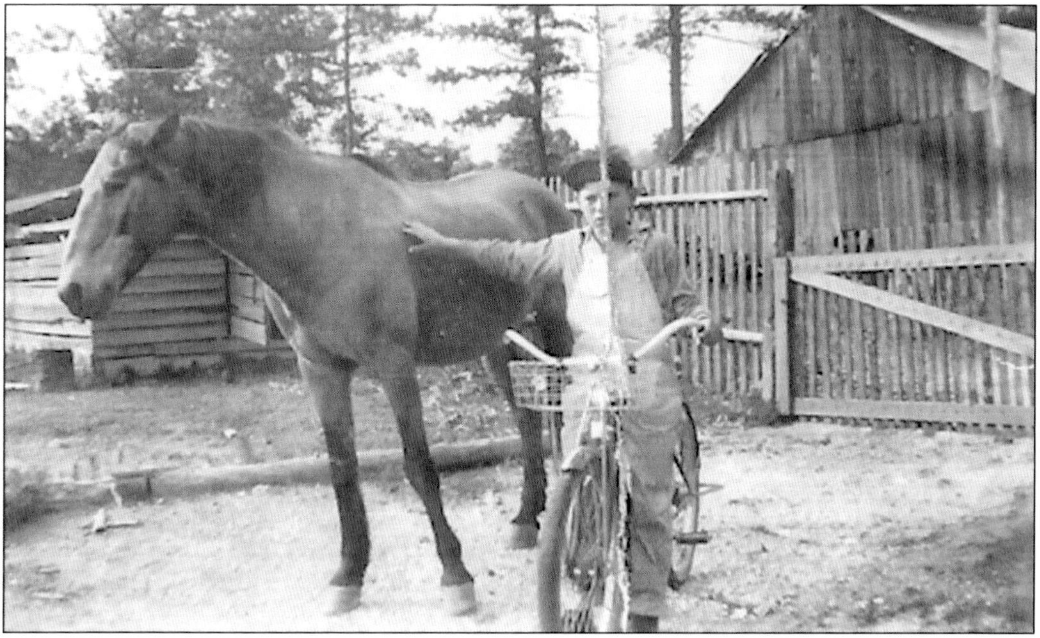

This 1937 photograph shows a farm scene on the stagecoach route in a bucolic valley that remains Leeds's quiet treasure. A strong sense of history remains throughout the Cahaba Valley at Leeds, where the silent pastures are interrupted only by the sound of distant trains reminding us that we are in the 21st century.

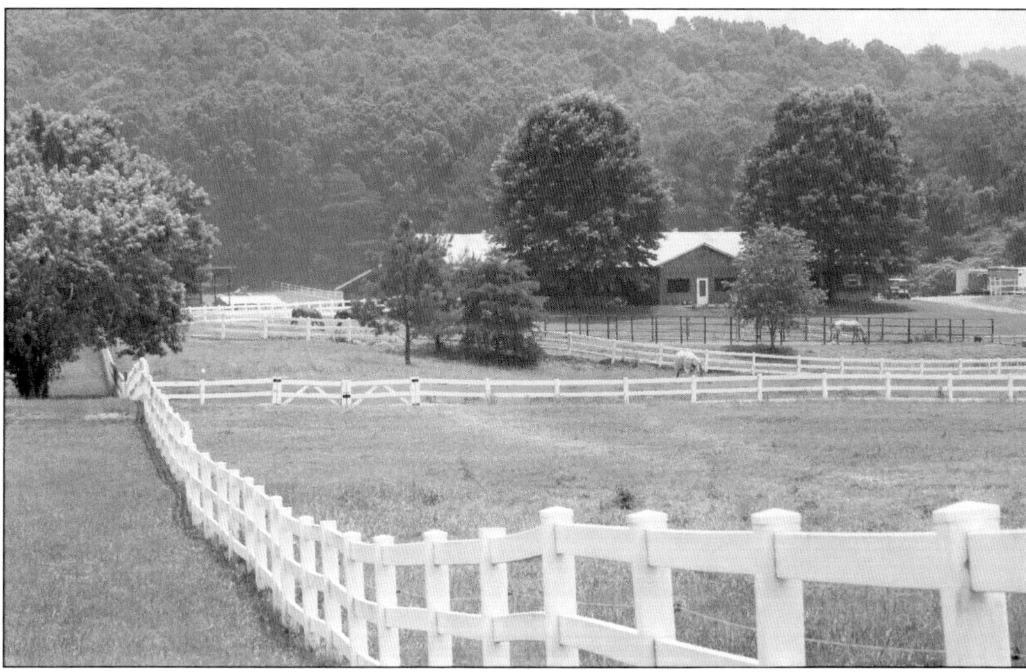

A visitor can spend an afternoon looking at white fences that seem to disappear into a mountainside and wondering where in the tangled woods is the screaming cougar heard the night before. Leeds children grow up with a sense of poetry and art, and Leeds shares its poets with the rest of the state. William Young Elliott, a former poet laureate of Alabama, is a native of Leeds.

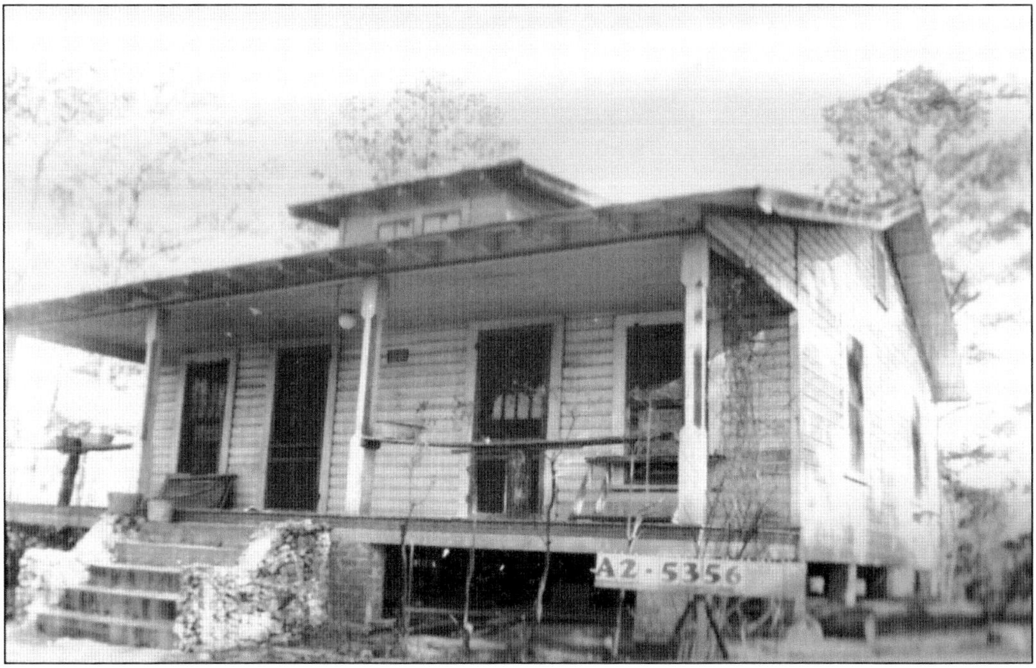

Bungalows, like this one built in 1919, are Craftsman-style homes. In Leeds, they have been occupied by families whose names have been on mailboxes here for almost a century. These names include DeShazo, McLaughlin, and Lee, all descendants of Civil War veterans. It was stylish to build this type of bungalow between 1925 and 1949, and the DeShazo family built them as single-family dwellings in that time period. (BL.)

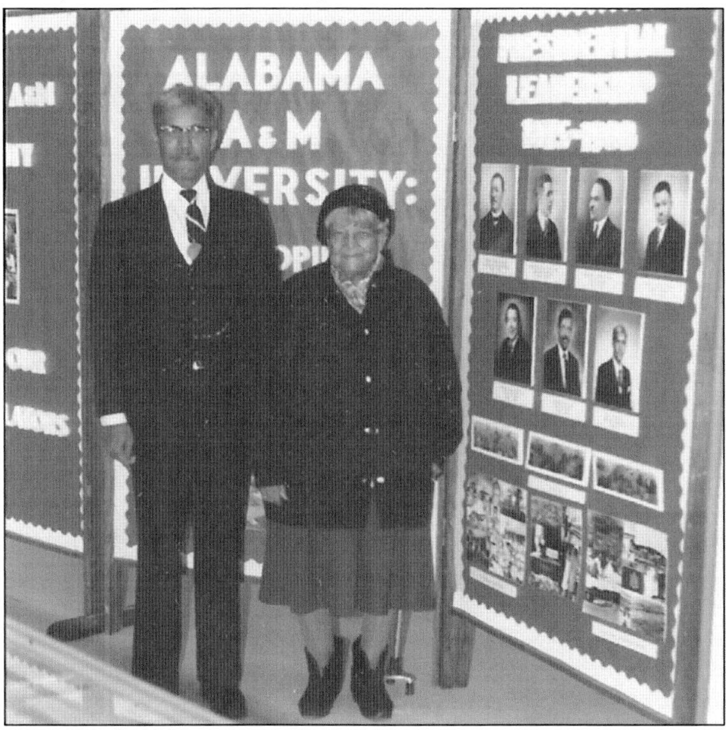

Carl Marbury and his mother, the daughter of Ciscero Davis and Melissa Hood Davis, posed for this photograph in 1988 when Carl was named president of Alabama A&M University. Marbury was previously a student at Alabama A&M and received a bachelor of science degree from that institution. (Photograph courtesy of Carl Marbury.)

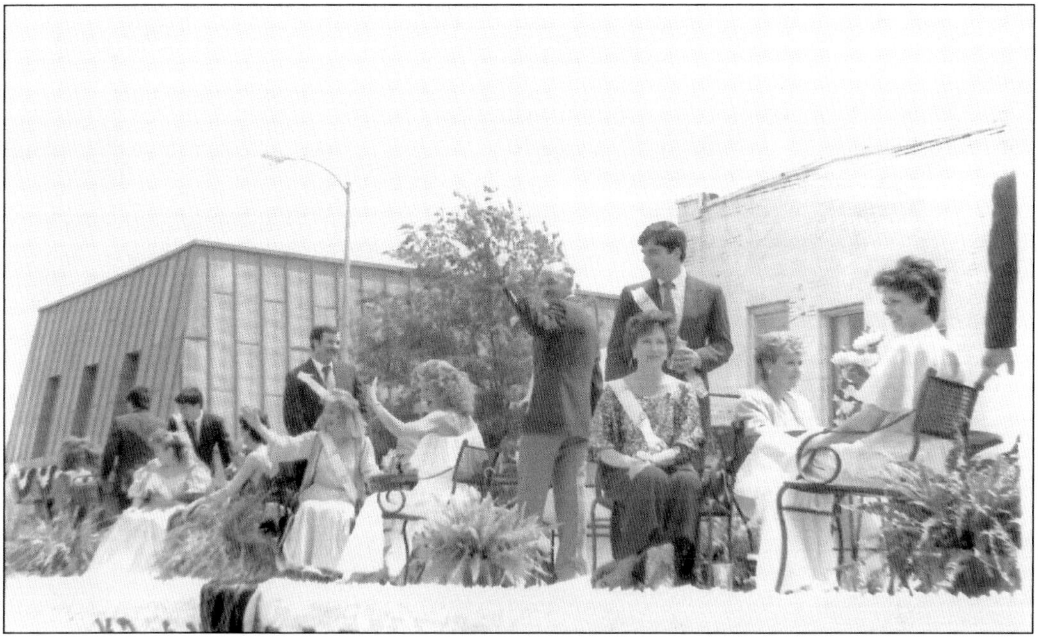

The Ninth Street buildings along this parade route look almost the same as they did during the parades that honored Alfred Lee McLaughlin, one of Leeds's Congressional Medal of Honor recipients; Paige Phillips (Parnell), Leeds's Miss Alabama; and Charles Barkley, Leeds's Olympian. Homecoming queens, Santa Claus, and stagecoaches have frequented the streets of Leeds at festive times of year. (LL.)

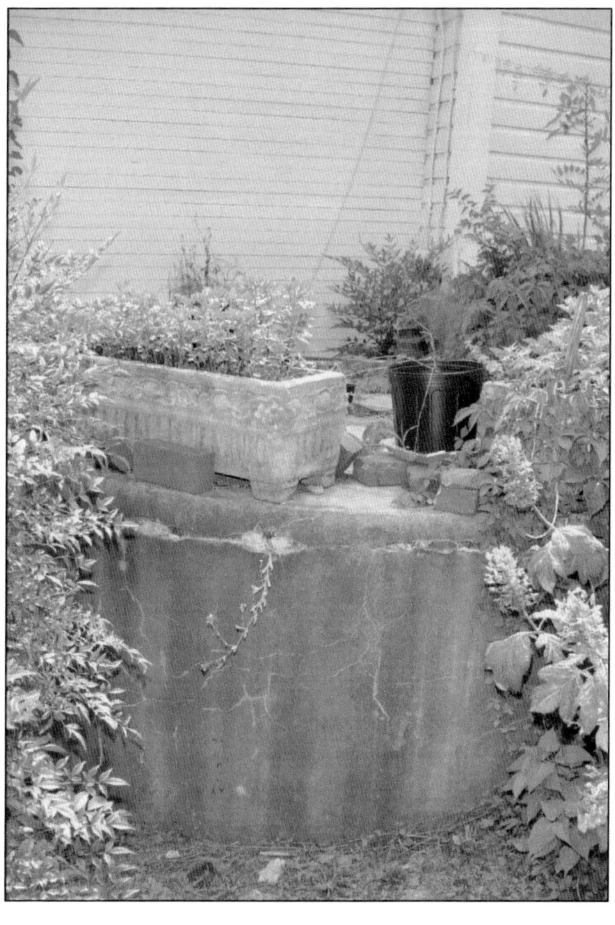

A cistern that stands beside the William A. Whitmire house still catches rainwater for household use. In 2005, Whitmire family members gathered in the home of Cecil Whitmire to receive a historic marker for the William A. Whitmire house, which was 100 years old. Cecil, who died in 2010, is remembered for restoring the Historic Alabama Theatre and Mighty Wurlitzer pipe organ in downtown Birmingham.

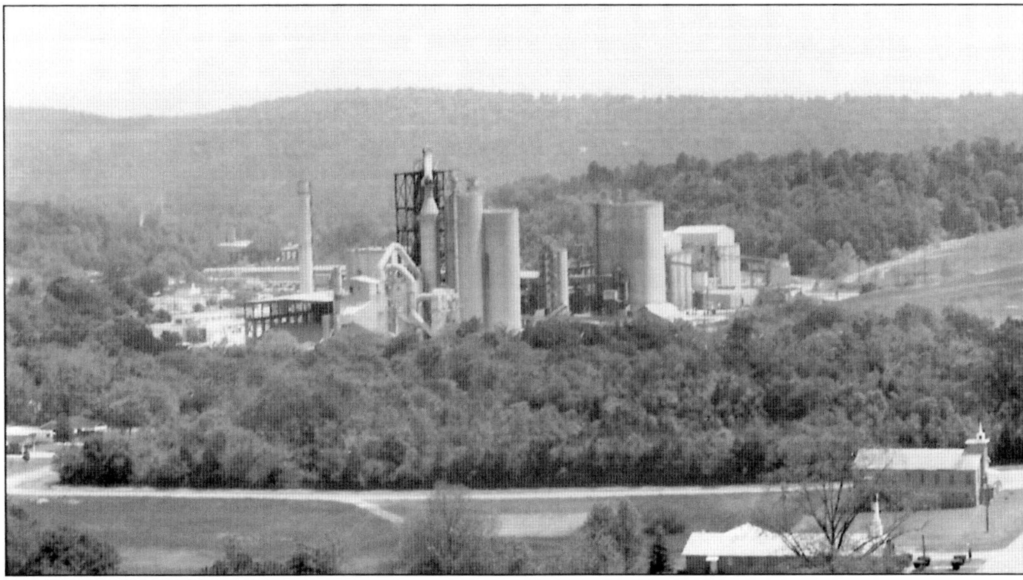

When Martin Luther King Jr. came through Alabama with the Southern Christian Leadership Conference in 1967, the group established a campground in Leeds near the cement plant, shown here. In the foreground of this aerial photograph, a site for such a campground can be seen near historic African American churches and schools. (LL.)

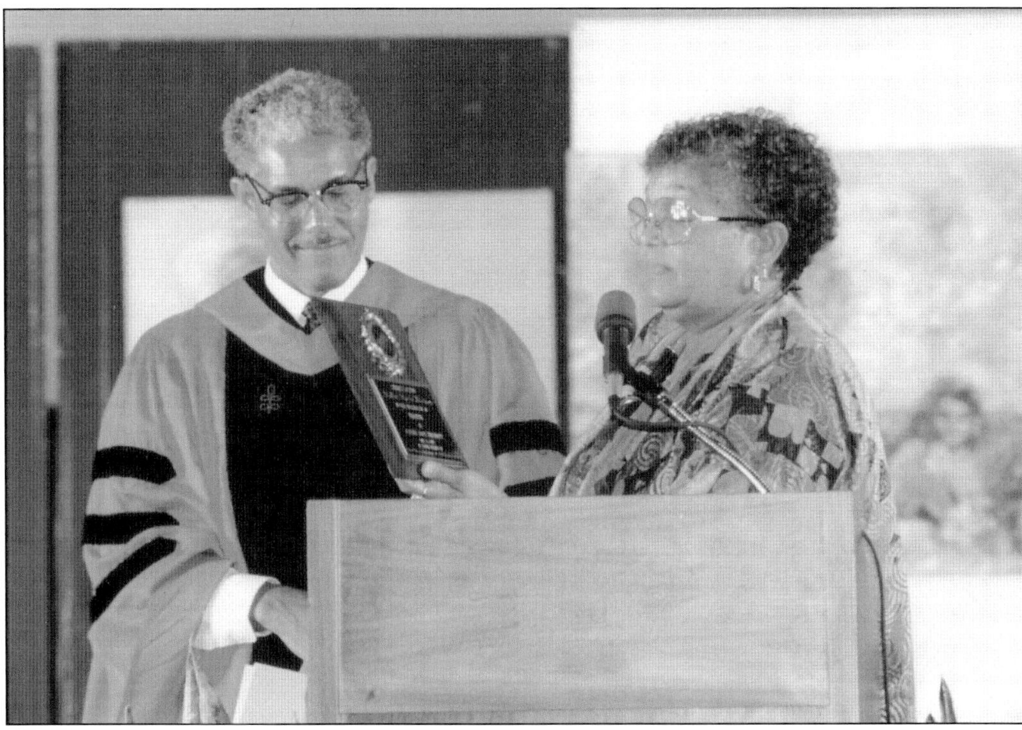

Leeds native Carl Marbury, shown here, is the grandson of Ciscero Davis and Melissa Hood Davis. Marbury received a bachelor of divinity degree and a master of arts degree from Oberlin College, a master of divinity degree from Vanderbilt University, and a PhD from Harvard University. (Photograph courtesy of Carl Marbury.)

A native and resident of Leeds, Paige Phillips (Parnell) was selected as Miss Alabama in 1980 and as first runner-up in the Miss America pageant the same year at the age of 17. She donated her Miss Alabama crown to the Leeds Historical Society, and it is on display at the society's Bass House Museum. In 2011, she was a candidate for the Alabama House of Representatives District 45 seat. (BM.)

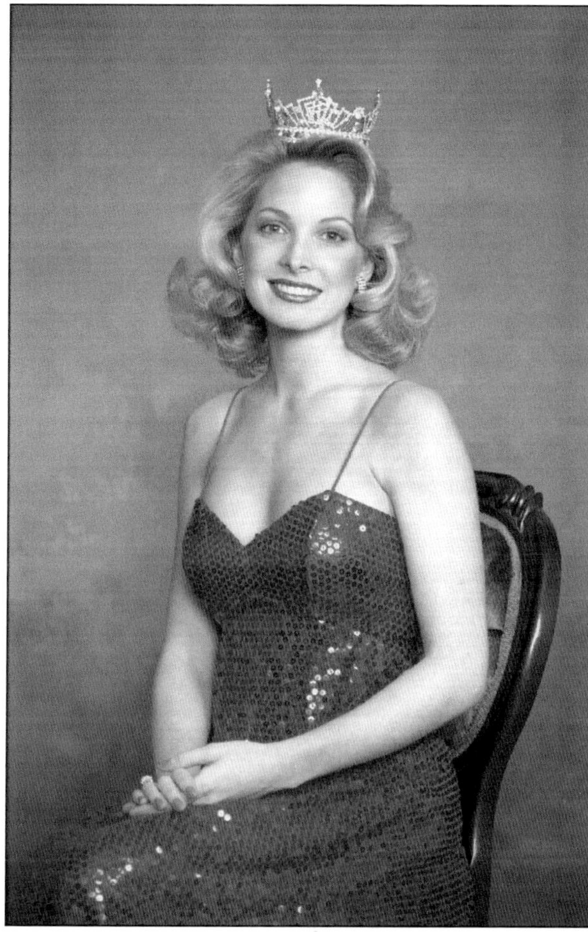

This building, pictured in 1937, now houses the library. In 1998, the name was changed to the Jane Culbreth Leeds Library in honor of Culbreth (1918–2009), who chaired the library's board of directors for 40 years. The first woman on the city council, she served as a councilwoman for 24 years. Her dream was for a larger library for Leeds, which is now in development. (Courtesy of Frank Little.)

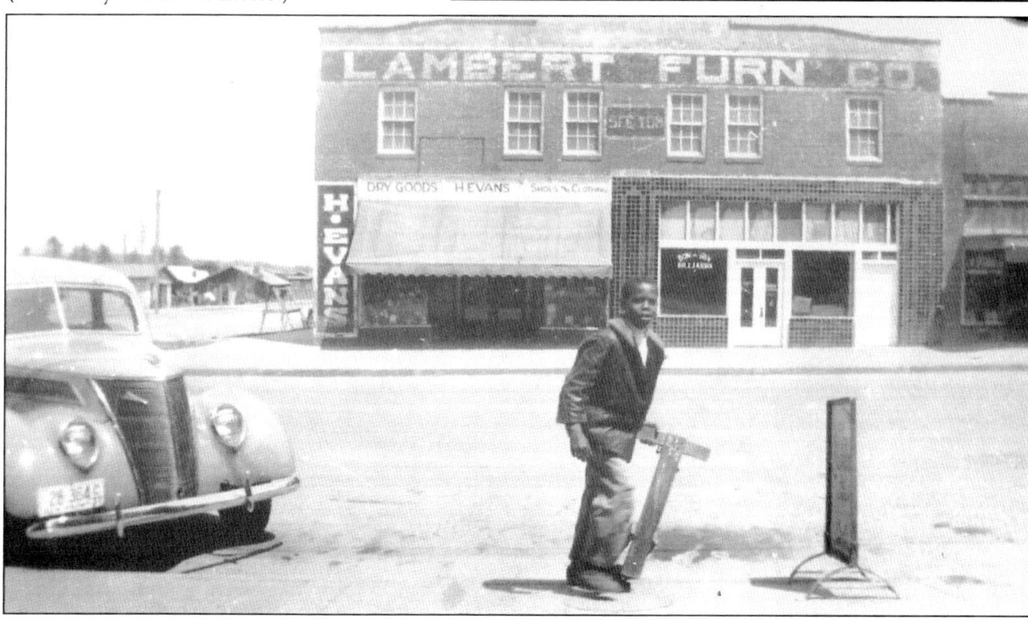

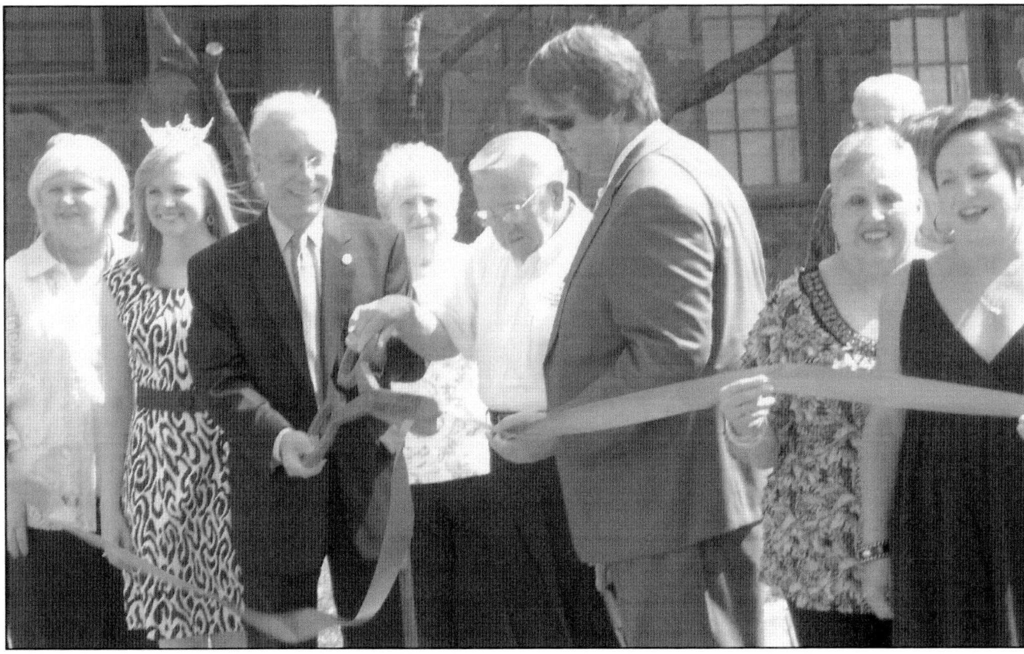

Alabama Tourism director Lee Sentell and Leeds mayor Eric Patterson open the Leeds Scenic Byway. Other dignitaries at the event included Sandra McGuire of the Leeds Area Chamber of Commerce, the reigning Miss Alabama, Liz McCormick of the Woman's Literary Club, and Charlotte Earnest and Susan Carswell, city council members.

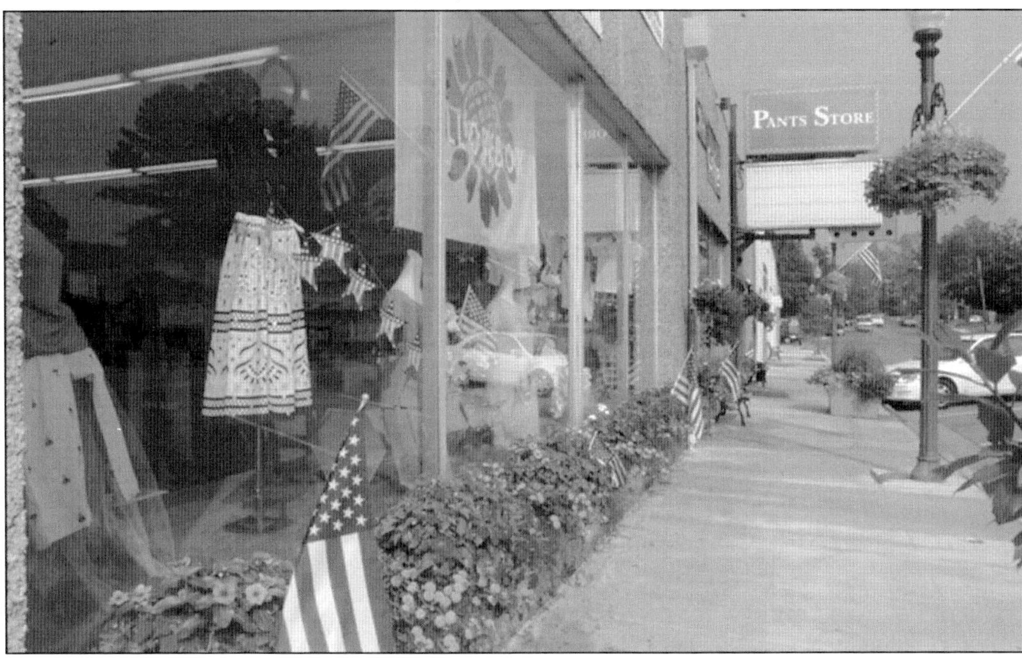

Mickey Gee's father brought the Pants Store to Leeds in 1950. The store was a hit from the beginning. People came to shop there from three counties, and their cars filled Parkway Drive in front of the store. The Gee family has been consistently supportive of Leeds during good times and bad.

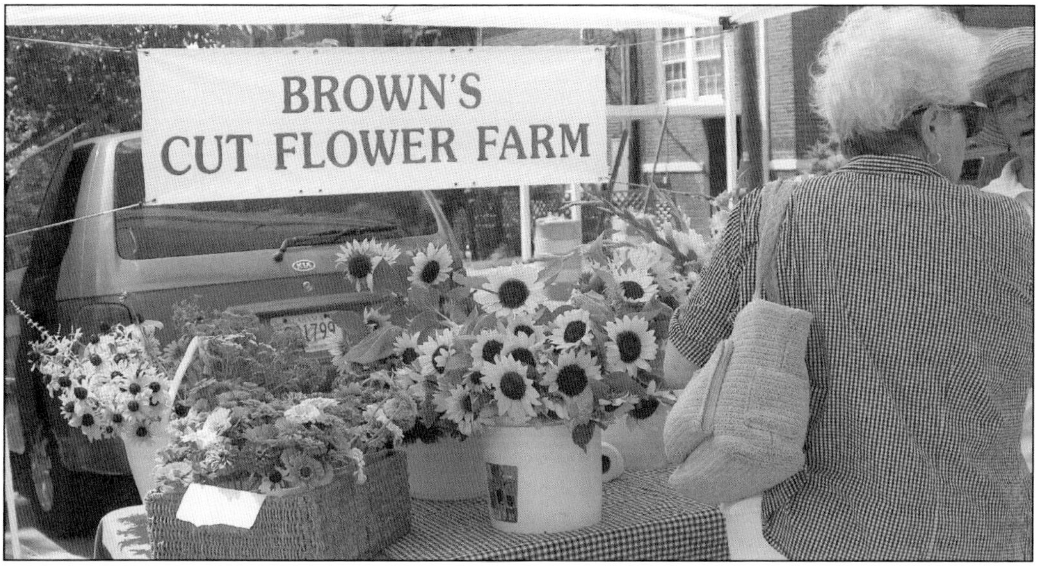

Leeds's farmers market, which draws farmers from two counties, is a favorite destination for Leeds residents. The flowers pictured are from St. Clair County. The farmers market, which is sponsored by the Leeds Chamber of Commerce, is open each Friday afternoon from the beginning of June until the end of August.

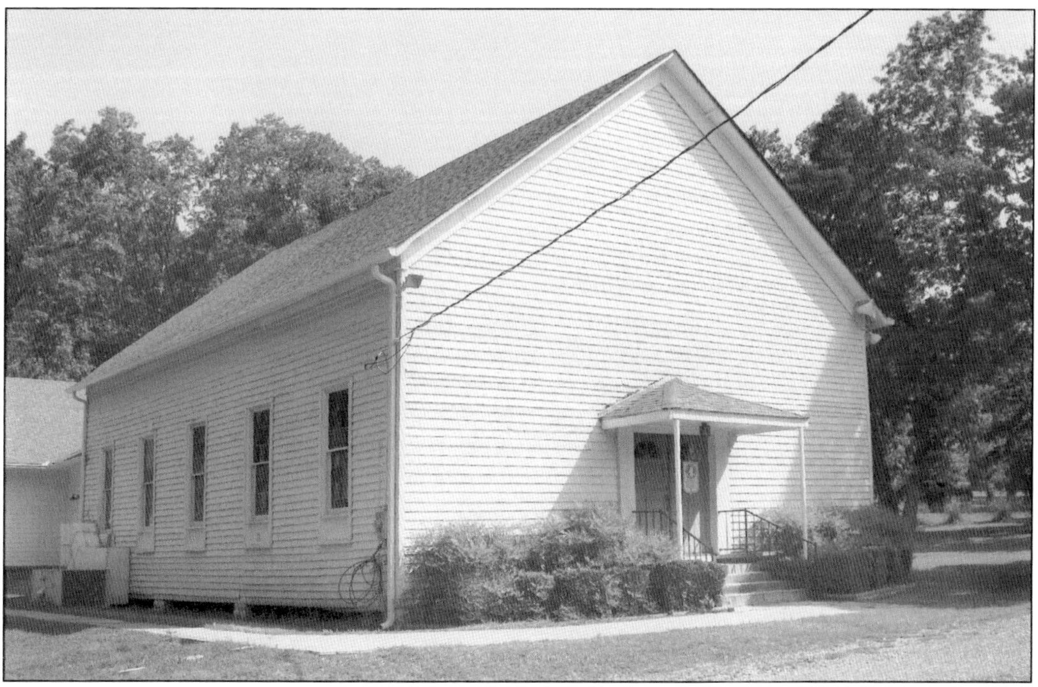

Historic Cahaba United Methodist Church, established in 1896, exemplifies churches of the period. The current congregation has restored the church building and keeps it maintained. The cemetery behind the church is significant. Names from important families in the area are found on gravestones there.

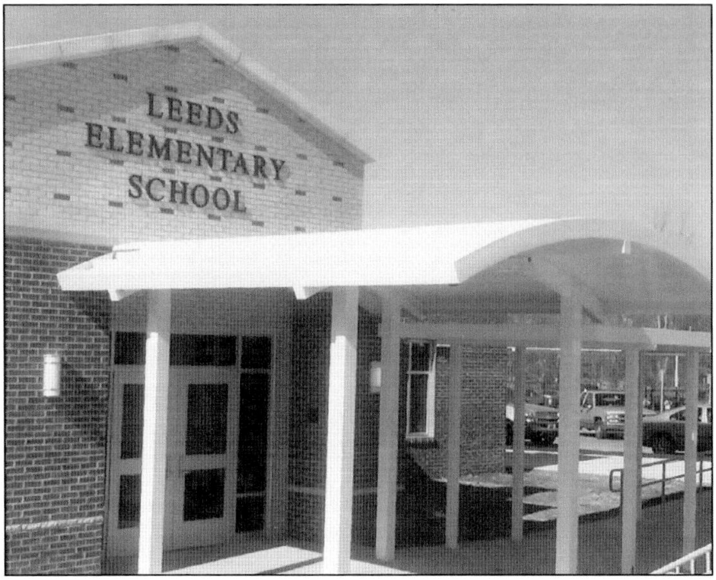

Leeds Elementary School, which is located at the corner of Alabama Highway 119 and US Highway 78, has been renovated since the Leeds City Schools began operations in 2008. The mission of Leeds City Schools is to develop confident, productive young people and enable them to become independent lifelong learners. (LCS.)

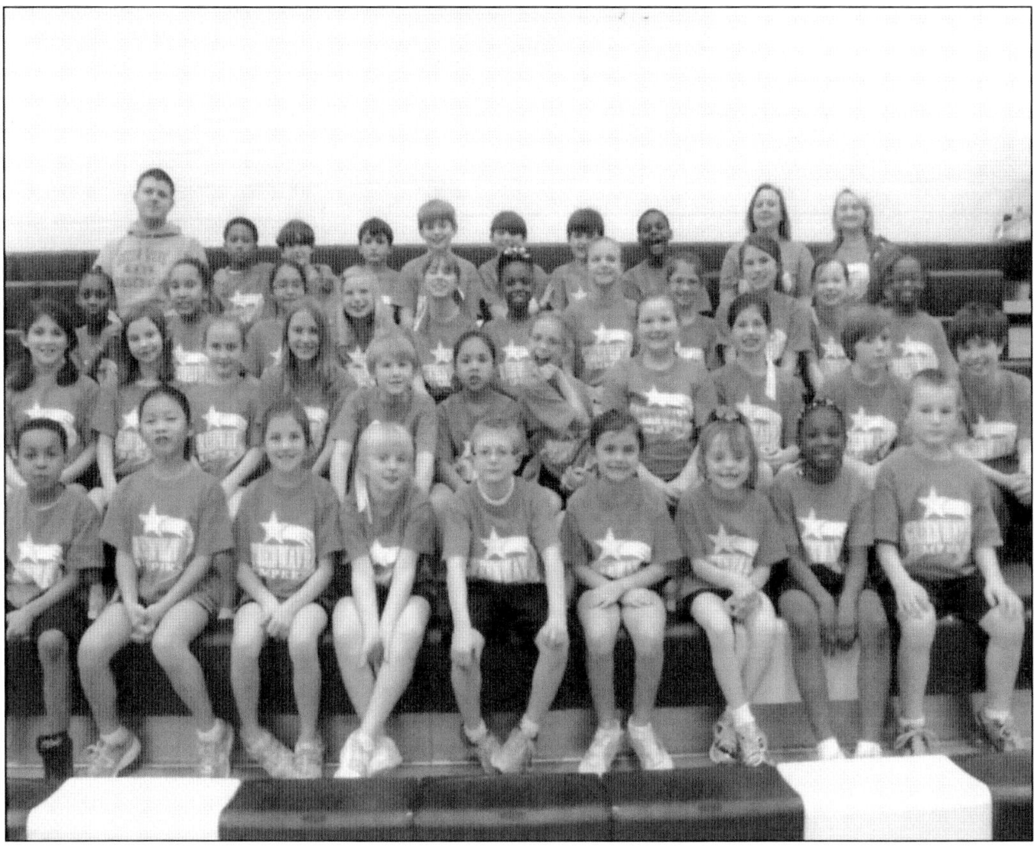

This group of multitalented students at Leeds Elementary School has performed at halftime during high school and collegiate sports events and at exhibitions for diverse audiences, from the Leeds Area Chamber of Commerce to Alabama governor Robert Bentley. The jump-rope team also serves as ambassadors for the city of Leeds.

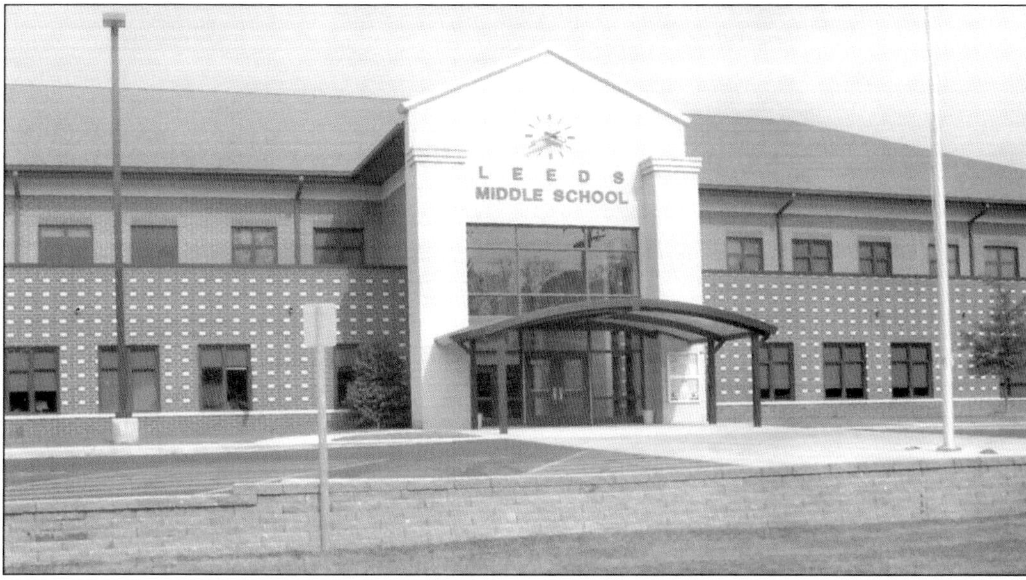

Leeds Middle School, a state-of-the-art facility, claims many successes, including nationally accredited teachers, such as librarian Susan Hutto. The school offers an atmosphere that provides students with an encouraging, challenging, and comfortable learning environment. The school's athletic program is enhanced by an Olympic-quality track on campus, originally built for the high school. The number of students at the school has increased significantly since it opened in 2008. (LCS.)

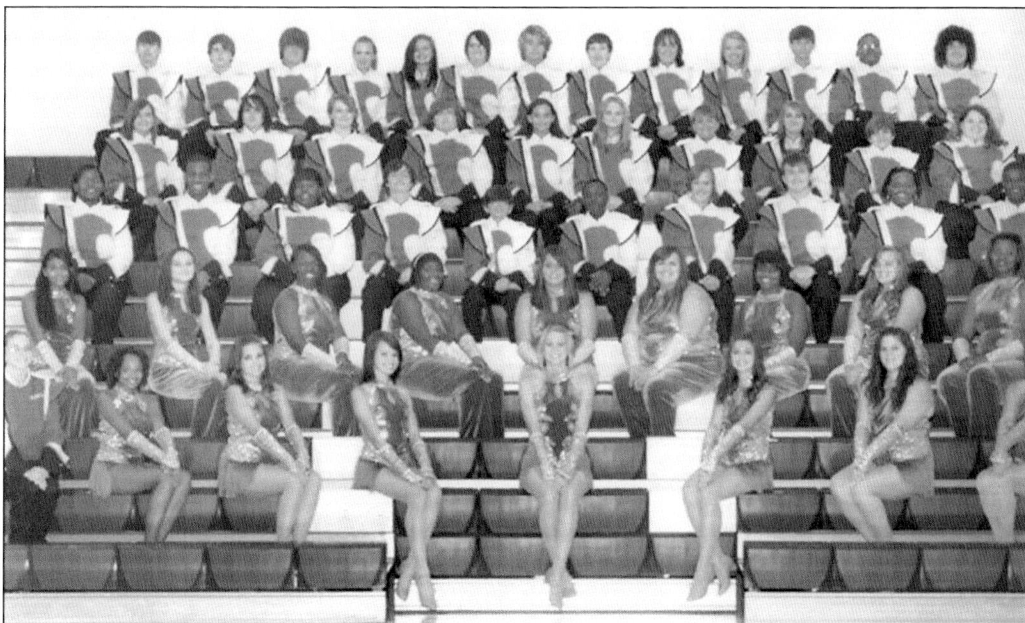

The Pride of the Green Wave, Leeds High School's marching band, has distinguished itself by receiving invitations to competitions and parades. It is experiencing a comeback since the school system reorganized into a small city school system rather than a large regional system. Members of the band have a tradition of receiving medals in the Alabama State Band that dates back to the 1950s.

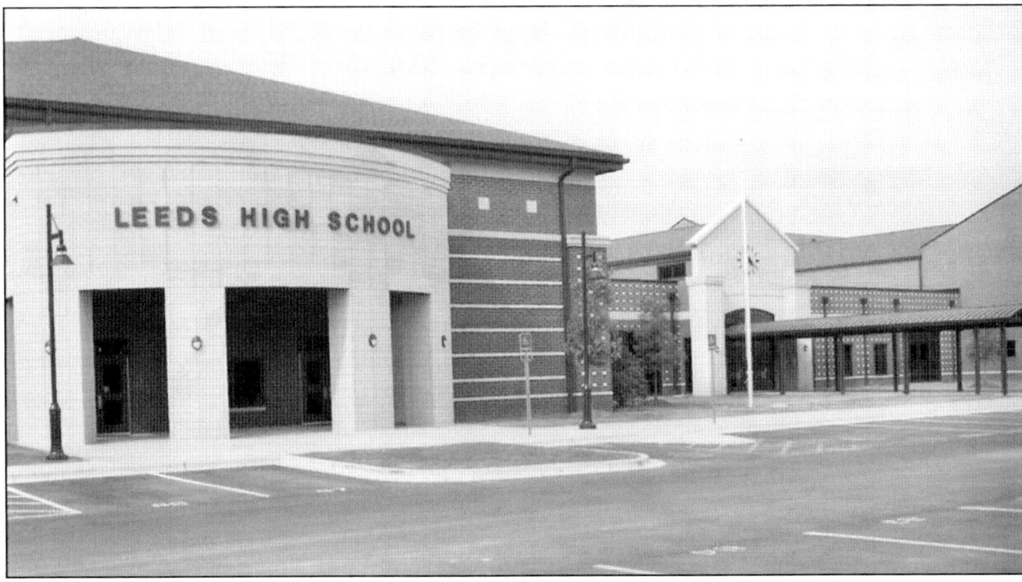

Leeds High School is a state-of-the-art facility located at 1500 Greenwave Drive. It is known for high academic standards and an award-winning athletic program. The chairman of the Science Department, Brian Swift, has received grants for planning and building outdoor classrooms on the school's expansive campus. Its up-to-date curriculum features dual enrollment and honors programs. (LCS.)

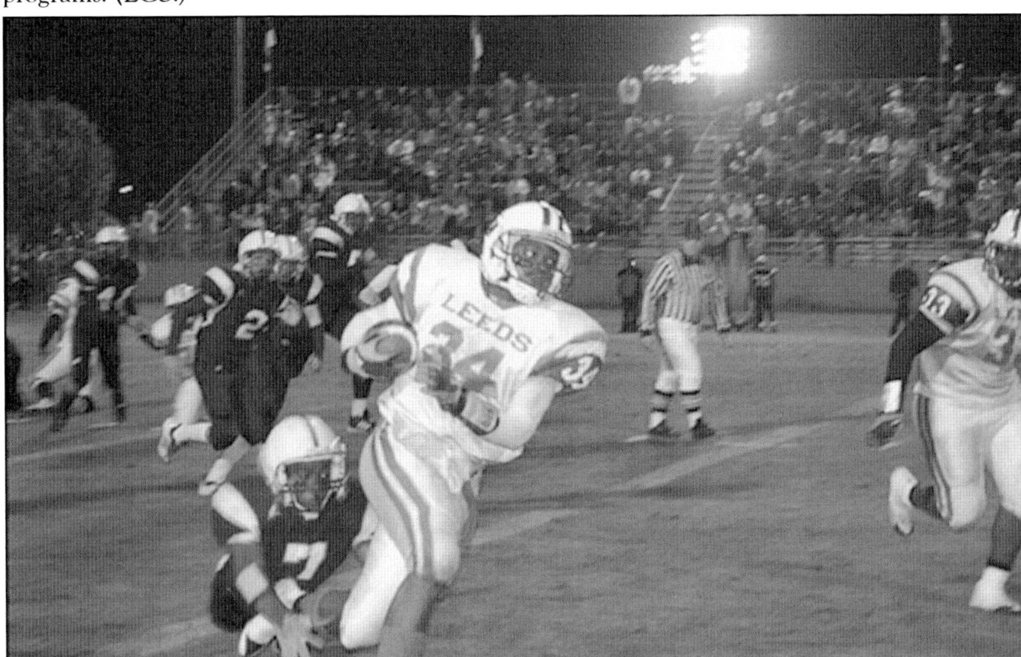

Leeds High School's celebrated football program has won two recent state championships, not unlike the school's first football team of 1923, which distinguished itself by winning six of the seven games it played that first season. The football program requires that players perform community service, such as building houses and mowing lawns for low-income and elderly people in Leeds. (LCS.)

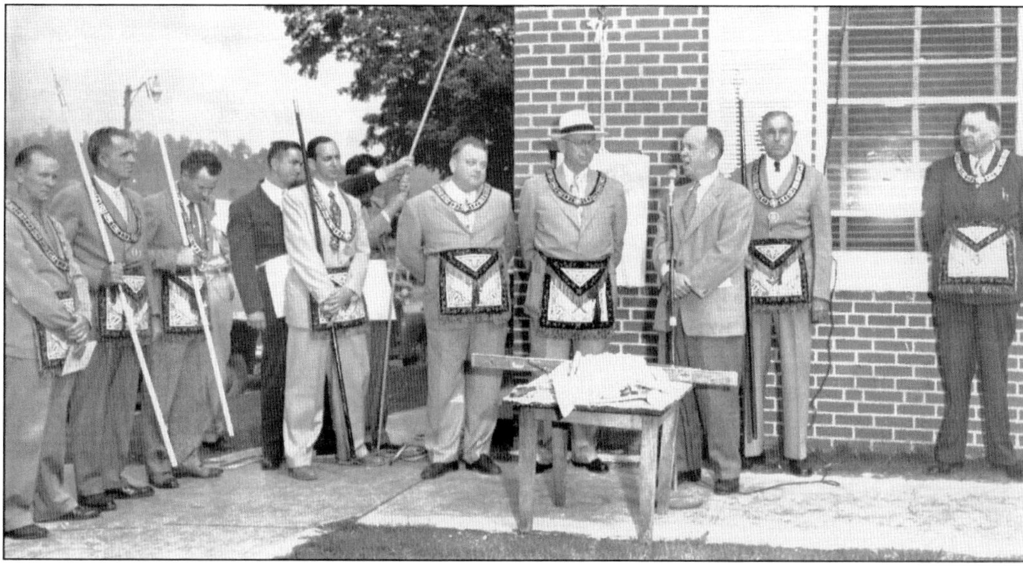

The laying of a cornerstone at the 1950s city hall was a full Masonic ceremony led by Bill Dorrough. Lodge No. 446 can claim almost every mayor of the city as a member. The lodge, which was established before Leeds was incorporated, has an active philanthropic program. (BM.)

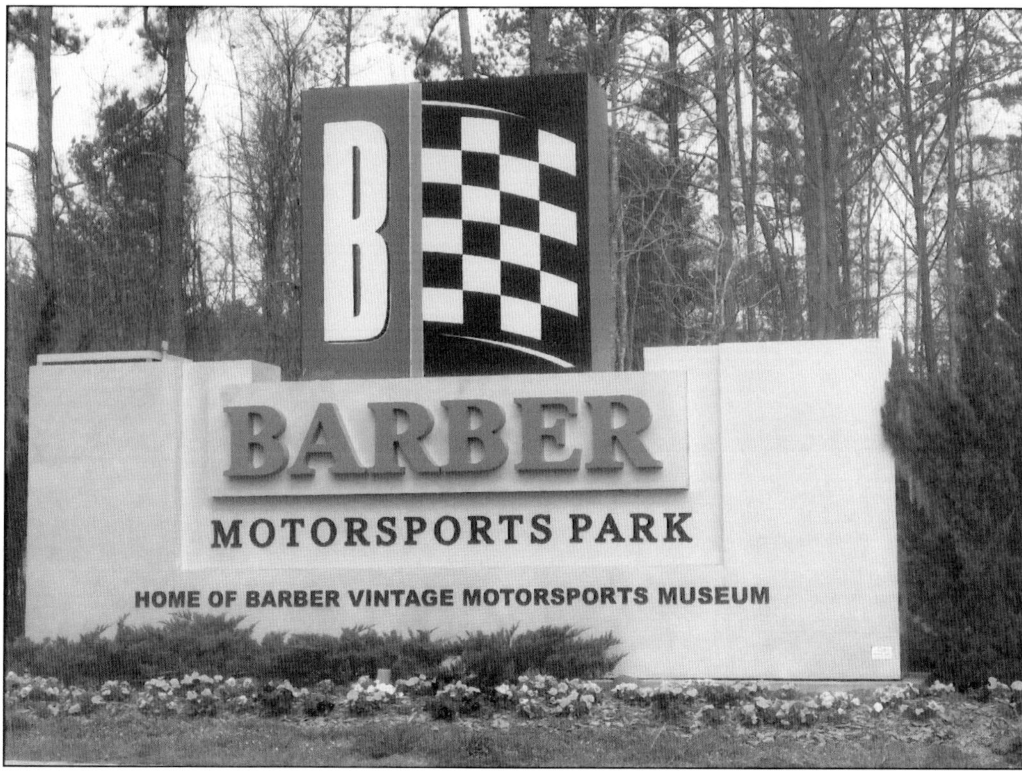

Barber Motorsports Park holds world-class automotive and motorcycle racing events. This venue is hailed as one of the most popular tourist attractions in the state of Alabama. A motorsports museum at the site holds more than 1,200 vintage and modern motorcycles and racecars. The collection is the largest of its kind in the world.

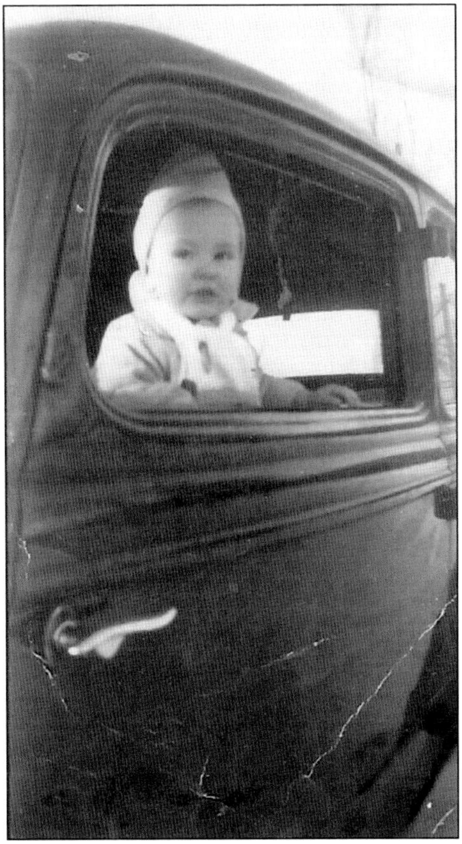

In 1938, there was no better way to celebrate with baby than to bundle her up in cotton clothing and take the family car for a spin. Samples of the old crafts, such as knitted and crocheted baby clothes, can still be found at the Leeds Creek Bank Festival, held annually in the spring at Leeds Memorial Park. The festival also includes a dog show, a flower sale, and Appalachian music.

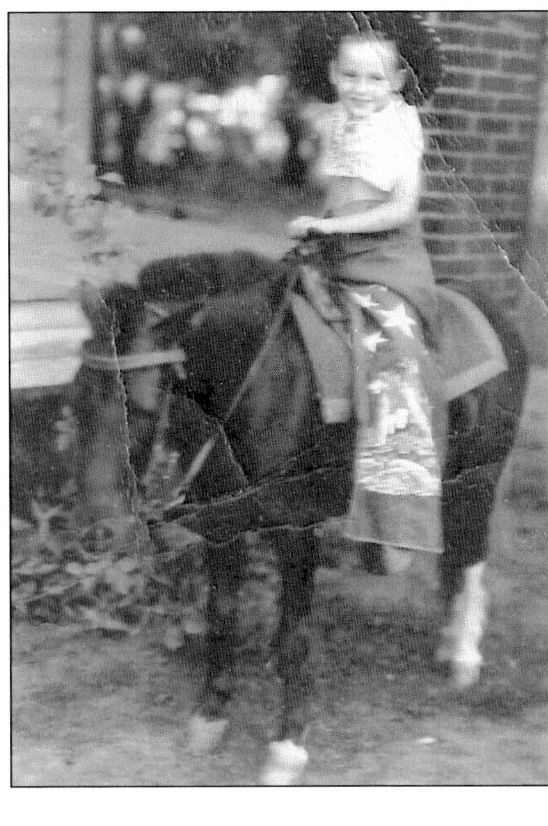

In the mid-1940s, cowboys served as role models for little boys, including Sonny Nelms, who plays on a pony in his front yard. Leeds is known for its horse farms that can be seen when traveling on Alabama Highway 119.

In the 1920s, Ray Little sits in front of his transportation, a wagon styled like a stagecoach. For decades, wooden vehicles have been enjoyed by Leeds children and train rides in Memorial Park have entertained them, while educating them about safety around railroads. For many years, wooden trains have been a main attraction for festivals and celebrations in Leeds. (Courtesy of Frank Little.)

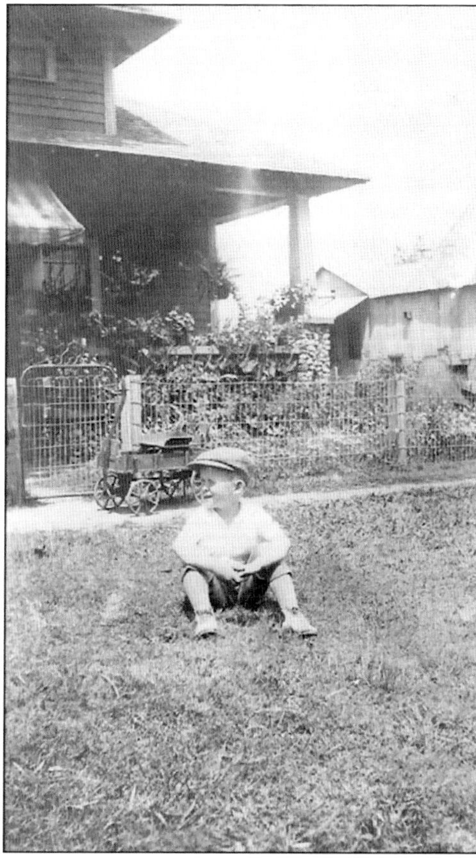

A Southern Railway X245 caboose is parked adjacent to the Leeds Historic Depot. In 2008, volunteers from the Leeds Masonic Lodge 446 painted the exterior of the caboose. At the same time, members the Leeds Historical Society and Leeds Scenic Byway Management Team partnered to landscape the grounds of the depot in preparation for the inaugural Leeds Downtown Folk Festival and John Henry Days.

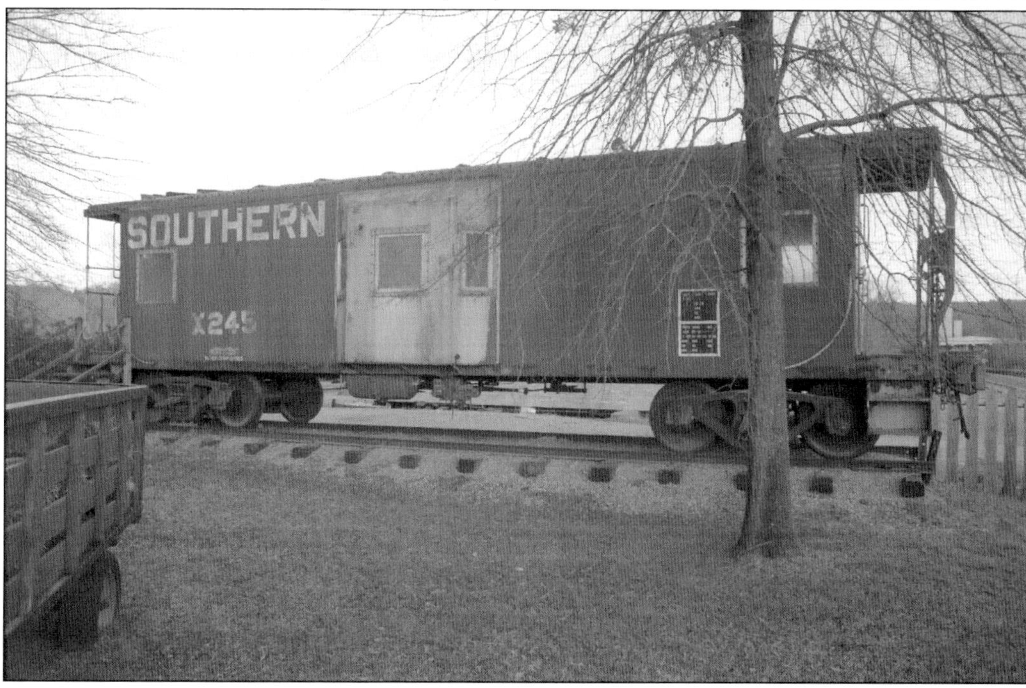

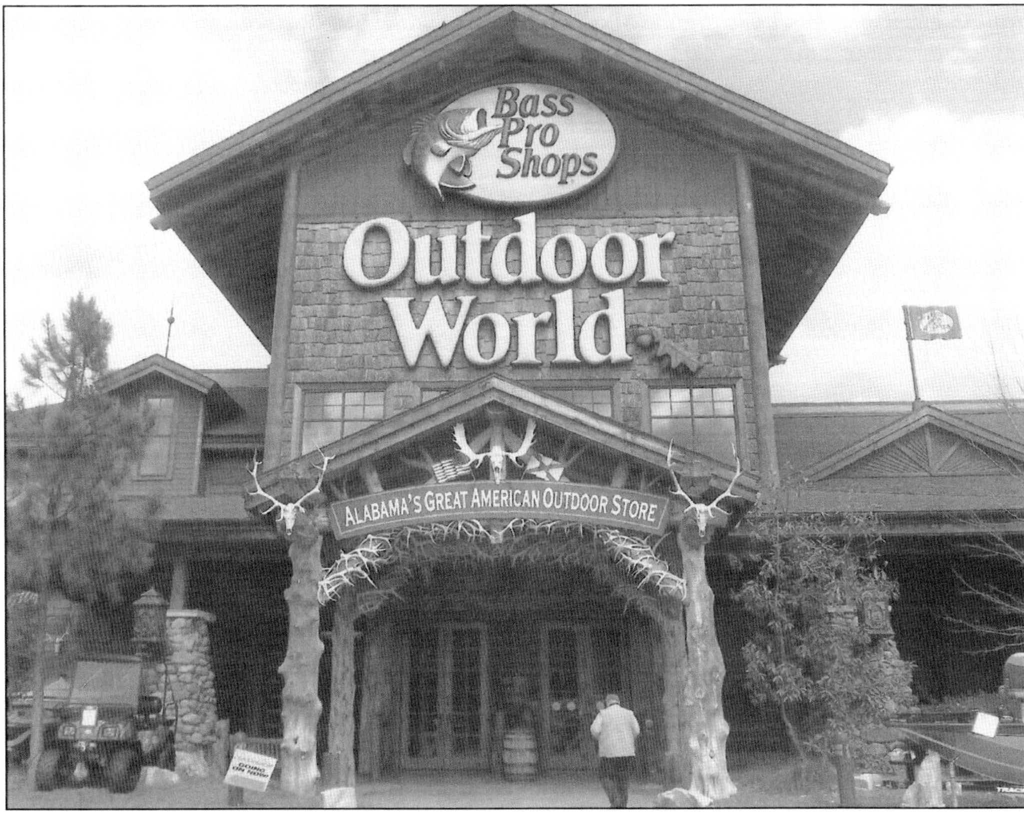

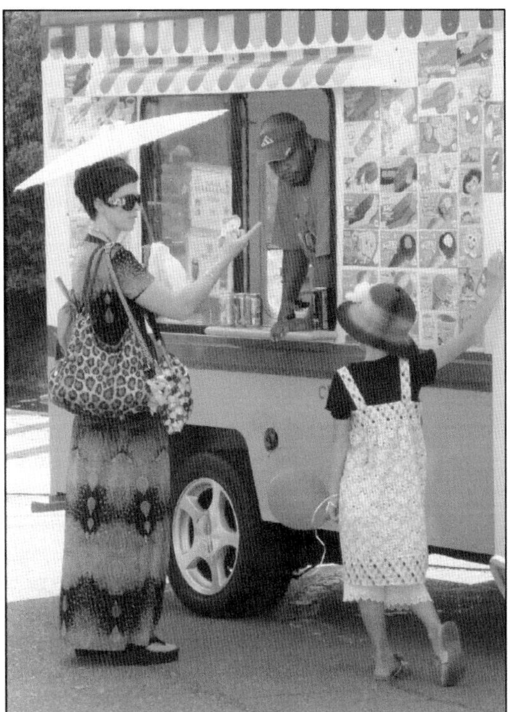

From the quaint sidewalk-bordered streets of downtown Leeds to the exceptional shopping at the Shops of Grant River outlet center and Bass Pro Shops, Leeds, with roots planted deeply in history, has an eye to the future and a plan that includes economic development, tourism, educational excellence, and fiscal stability.

Members of the Leeds community come together at the annual Leeds Downtown Folk Festival and John Henry Celebration. This festival, first held in 2008, celebrates the roots, richness, and variety of Alabama culture in the heart of historic downtown Leeds. The festival, which is held annually on the third weekend in September, includes an outdoor play or symposium about John Henry, an art show, musical entertainment, Southern-style food, and a special area set aside for children's activities.

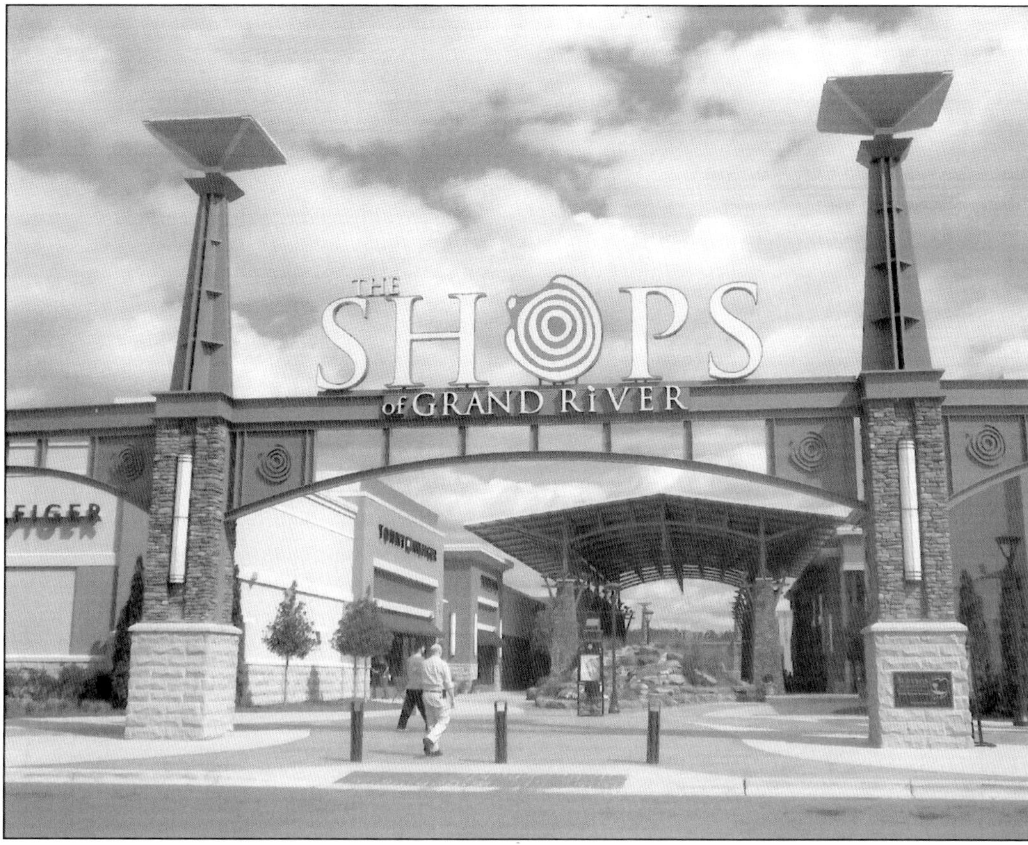

The Shops of Grand River, a major part of Leeds's growth at the Intersection of Interstate 20 and US Highway 78, is an upscale, 330,000-square-foot outlet mall. It has the Gold Seal Bond of the Audubon Society for ecological excellence in the implementation of the center's master plan.

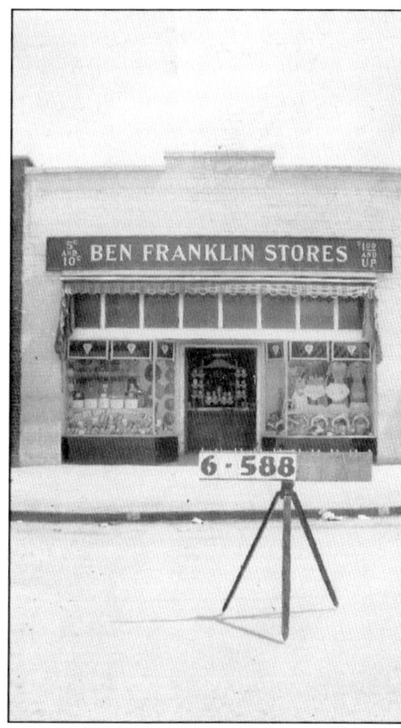

Several five-and-dime stores, including a Ben Franklin Store, shown here, were open in downtown Leeds during the 1930s and 1940s. Found in small towns throughout the country, Ben Franklin Stores are named for Ben Franklin, whose philosophy was summed up in his saying, "A penny saved is a penny earned." (BL.)

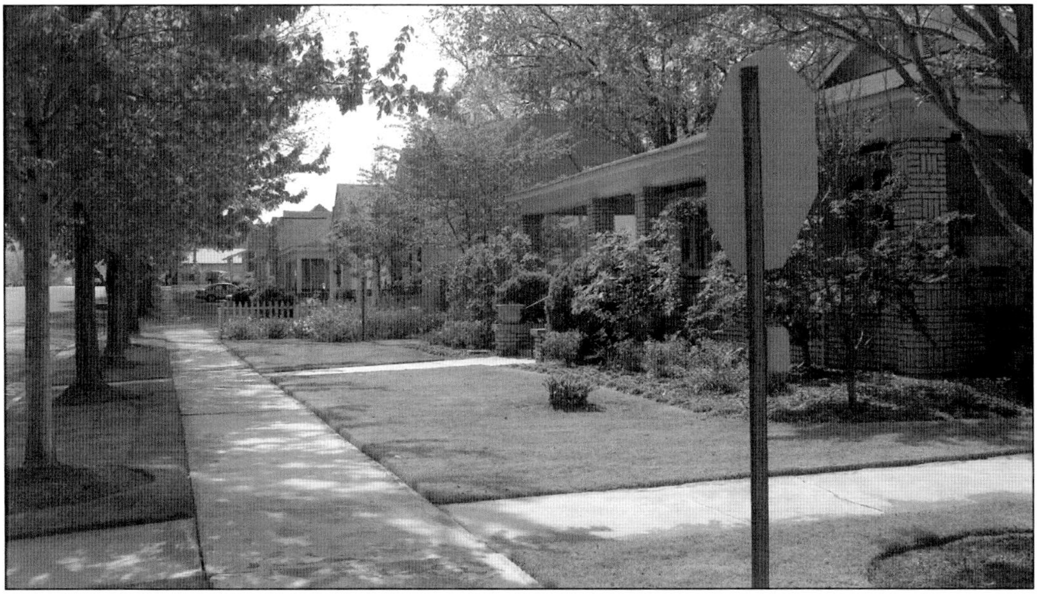

In the summers, elementary school–age children walked a sidewalk circuit from one Bible school to the next. They strolled to Leeds Presbyterian Church, the First Methodist Church, and the historic First Baptist Church to enjoy their nearby swimming hole on the Little Cahaba River. After a swim, they might take other sidewalks to Rowan Springs and other artesian springs in different parts of town.

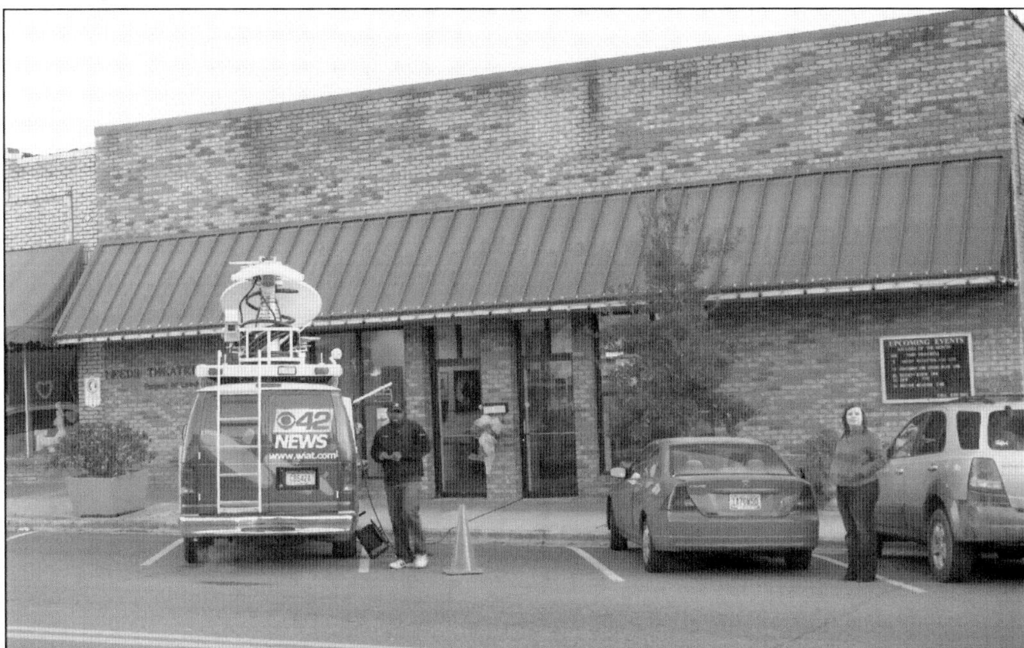

A reporter and cameraman from a Birmingham television station arrive at the Leeds Theatre and Arts Center on Parkway Drive to cover one of the many events held there. The center is operated by the Leeds Arts Council, which was formed in 1985. The center, which opened in 2000, is home to poetry readings, art exhibits, a concert series, and theatrical productions.

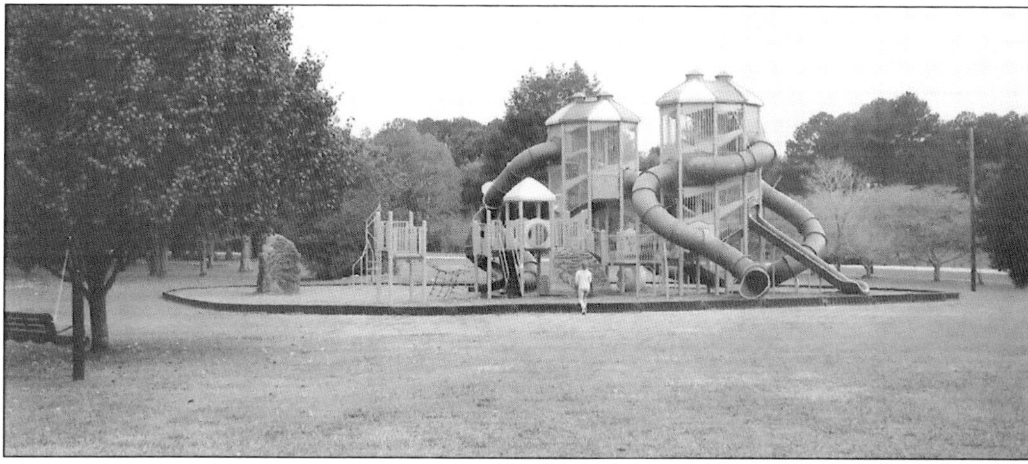

James Whitfield's mayoral administration was responsible for the playground in Leeds Memorial Park. Councilor Carol Phillips campaigned for the playground and raised the necessary funds. The playground is a legacy left by that administration. The Eric Patterson administration has placed a full ball complex in the park, including baseball, softball, and soccer fields.

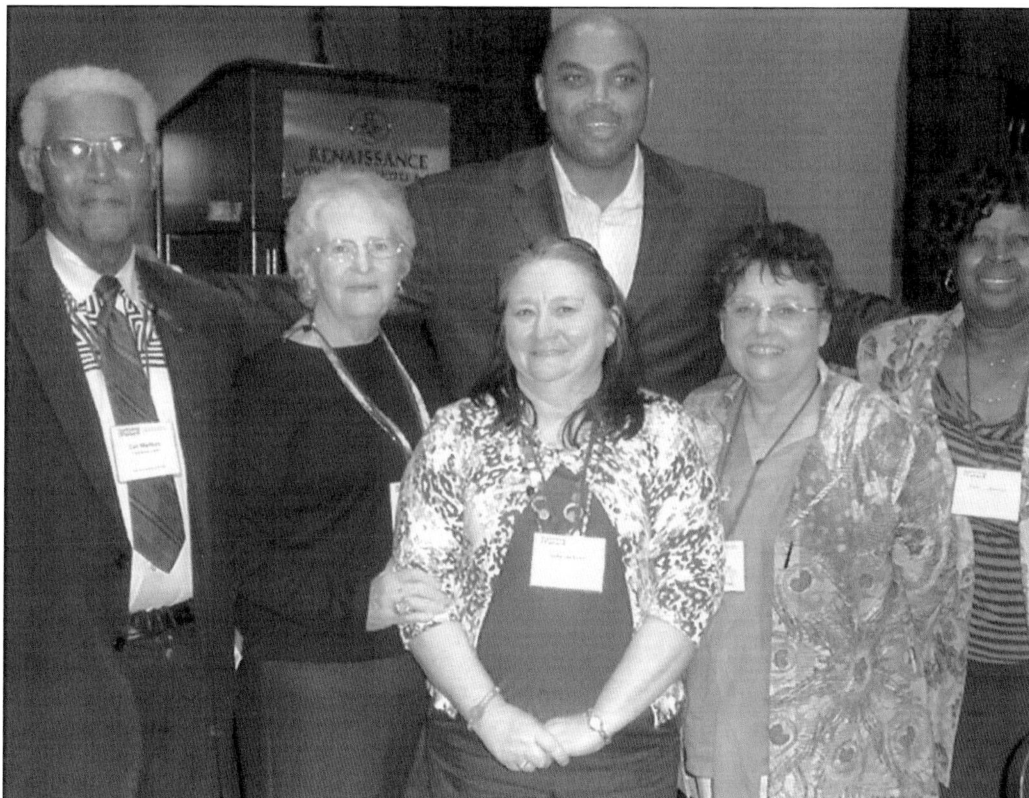

Olympian Charles Barkley, a basketball Hall of Famer, is a Leeds native. He is shown with the Leedership Leeds planning team after he spoke at a statewide workshop, where he urged Alabamians to become leaders. Leadership Leeds is part of the Alabama Community of Excellence program, which encourages excellence in government, education, and culture, for the purpose of marketing Alabama's best cities to business and industry.

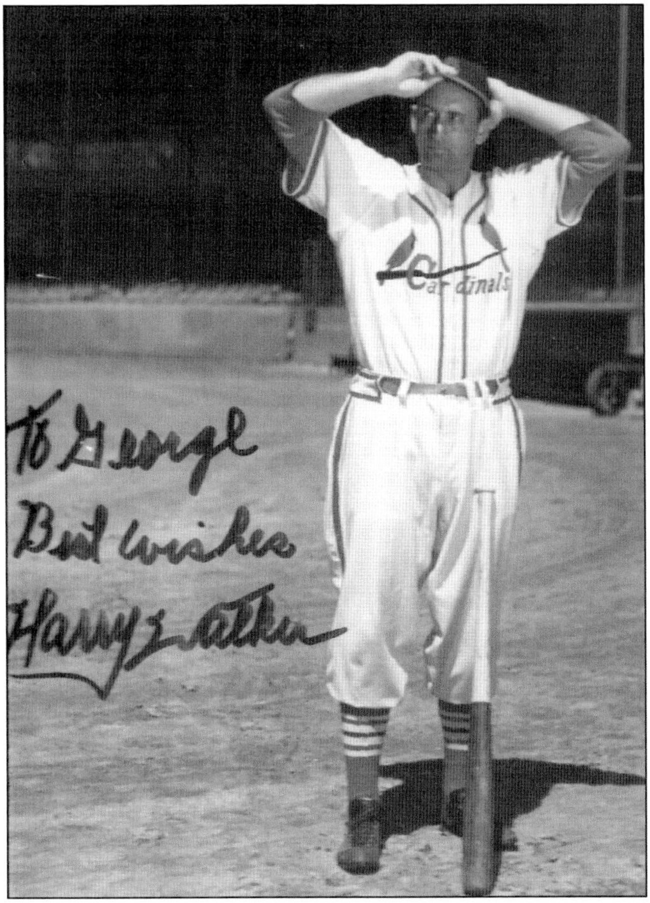

Harry "The Hat" Walker became a Leeds resident when he married his wife, Dot, who was a member of a Leeds family. Walker played, managed, and coached professional baseball, and was a one-time National League batting champion. He started the baseball program at the University of Alabama in Birmingham. (Courtesy of Golden Rule Barbecue.)

Members of the military lend dignity to one of Leeds's many Veterans Day ceremonies. These events have as big a turnout as any other Leeds events, because many veterans have retired in Leeds, and the city's population has distinguished itself with prominent veterans of war. The phenomenon of Leeds's three Congressional Medal of Honor winners attracts veterans who pass through Leeds.

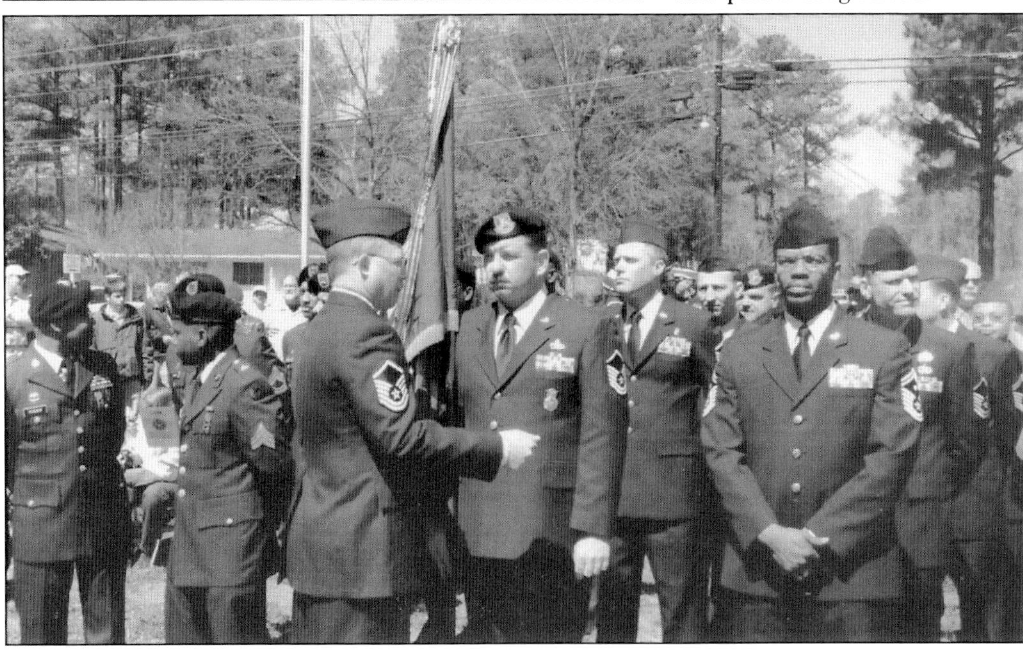

Ten

Twenty-three Square Miles of Living History

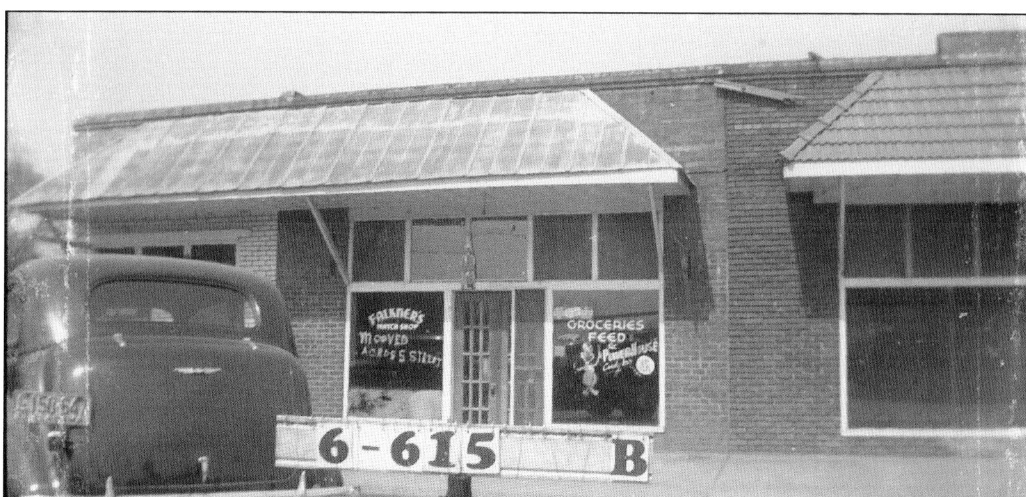

Grocery stores such as Falkner's grocery and feed store in downtown Leeds, shown here, sold bread in 1939 for 5¢ a loaf, cheese for 23¢ per pound, and peanut butter for 23¢ a quart. During the Great Depression, grocery stores bought produce from farmers in exchange for groceries and allowed townspeople to buy items on credit. (BL.)

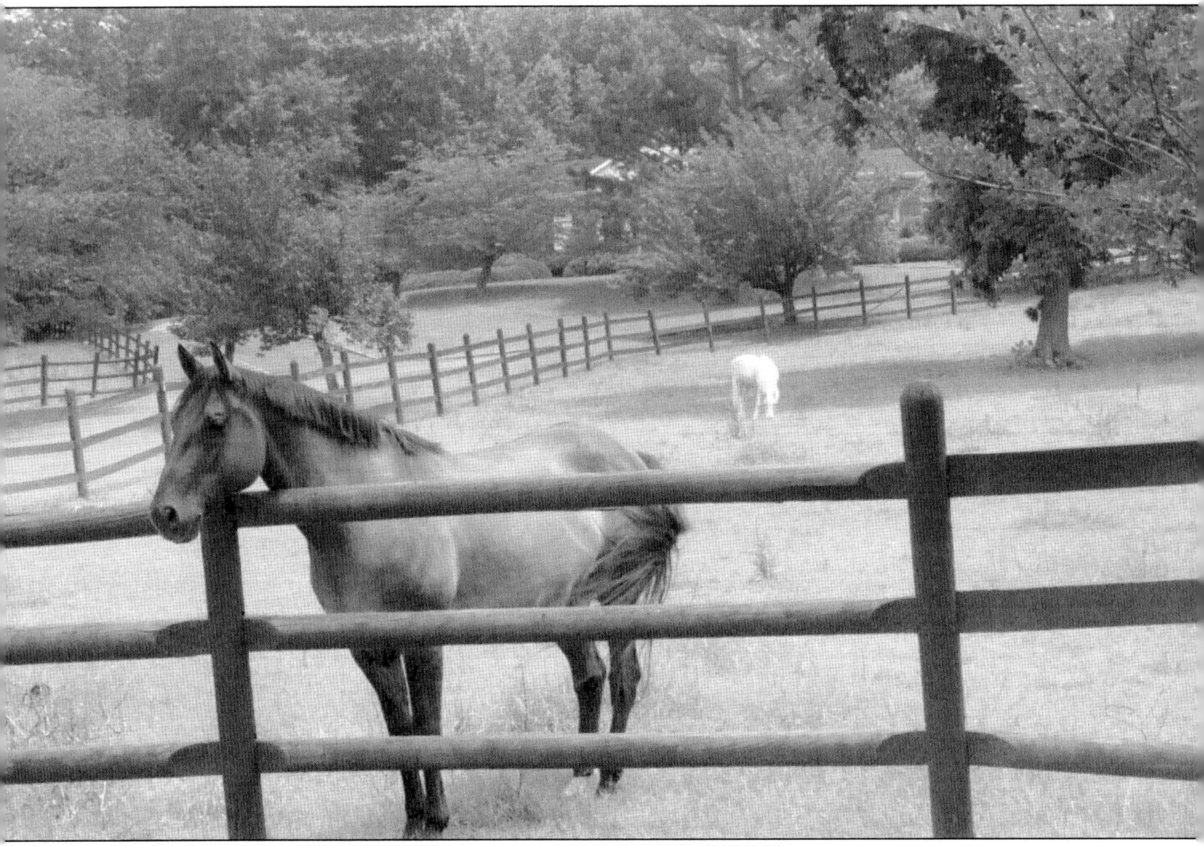

The calm setting of a Leeds horse farm on Montevallo Road (Alabama Highway 119) was the site of a royal and vice presidential visit. In 1992, a Saudi prince came to the University of Alabama in Birmingham Hospital for surgery. He brought an entourage with him. The Leeds horse farm district was selected as the best site to house the family during the visit. People in the area knew something was going on, because some residents were relocated by the Secret Service. Then, Vice Pres. George Herbert Walker Bush slipped into the quiet countryside of Leeds and visited with members of the Saudi royal family. Not only did Bush make this visit to Leeds, he sent a special video greeting to the Leeds Historical Society in 2001 congratulating the society for Leeds's Congressional Medal of Honor winners.

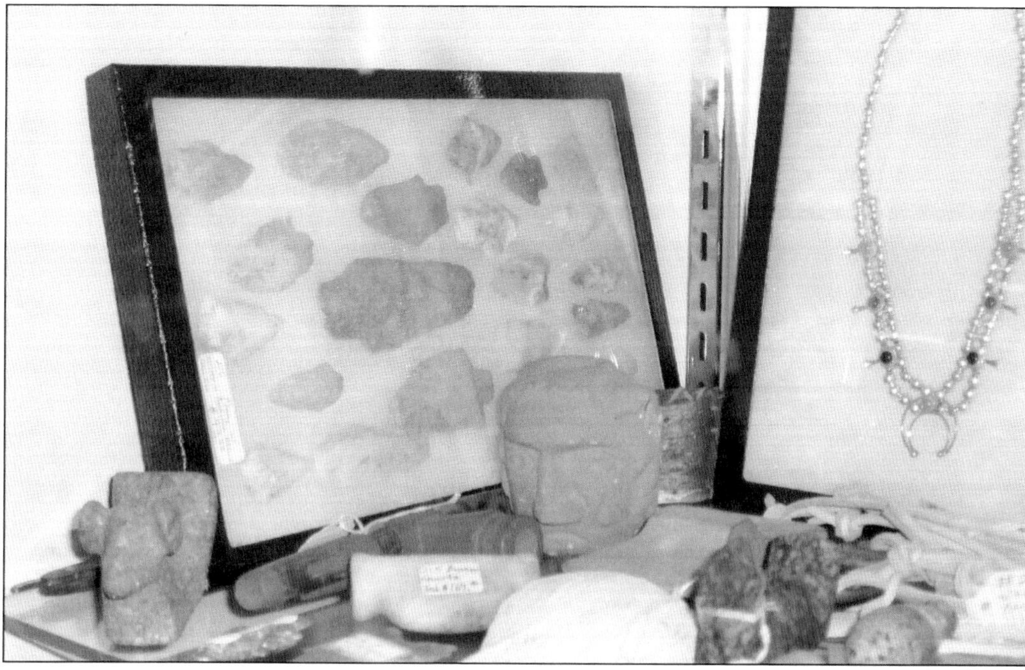

The antique mall in Leeds is a favorite destination for antique and collectible buffs and artists. The mall sells collectibles including Native American artifacts. The case shown here is exceptionally interesting, but any resident of the horse farm district can tell the story of arrowheads he owns. It is not unusual to see rare Cherokee arrowheads at farms tucked into the nearby mountains.

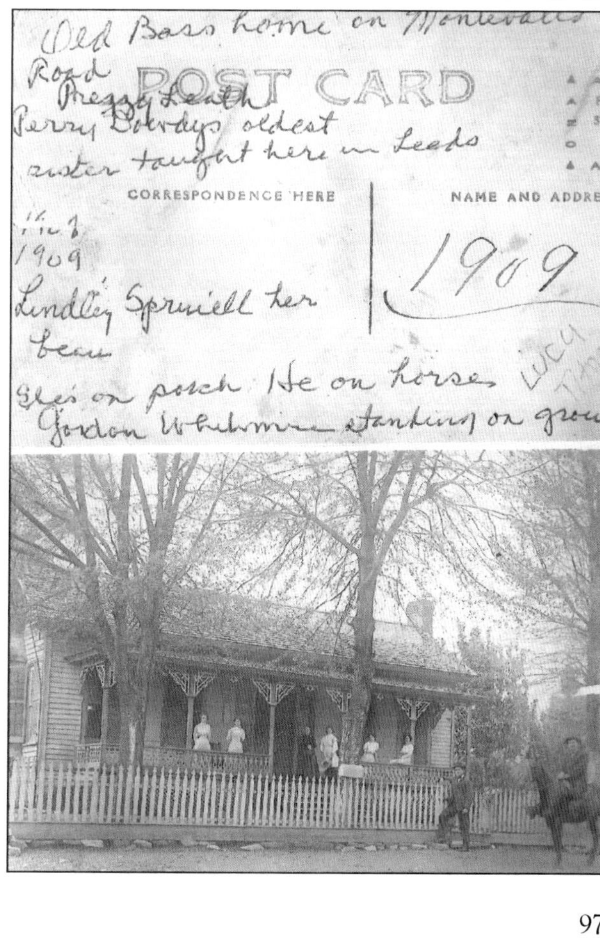

The Leeds Historical Society purchased the Jonathan Bass House (1863–1865) from Bold Springs Church in 2003 and restored the home. Today, the farmhouse showcases a museum of local history. In 2006, the Bass House received a historical marker from the Alabama Register of Landmarks and Heritage organization. In 2008, the house was listed in the National Register of Historic Places. (LHS.)

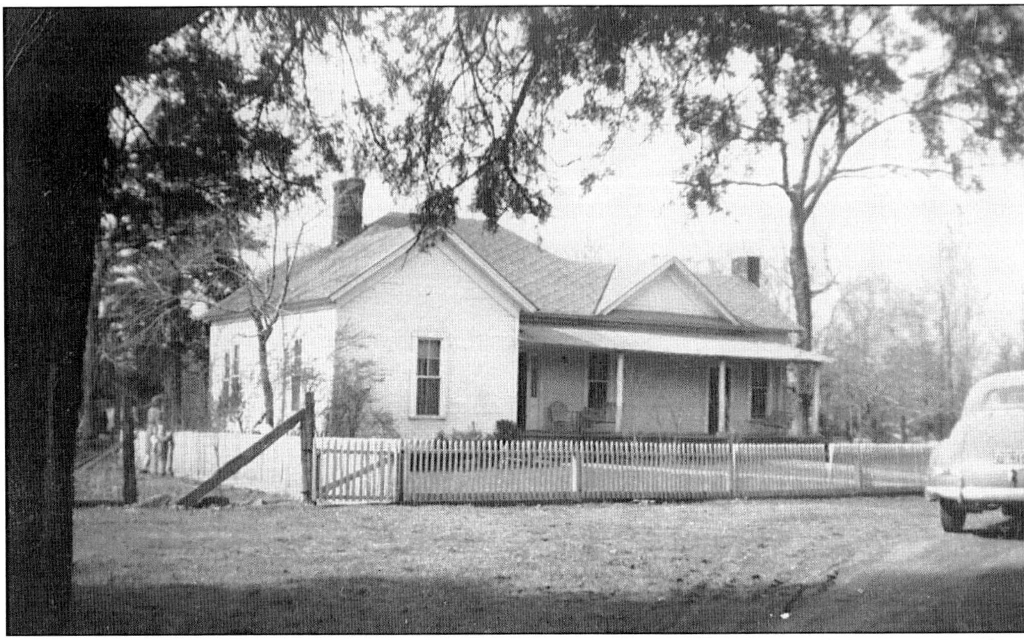

This photograph of Arthur Mason and Martha Jane Spruiell's house was taken in 1930. Three generations of Spruills-Spruiells lived in the house, which was built in 1903 and wired for electricity in 1910. The family is descended from John S. Spruiell, who moved to the St. Clair County area of Leeds in the mid-19th century. (BM.)

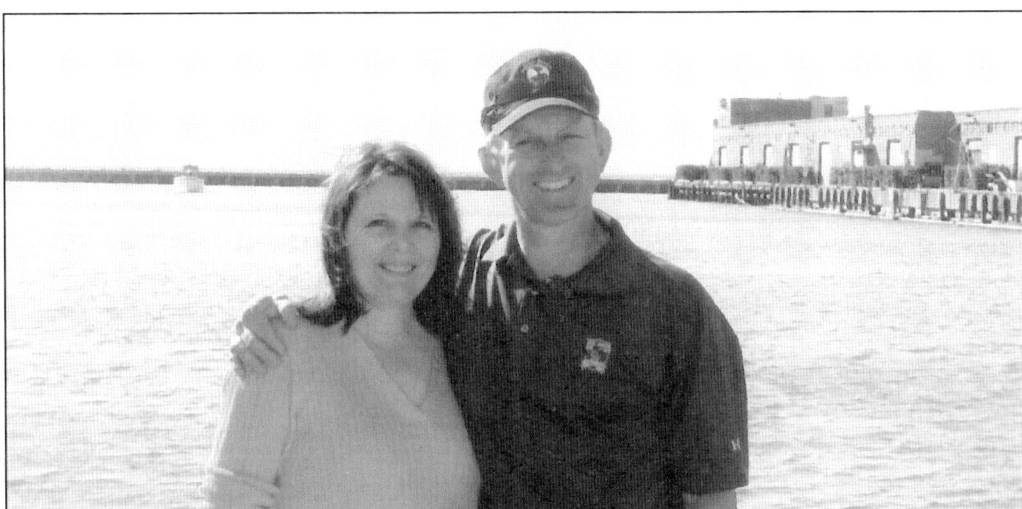

Former Leeds resident George A. Little is a member of the Alabama Engineering Hall of Fame. George's wife, Anna, also pictured, is a descendent of Lyman Hall, a signer of the Declaration of Independence. George is chief executive officer of HDR Engineering, a firm whose project won a place in the Alabama Engineering Hall of Fame. Both George and Anna have relatives remaining in Leeds.

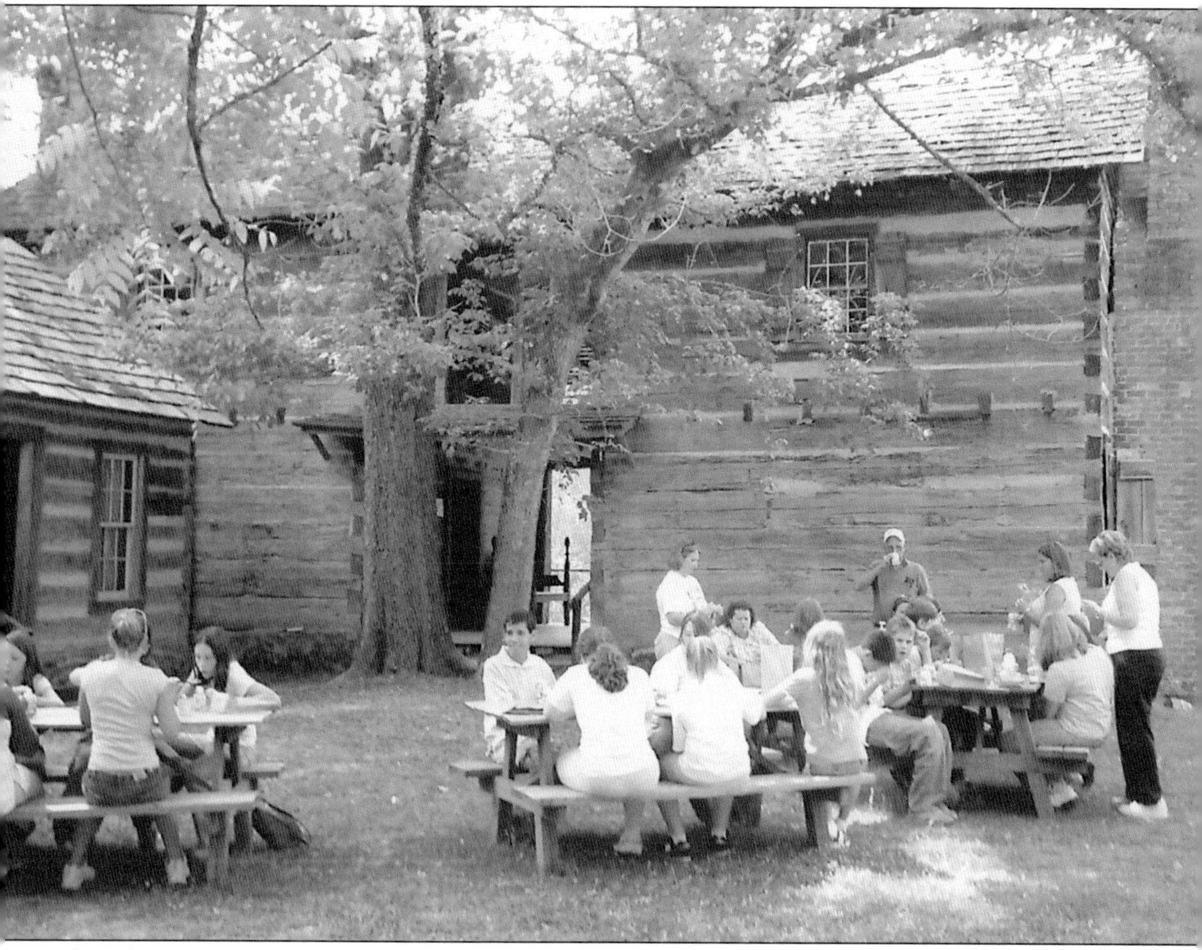

The John Looney House, a two-story log house in Ashville, Alabama, is listed in the National Register of Historic Places. Both the John Looney House and the Henry Little log cabin in Leeds are located on a stagecoach route that was marked in the 1990s in a joint effort by the Leeds Historical Society and the St. Clair Historical Society. The leadership for this project was provided by Marie Cromer, a Leeds native. Cromer served as president of both the St. Clair Historical Society and the Leeds Historical Society. She is recognized as an authority on the stagecoach period in St. Clair County and in Leeds. Cromer contributed articles to newspapers and journals discussing postal routes and the stagecoach stops along the way. Her work established the basic information about the Cahaba Trail and the stagecoach era that later Leeds preservationists successfully used to support a request to have the Leeds Stagecoach Road named an Alabama Scenic Byway.

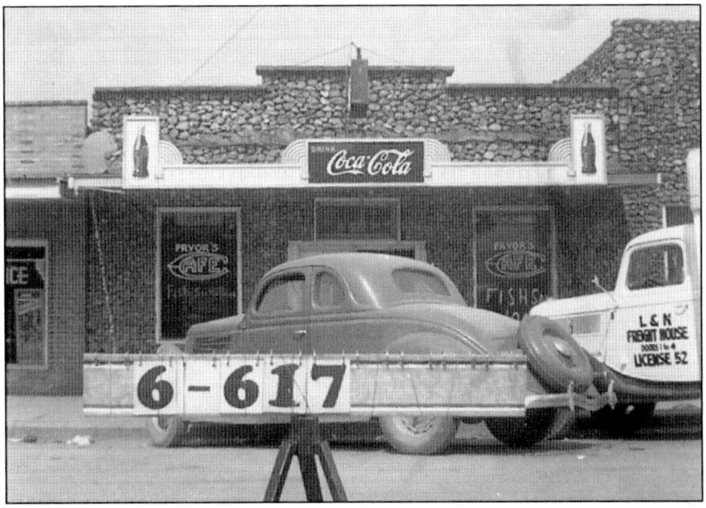

One of downtown Leeds's restaurants, shown here in 1939, appears to have customers. Americans who frequented restaurants during the Great Depression ate familiar American food such as a "bunny salad" made from a canned pear half, shredded cheese, and mayonnaise. They were more likely to order coffee or a sweet, inexpensive soft drink, such as a Coca-Cola, rather than an unfamiliar and expensive wine. (BL.)

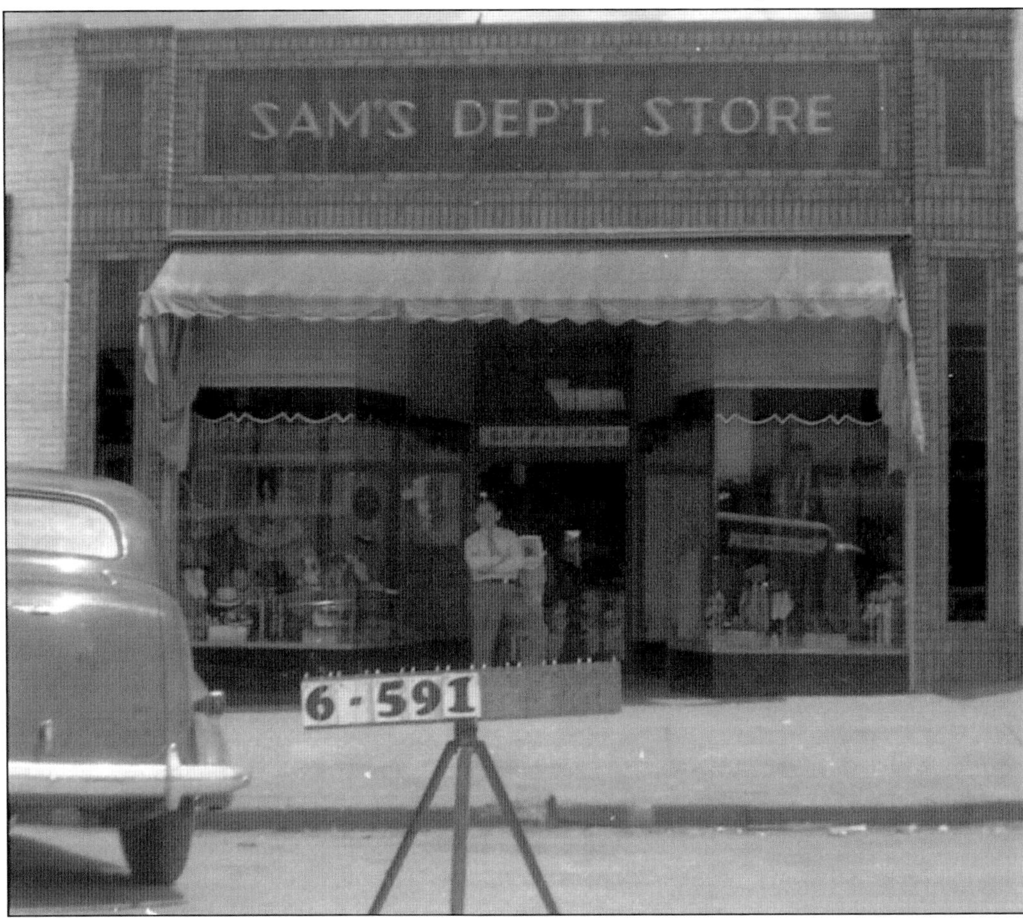

Sam Halpern's department store, shown here in 1939, was typical of the time period. Department stores changed the business world, and their window displays promoted their stock. Other department stores in Leeds have included Asman's, H. Evans and Son, and, most recently, the Pants Store, which began operations in 1950 and is still located in the downtown area. (BL.)

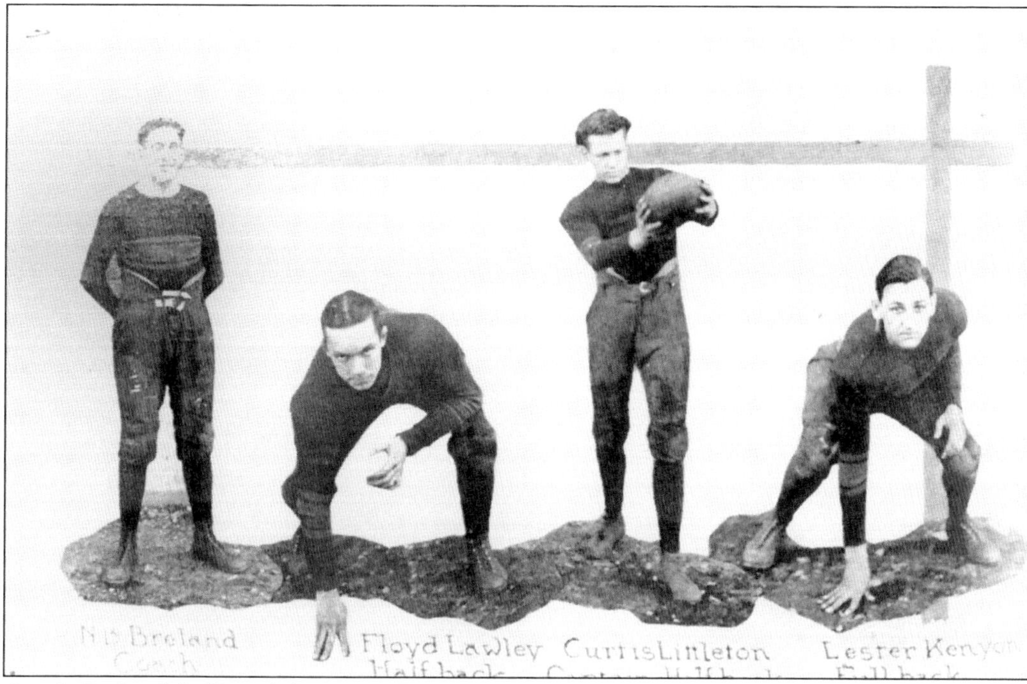

Coach Breland (left) and three members of the 1923 Leeds Leeders, photographed for the 1924 Leeds High School annual, had a 6-1 record and started a winning sports tradition that has continued into the 21st century. Names of team members included Lawley, Whitmire, and Powers. In 1949, the Leeds Memorial Stadium grandstand would be built and dedicated to soldiers from Leeds who had been killed in World Wars I and II. (BM.)

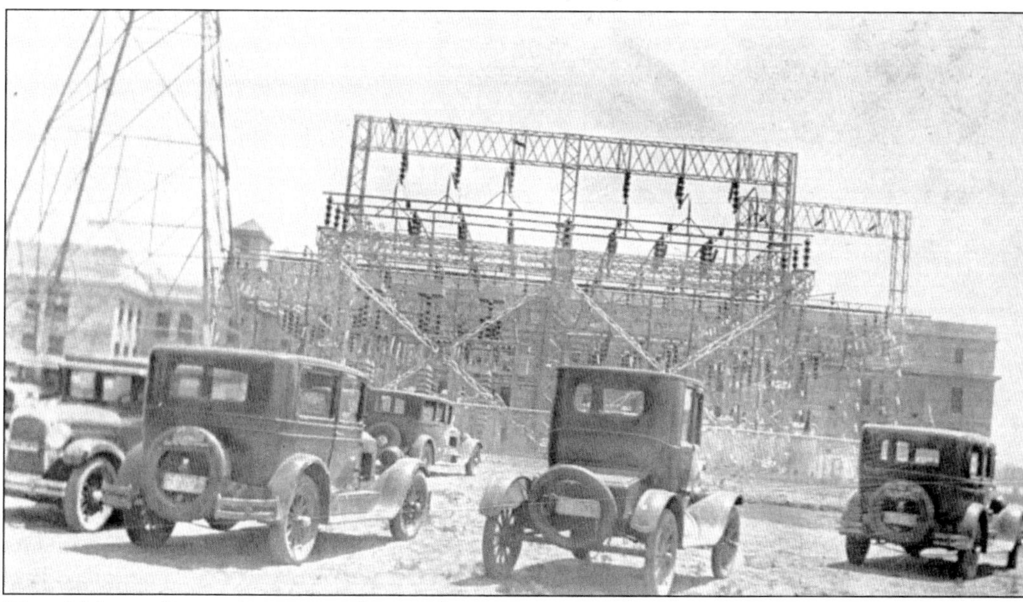

This Alabama Power Company electrical transmission substation has been located on Alabama Highway 119 in Leeds for nearly 100 years. In 1914, Lock 12 (now Lay Hydroelectric Generating Plant) began operations on the Coosa River in Chilton County. Transmission lines were strung from Lock 12 to Leeds and points west, and electricity was provided to Leeds in 1915. (BM.)

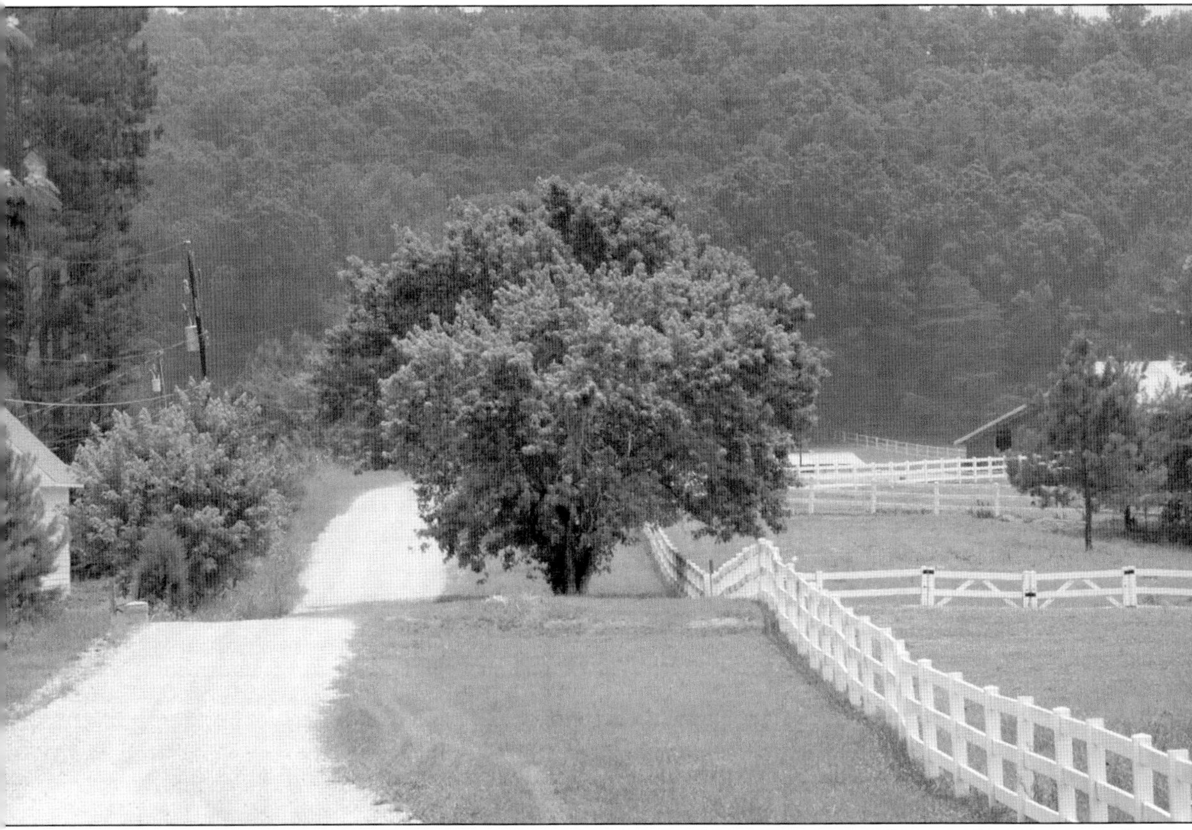

The business card and other official forms for the Leeds Scenic Byway feature this photograph of a winding road that leads to the base of Oak Mountain. This scene is an asset of the byway. More than 33 homes, businesses, and churches along the eight-mile byway through Leeds display county, state, or national historic markers. Five interpretative facilities along the corridor promote the historical theme in Leeds. The exhibits include the Leeds Depot, Rowan Oaks Historic Home, the Bass House Museum, the Imogene Wright Falletta Visitor Center, and the Historical Park. The park displays information about Leeds's three recipients of the Congressional Medal of Honor and lists Alabama's recipients of that award. On September 17, 2011, volunteers from more than 21 civic organizations and guests witnessed the unveiling of a historic marker for the city of Leeds at the visitor center. The marker was given to the city by the state department of tourism during the Year of the Great Alabama Homecoming.

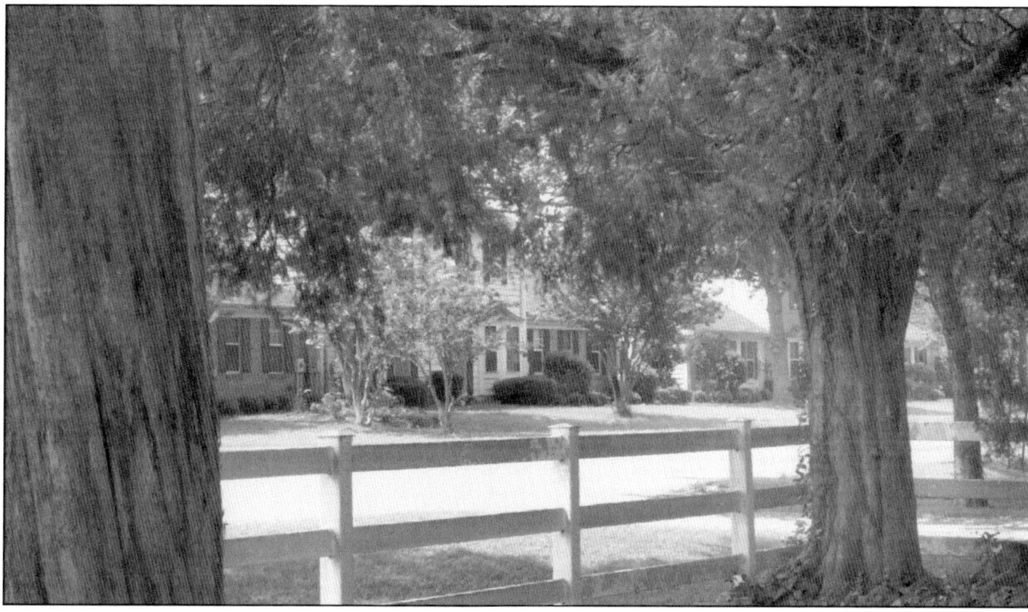

This view along the Jefferson/St. Clair County line, through the fence of a Spruiell ancestral home to condominiums across the street, brings back memories of confusion about the location of county lines. Leeds is the only tri-county city in Alabama. While the first sheriff of Shelby County never moved from his home, the change in the location of the county line in 1830 made him a Jefferson County resident.

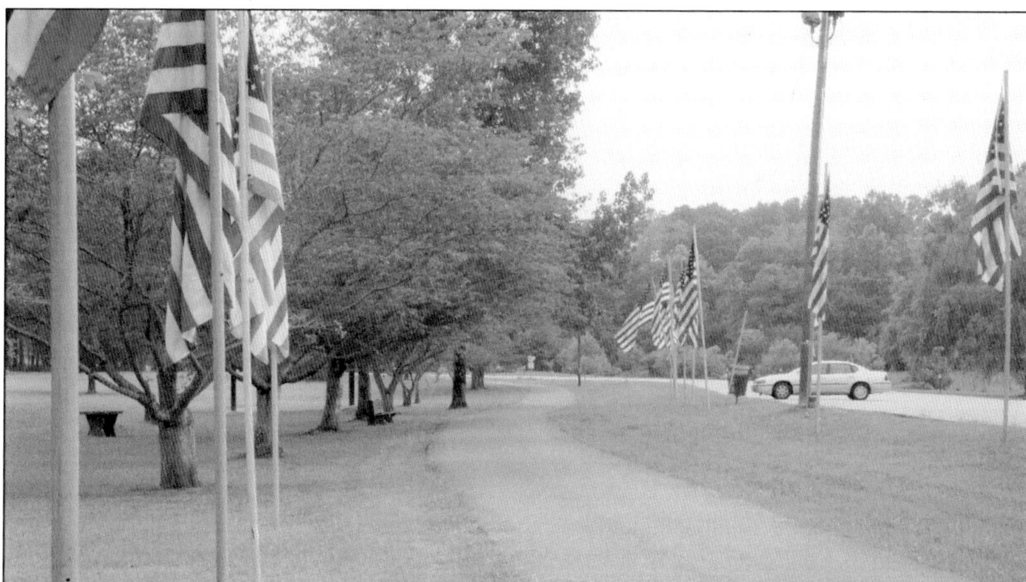

The walking track at Leeds Memorial Park is lined with flags, indicating the continuing patriotism of Leeds residents. American Legion Post 400 and VFW Post 6440 provide the flags. The Cahaba Valley and Dirt Dabbers garden clubs provide and maintain flower gardens in the area. The Castalian Literary Club and Woman's Literary Club provide memorial benches. The Leeds Tree Commission is in charge of horticulture. All of Leeds's civic clubs work to improve Leeds Memorial Park.

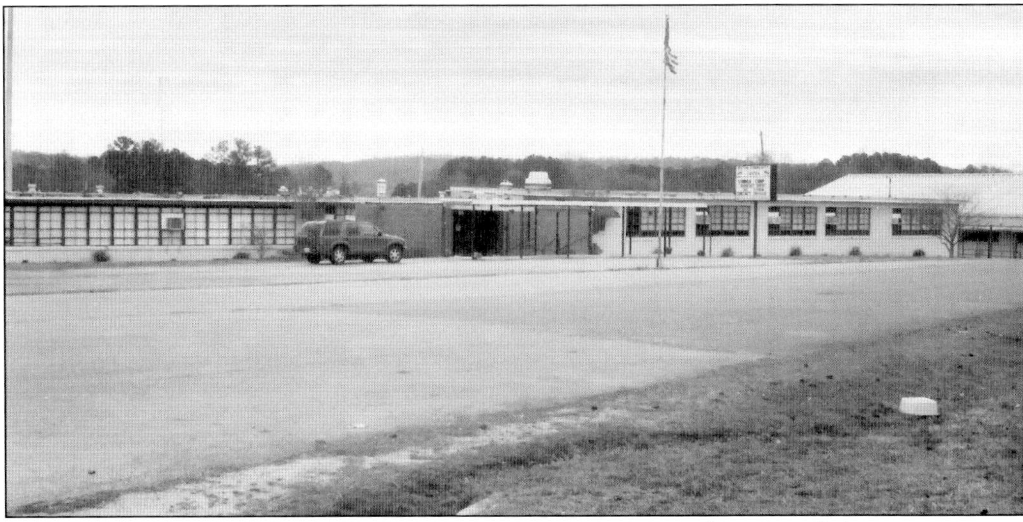

Recently renovated, the Robert R. Moton Community Center has served the community as Leeds Middle School. The gym is part of what was once Robert Russa Moton High School for black students in a segregated community. The center serves children (especially at-risk youths), adults, and seniors. Its programs complement the work of Leeds City Schools to help lower the dropout rate. (Courtesy of Dan Marbury.)

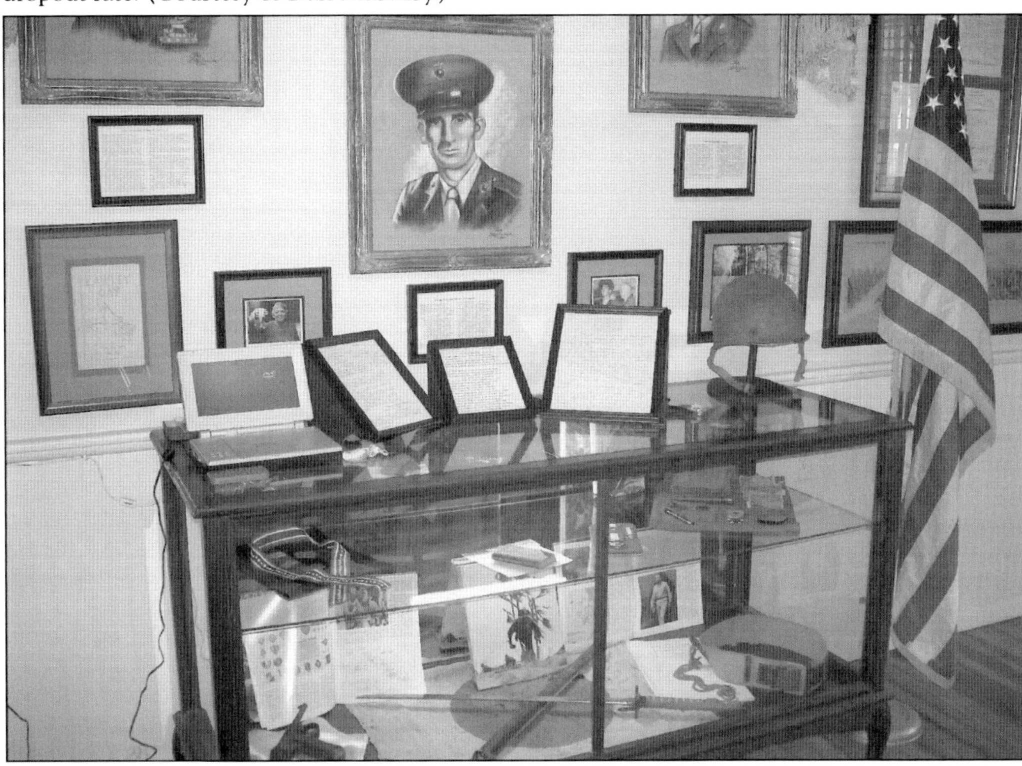

This exhibit, located in the Bass House Museum on Montevallo Road (Alabama Highway 119), tells the stories of men and women of Leeds who have served in the military. The display includes information about Leeds's three recipients of the Congressional Medal of Honor and other Leeds residents who have distinguished themselves while fighting for our country.

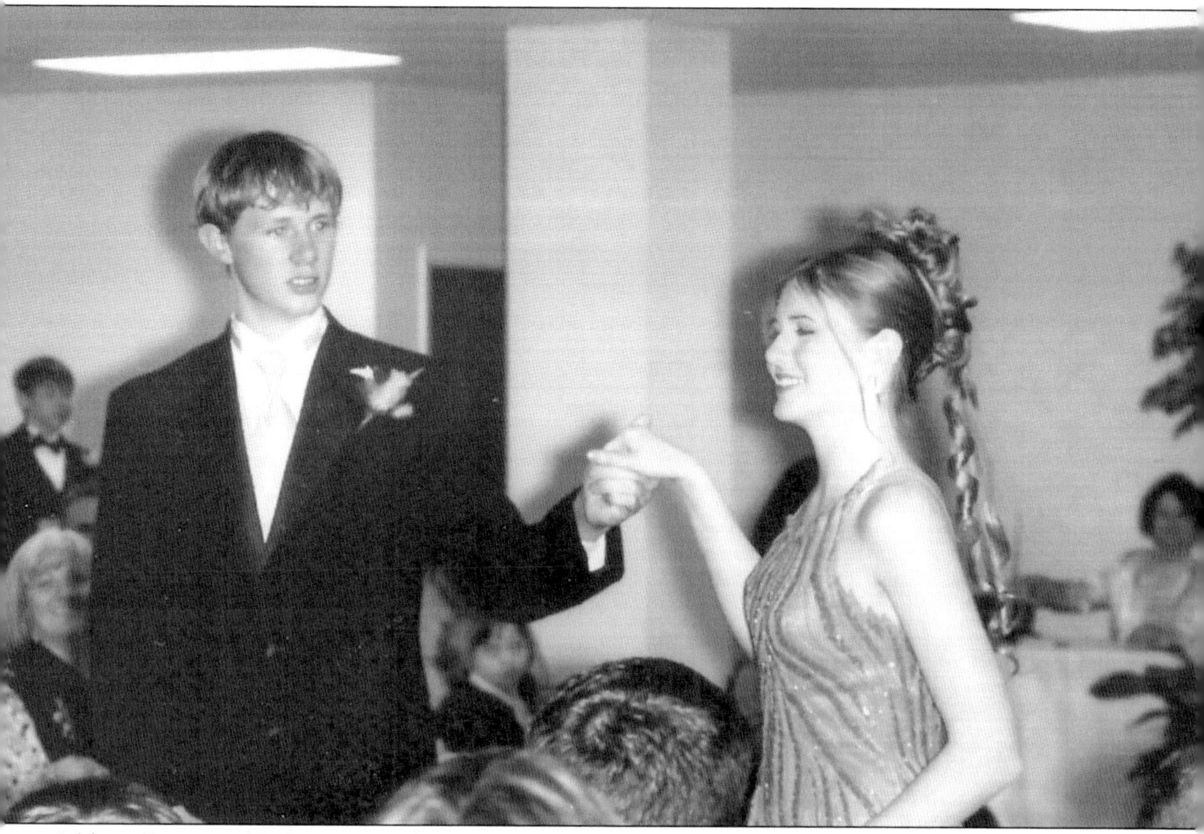

Siblings Larry and Rebecca Nix, descendants of John Richard Ingram Paschal Stewart, represent the remnants of Cherokee royalty in Alabama. These Leeds natives are among Pat Hall's student interns who worked to research and record photographically the archival elements of the Leeds Stagecoach Route. These students and others spent four years collecting the research on which to base Leeds's proposal to be named an Alabama Scenic Byway. In the photograph, they are celebrating their achievements at a charity fashion show. The suit modeled is from the Pants Store, Leeds's oldest retail clothing store, owned and operated by the Gee family since 1950. The dress is from a shop on Parkway Drive that specialized in pageant dresses. The celebration was only a slight reprieve from the research that these students would continue. Field trips to other parts of Alabama were part of the work. Students worked with archaeologists, park rangers, and trail experts to compare the Leeds experience to the overall Alabama culture.

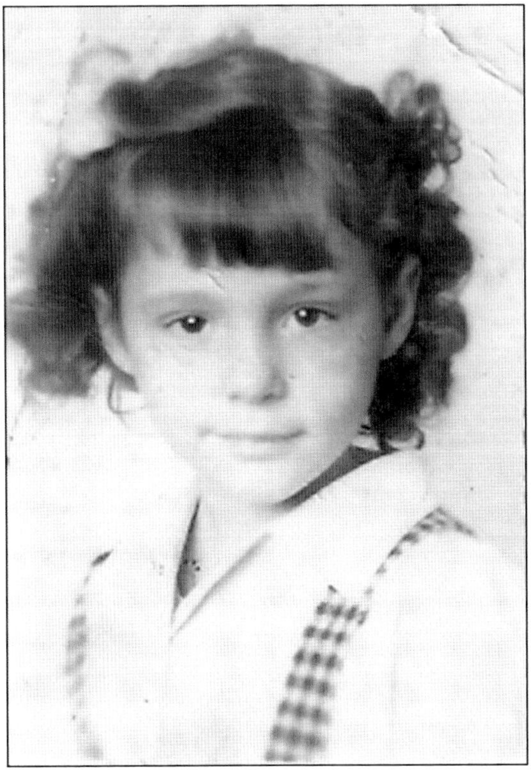

The thrill of watching an honor guard pass by is a mainstay of Memorial Day parades and celebrations in Birmingham and, now, in Leeds. This Leeds child, seven years old in 1945, visited Birmingham with her father to see military pomp and circumstance. In recent years, retired Marines have donned dress uniforms and provided military protocol for Veteran's Day ceremonies at Leeds Memorial Park.

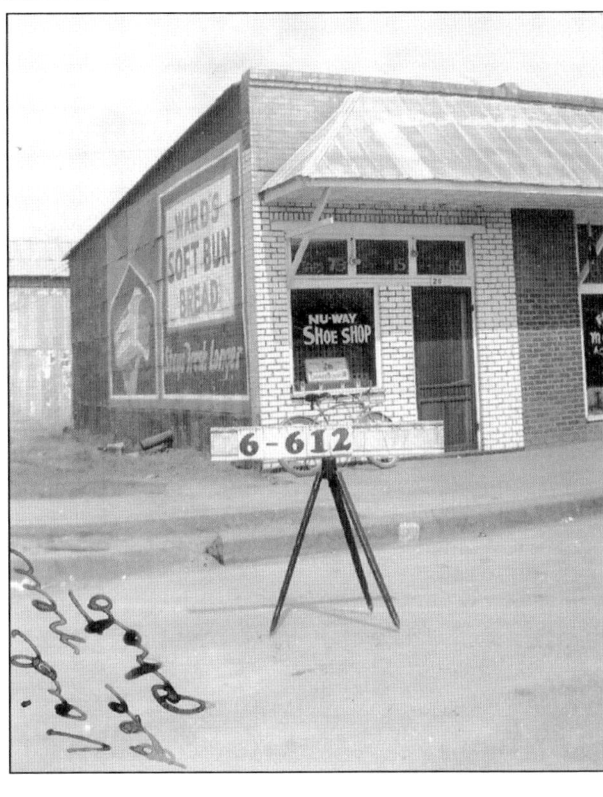

The Nu-Way shoe repair shop, located on Parkway Drive near Seventh Street, is shown here in 1939. The building's side wall featured an advertisement for Ward's Soft Bun Bread. During the Great Depression, three-fourths of the demand for shoe repair had vanished. Such shops were gone from Leeds by the 1970s when McKinnon's Pharmacy moved into this building. (BL.)

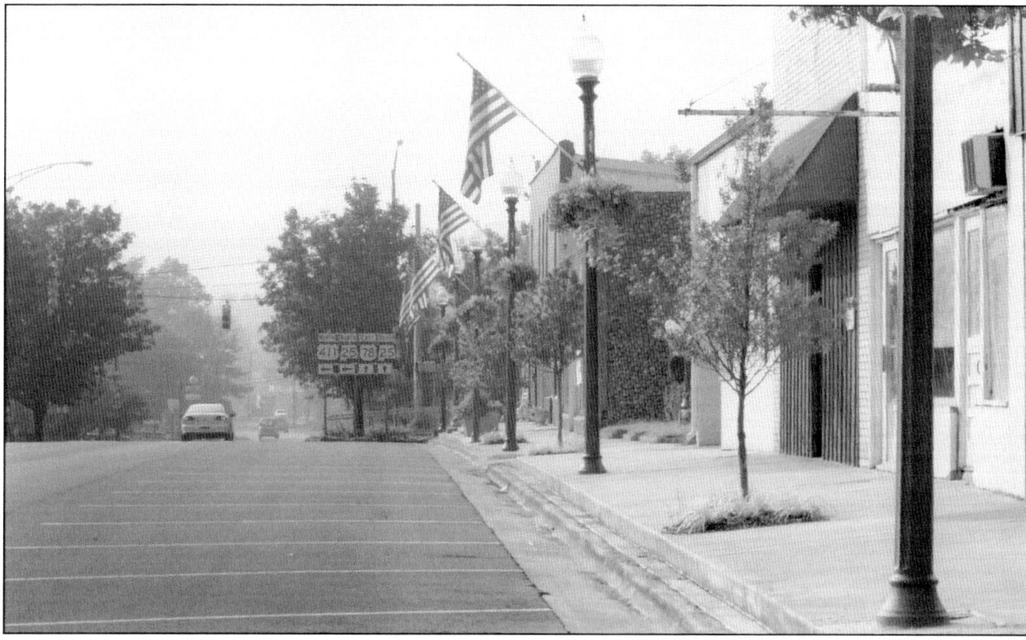

Flags fly each summer on Leeds's downtown streets. The sidewalk pictured is on a street that connects to the rest of Alabama to the north, south, east, and west. Leeds lives up to its designation as a gateway to a region. The car in the background heads east toward Atlanta while oncoming traffic would head west toward Birmingham.

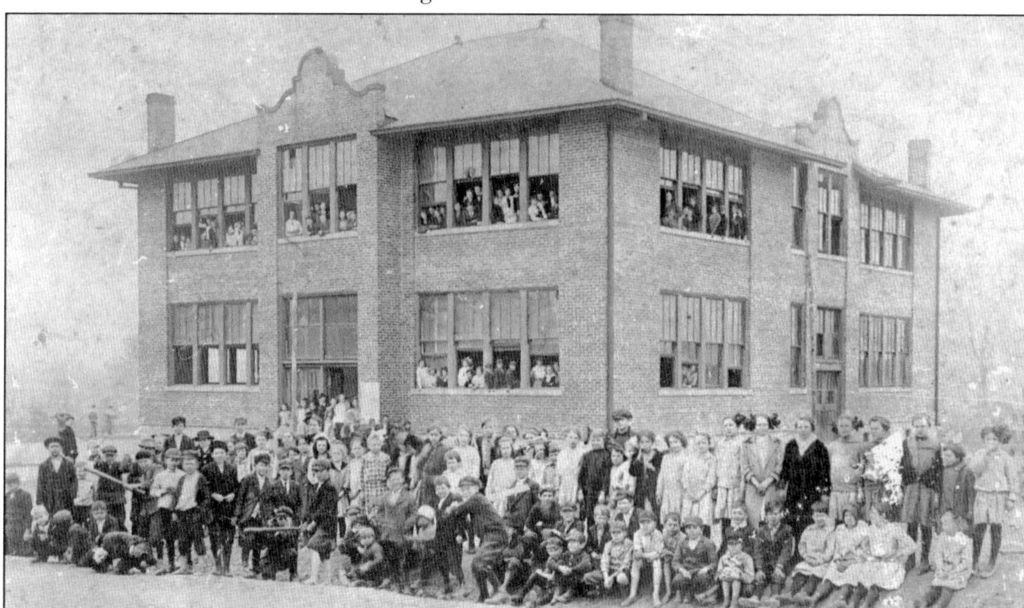

The first Leeds High School building was finished in 1911. At the time, it was a modern, two-story building on Ashville Road (Alabama Highway 119) adjacent to the present teachers' parking for Leeds Elementary School. This building no longer exists. A new high school was built in 1926 next to the old high school building. The 1926 building housed Leeds Elementary School until recently. (BM.)

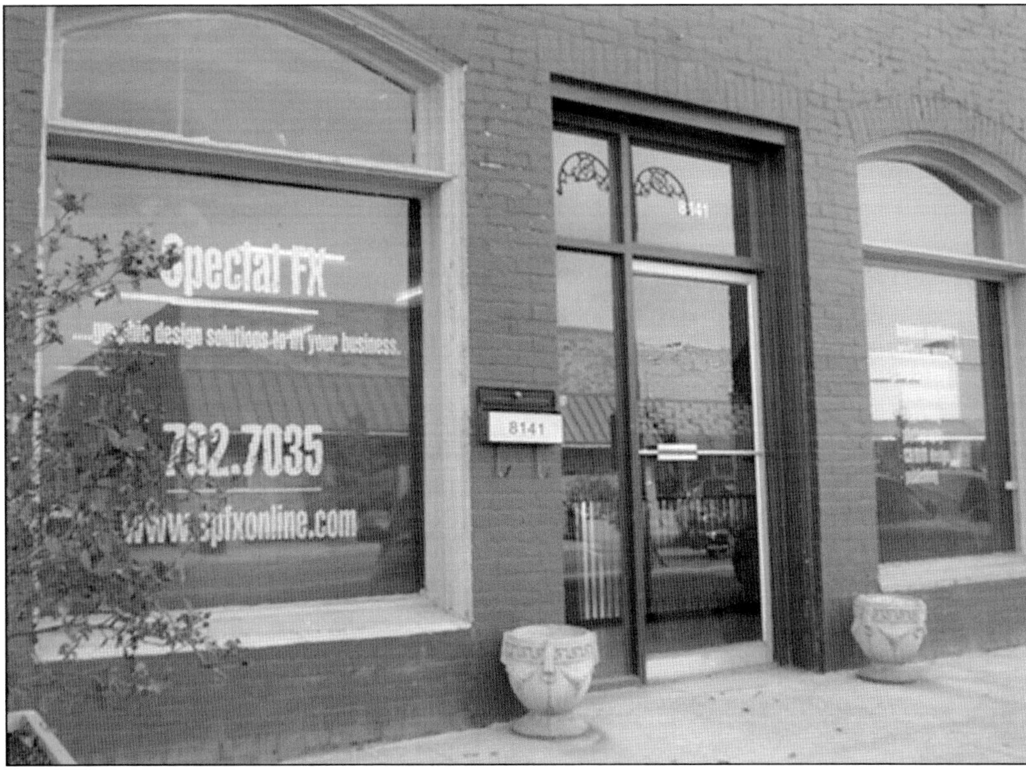

The Sharp building in downtown Leeds is owned by descendants of Michael J. Sharp Sr. He established and owned Sharp Furniture Company, which operated here between 1910 and 1978. He left the company to Michael J. Sharp Jr. The younger Sharp married Mattie Will, who had come to Leeds to teach school. By 1978, the building also belonged to her.

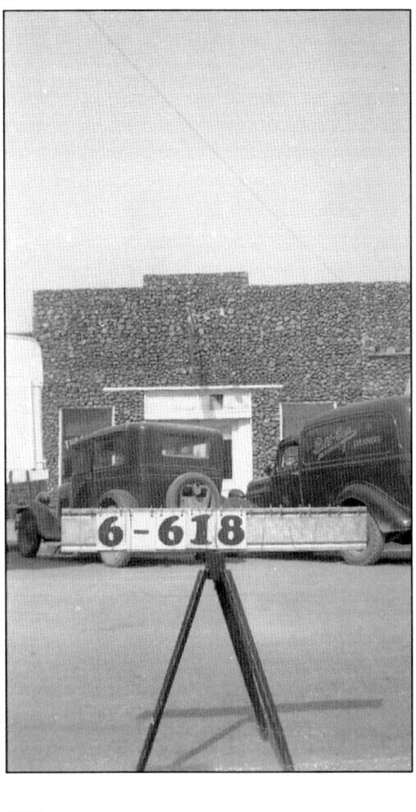

Bill-Cop Cleaners, shown here in 1939, was located at the corner of Parkway Drive and Eighth Street. During the Depression, the cleaners anchored a row of shops that now includes the Monkey's Uncle, a high-quality specialty shop that sells clothing and gifts, collectible items, and items of local and regional interest. Its owners also have a Christmas shop that opens seasonally in the downtown area. (BM.)

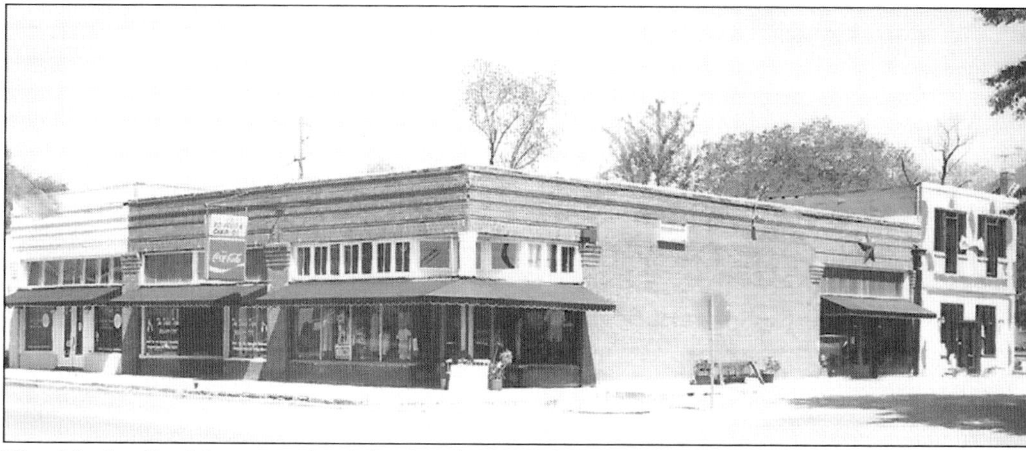

This block of buildings north of the Southern Railway tracks has been restored by Kelly Love, former president of the Leeds Area Chamber of Commerce. One of the early businesses in those buildings was owned by G.W. Hurst. His store sold candy and tobacco until the building was restored.

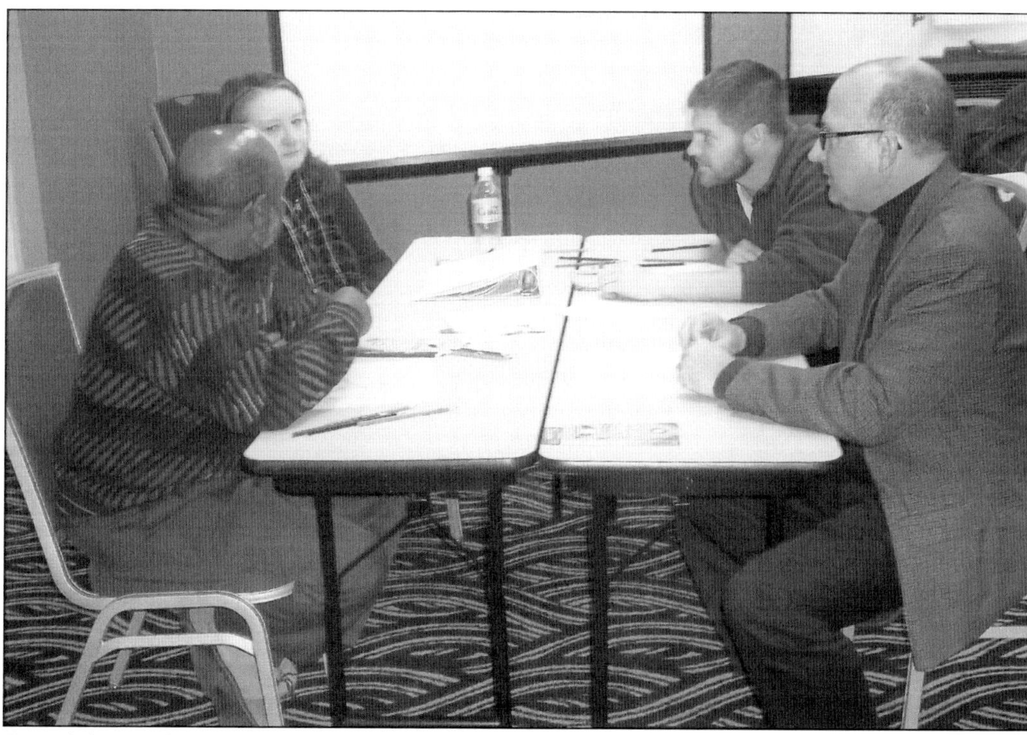

From left to right, Dan Marbury, Judy Jackson, Dane Boykin, and Kevin Fouts, members of the first Leedership Leeds class, participate in a problem-solving exercise. The program began in 2011 as part of Leeds's participation in the Alabama Communities of Excellence program.

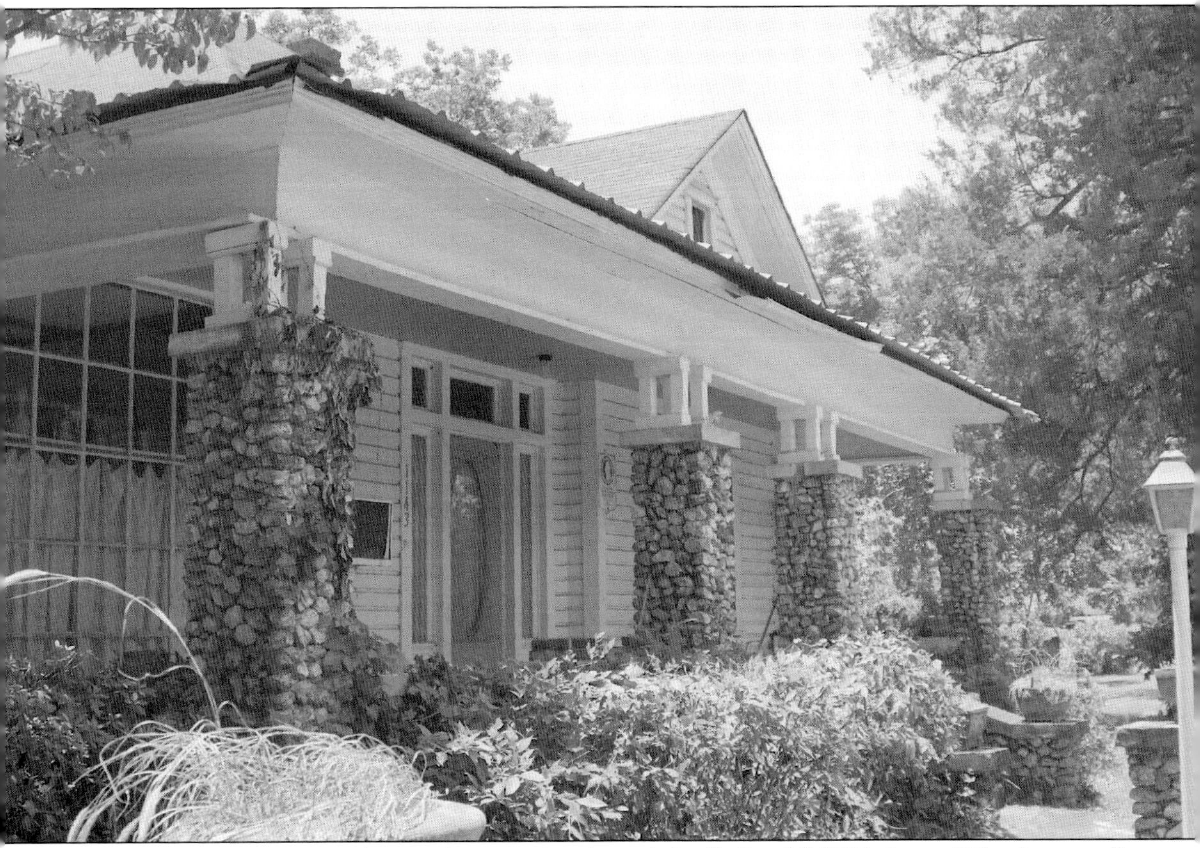

The 1913 William A. Whitmire house in Leeds on Ashville Road (US Highway 411) is historically marked. John Earl Whitmire's widow was the last occupant of this house. She flew a flag on each side of the front door—the American flag and the flag of the US Marine Corps. She was the wife of a Marine who had a son and grandsons in the Marines. The nearest house to hers was that of John Earl's brother T.B. Whitmire. A Leeds newspaper account of the death of T.B. Whitmire tells of the importance of the family to Leeds history. T.B. was survived by three sons, Bryant, McCoy, and John Earl Whitmire. The late Cecil Whitmire, a historic preservationist in Birmingham, was a member of this family. Cecil Whitmire recalled the times when he sat on a Whitmire porch and watched people at the train station.

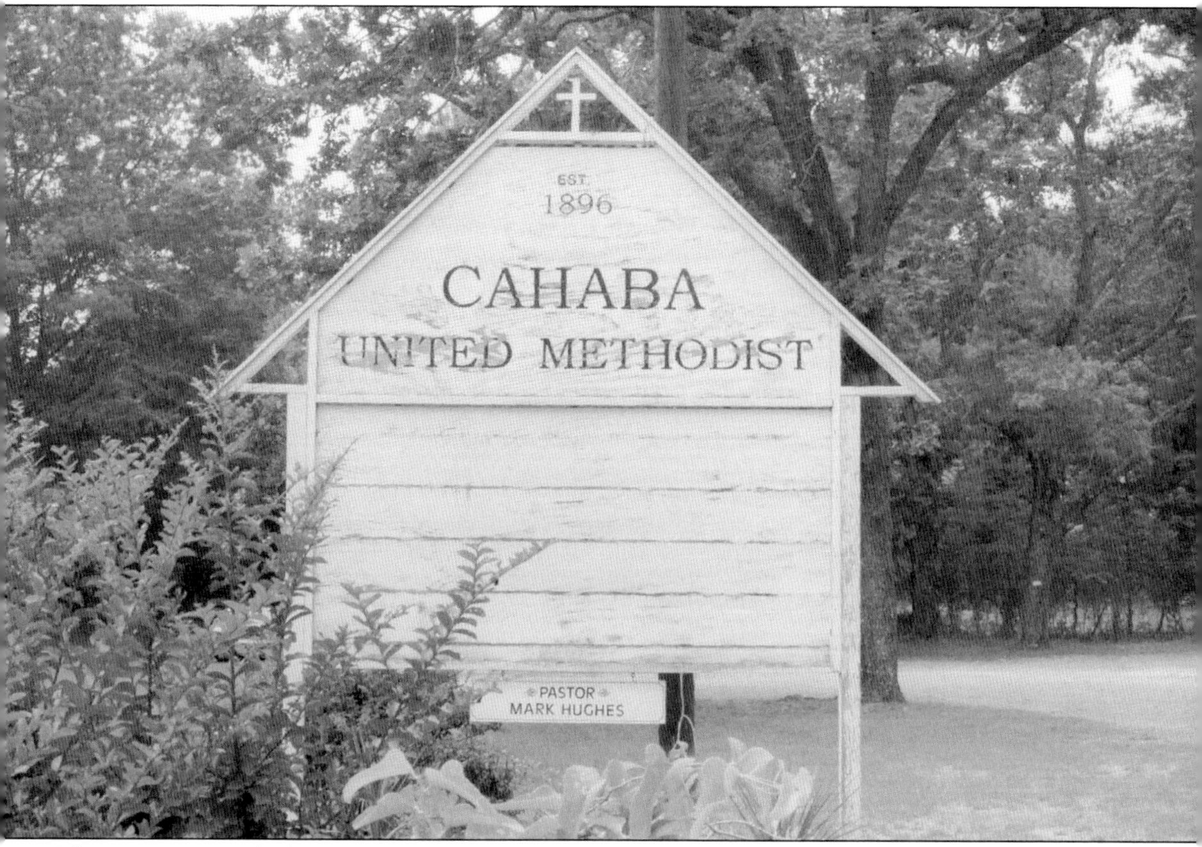

This rustic sign, which marks the Cahaba Methodist Church, greets commuters daily. The sign is on the Leeds Scenic Byway, where it is a constant reminder to drivers that this road has been traveled by horses, wagons, and early automobiles. It now greets bicyclists and commuters as well. Leeds Scenic Byway chose this point as its approach to the section of the byway named the Road, River, Horse Farms, and Home District. As the road meanders through the rural section of the Cahaba Valley, it arrives at Rowan Oaks Historic Home, the Stagecoach Stop, and Bass House District. The second district is named for its three important assets. In addition to the historical presence along the road in this district, the byway intersects with the Little Cahaba River for much of its three-mile run from Ziegler Road to US Highway 78 in the city of Leeds.

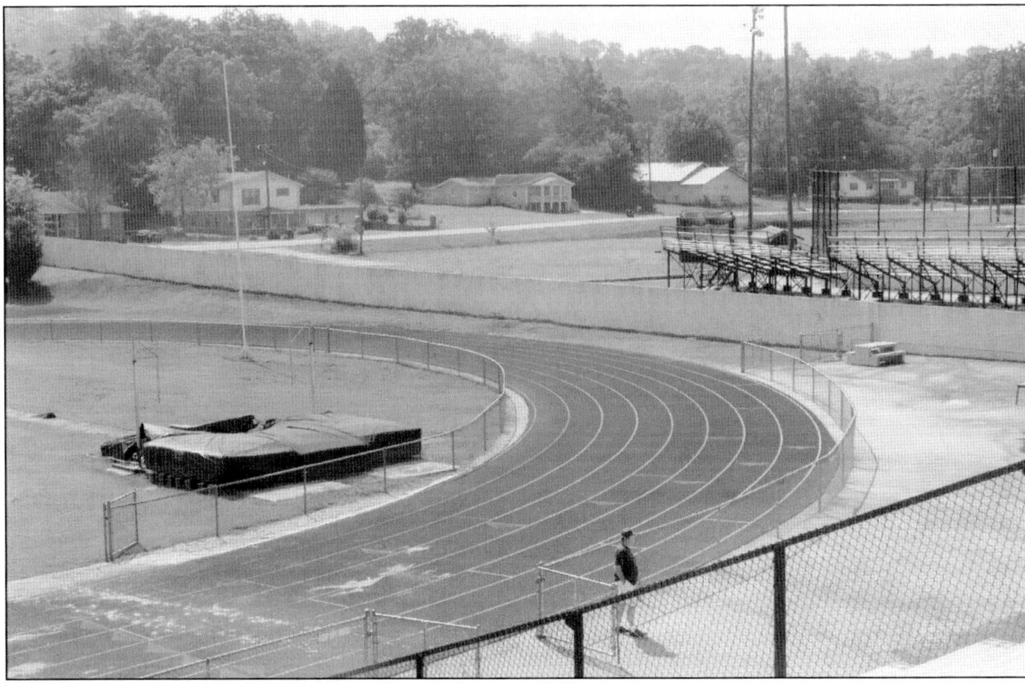

The people of Leeds built an Olympic-quality track to be used by an Olympic track team prior to the Atlanta Summer Olympic Games in 1996. The state-of-the-art facility enhanced Leeds High School's track and field program, which has won numerous state championships since that time.

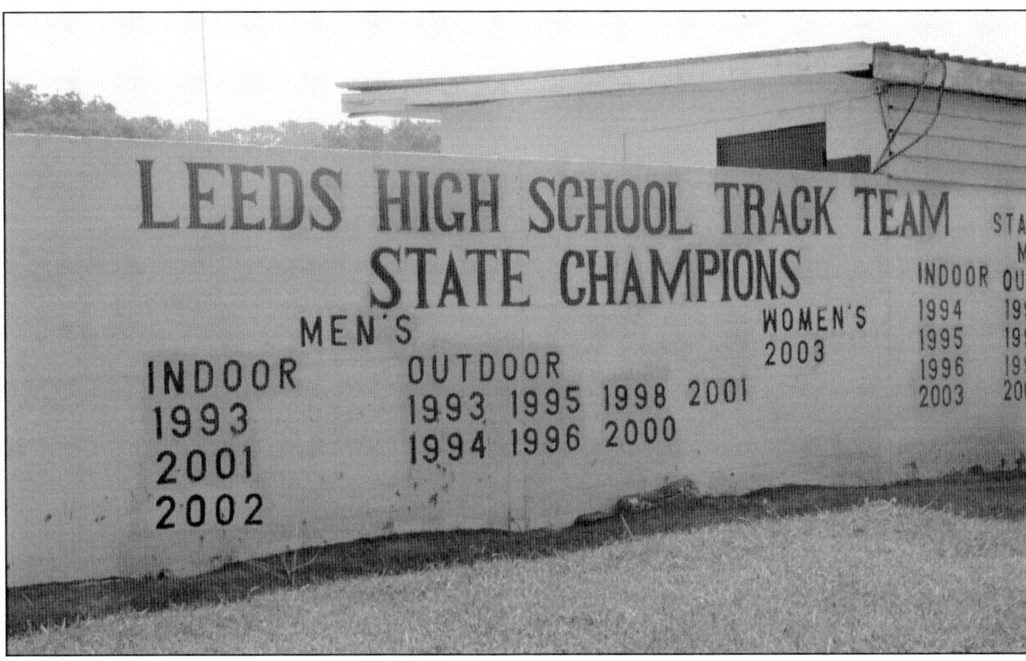

A wall that surrounds the track displays the dates that the track and field teams have won championships. The Leeds High School athletic program also includes football, basketball, baseball, softball, soccer, golf, volleyball, and wrestling.

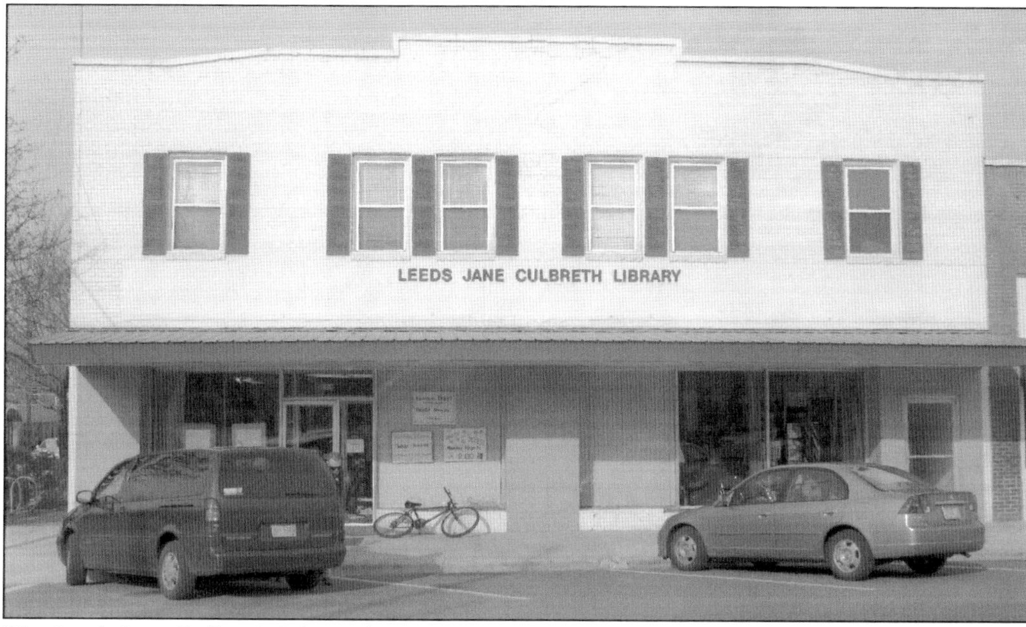

The Leeds Jane Culbreth Library began operations in about 1923 in two rooms above a building on Ninth Street in downtown Leeds. In 1971, the library moved to its current location on Parkway Drive, shown here. The library bears Culbreth's name as a tribute to her library work and other civic accomplishments.

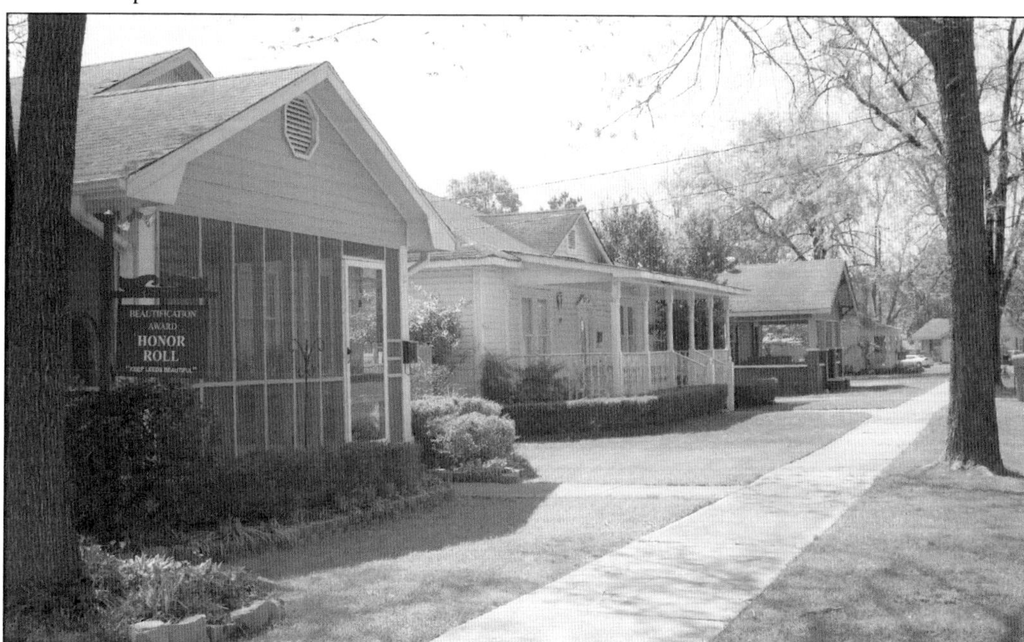

This permanent Beautification Honor Roll sign, seen here in the Spruiell subdivision, is a coveted award in Leeds. The town is a Tree City, a bird sanctuary, and the site of equestrian exhibits. It is located at the headwaters of the longest watershed in Alabama, which provides drinking water for the majority of Alabamians. Leeds deals responsibly with its natural assets, knowing they affect not only Leeds, but the rest of Alabama.

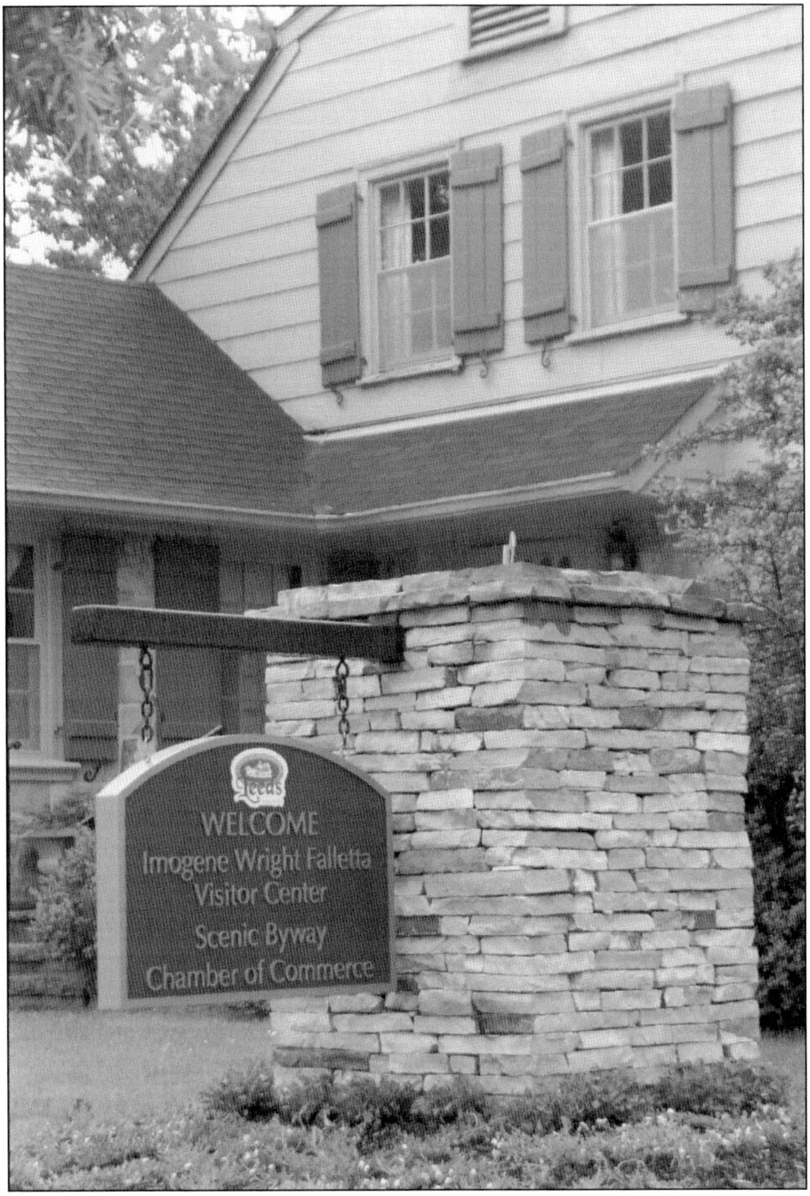

The architectural style of the Imogene Falletta house was the subject of a study for historical marking purposes. According to the study, Leeds-area craftsmen used locally quarried brownstone on the house's exterior to convey a sense of warmth in every season. The house was built by Leeds physician E.C. Clayton in 1938.

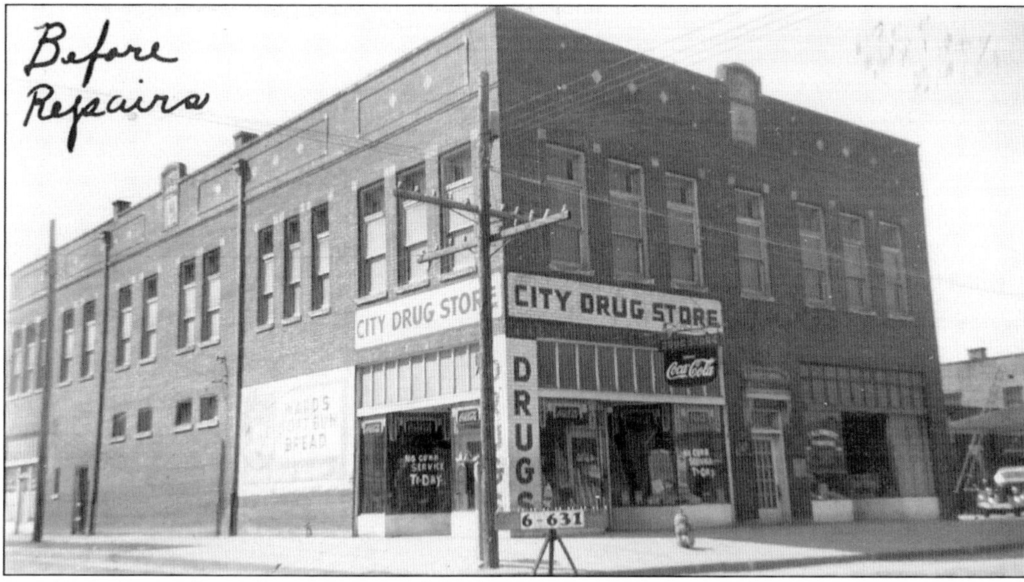

City Drug Store, shown here in 1939, sold soft drinks, medical equipment, and prescription drugs. Dr. A.E. Powers's dental practice was located on the second floor of the building, above City Drug Store. He was the father of Joe Powers and the grandfather of Jo Ann Powers, who met Elvis Presley at Power's Café, which her father owned when Presley visited Leeds in 1955. (BL.)

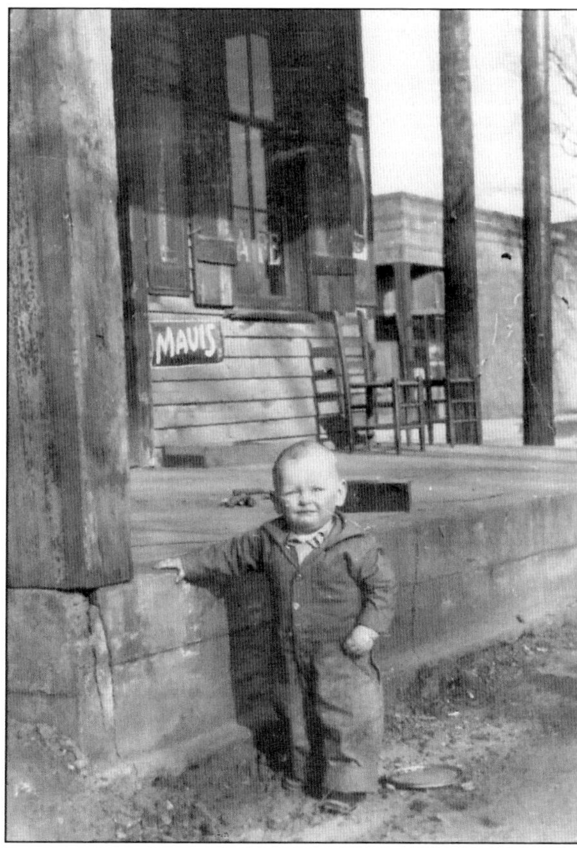

Leeds native Vernon Byars is pictured here as a child. More than one member of the Byars family was in Company C, 18th Alabama Regiment, known as the Cahaba Valley Rangers. The company was organized in the Cahaba Valley on July 4, 1861. They chose as their officers Leeds natives J.M. Oliver, Hezekiah Moor, and C.C. Coupland. (LL.)

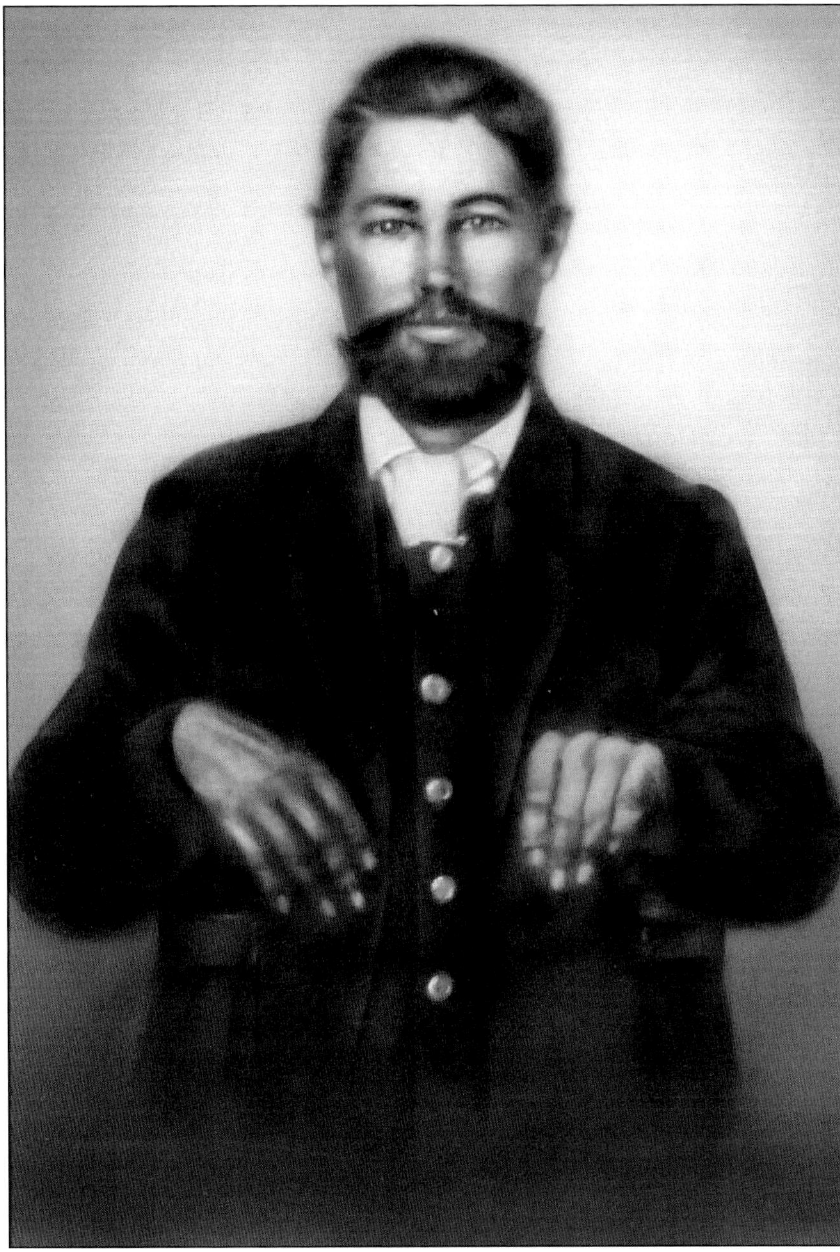

Hezekiah Moor was a surgeon and a celebrated founder of Leeds. The city's founders, their fathers, and progeny have fought in every war that the United States has fought. Some of the families are descended from more than one signer of the Declaration of Independence. While Dolley Madison was fleeing the burning White House with a photograph of Pres. George Washington, some forefathers of Leeds natives were fighting in the Indian skirmishes during the War of 1812. French and British forces had returned to America to fight over the land and were using Native Americans as their foot soldiers. With the same tactics used to help Washington win the Revolutionary War, ancestors of Leeds families were battling in the wilderness. In the 21st century, Leeds can celebrate not only those motivated warriors, but also three Congressional Medal of Honor winners from a population of less than 5,000. (BM.)

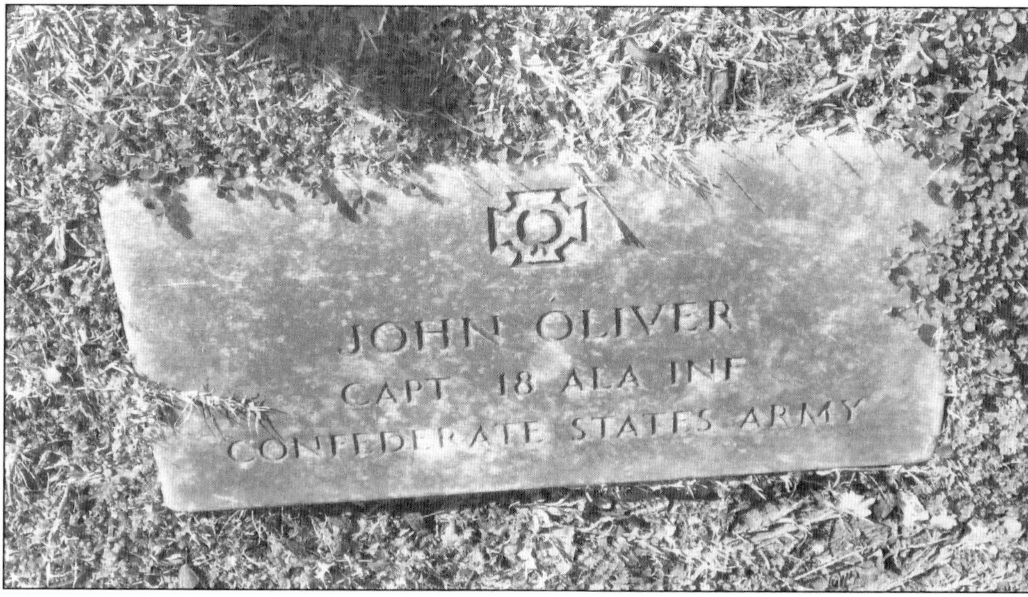

John Oliver and Hezekiah Moor had adjoining land grants. Oliver Crossing, a subdivision named in honor of John Oliver, is located on Oliver's land grant. Oliver was one of Leeds's early pioneers and was accorded the right to purchase land grants because he had served the United States in the War of 1812.

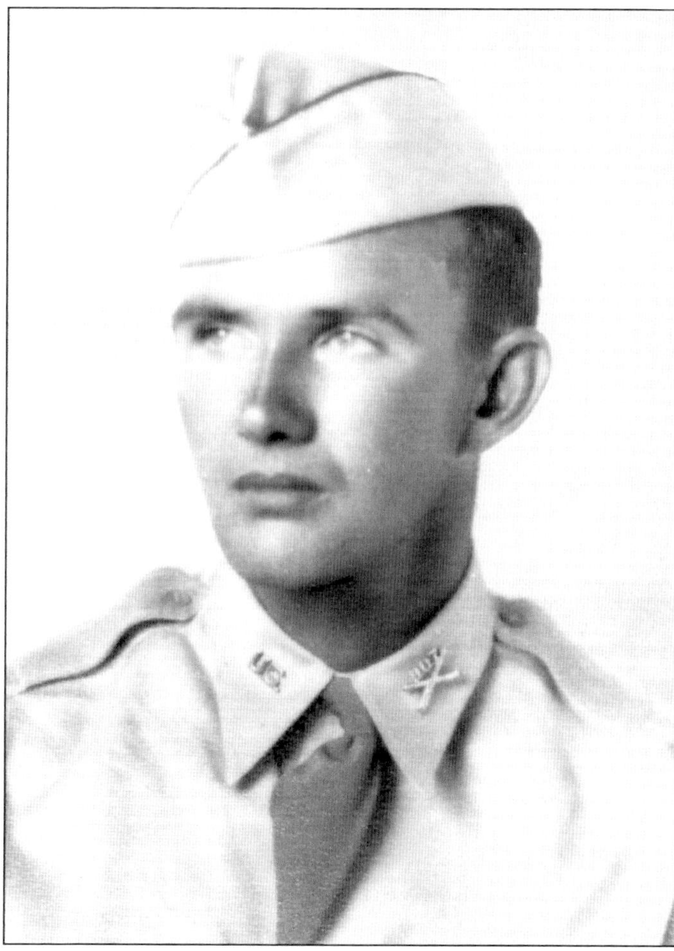

Morton Spruiell was killed by enemy fire on June 11, 1944, after parachuting into Normandy. The circumstances of his death remained a mystery until a collector of World War II antiquities purchased Spruiell's helmet (with a bullet hole in it) 62 years later. After discovering who the helmet belonged to, the collector presented it to Morton's brother, Glenn Spruiell, in 2007. Morton Spruiell was awarded a Distinguished Service Cross posthumously. (LL.)

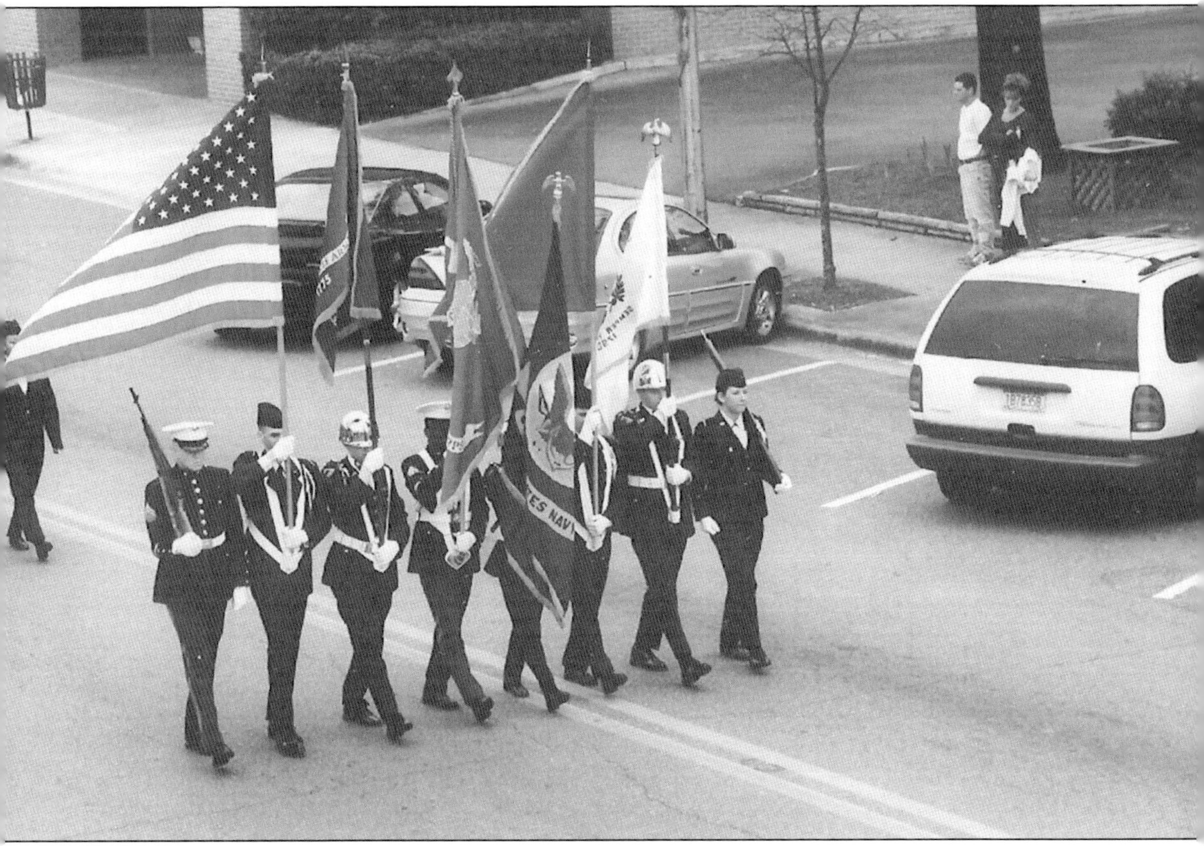

A military honor guard comes to Leeds for a celebration honoring all of Leeds's veterans, including veterans of the Vietnam War. The sorrows and price of this conflict are exemplified by meritorious acts of Army Platoon Sgt. James A. Bunn, who was killed in action on February 2, 1968. James's wife, Rachel, was notified by the Army that her husband had been awarded a Bronze Star Medal and a Purple Heart posthumously. He was killed during his second tour of duty in Vietnam, where he had already acquired one Purple Heart. The citation reads, in part: "Through his untiring efforts and professional ability, he consistently obtained outstanding results. He was quick to grasp the implications of new problems with which he was faced as a result of the ever-changing situations inherent in a counter-insurgency operation and to find ways and means to solve those problems."

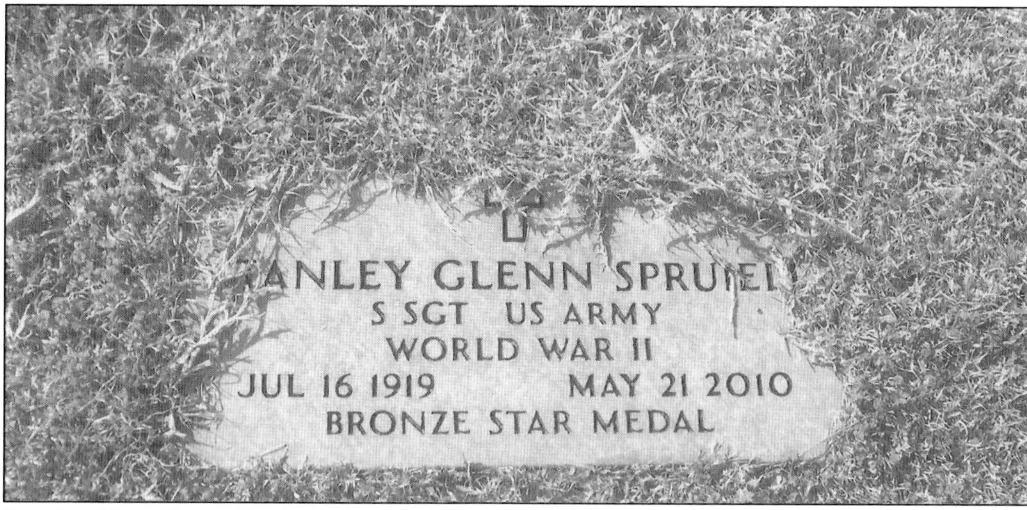

Stanley Glenn Spruiell is buried in Shiloh Cemetery. Glenn is the son of John Melvin Spruiell, a pharmacist whose forefather fought in the American Revolution. Glenn and his brother Morton Spruiell fought in World War II. John Melvin Spruiell was the mayor of Leeds from 1920 through 1924.

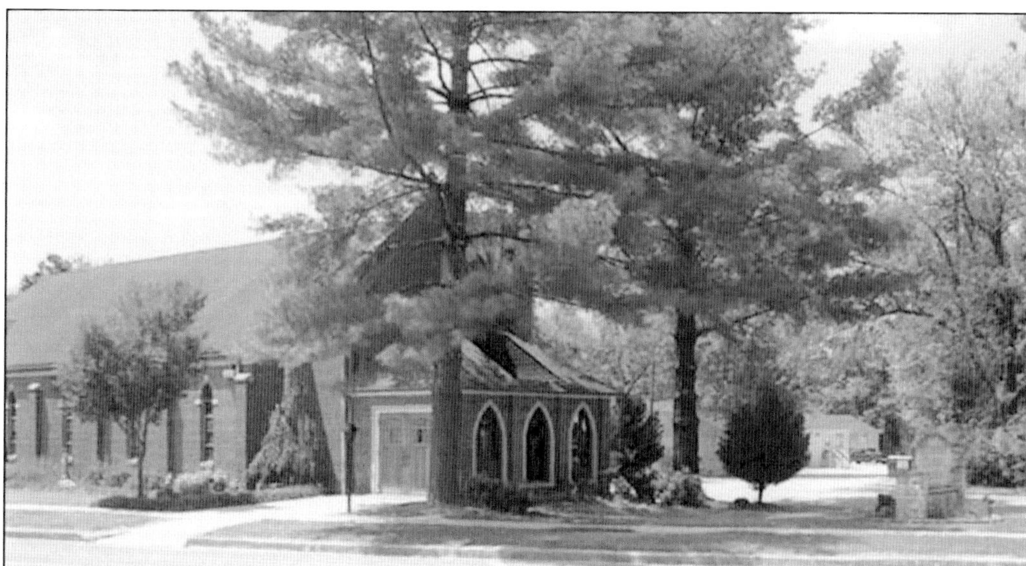

St. Theresa's Catholic Church was built in 1952 at a cost of $19,600. Rev. James Gallagher was appointed pastor and offered the first Mass on July 27. A parish house was built in 1960, a church hall in 1987, and a bell tower in 1989. In 2011, the church completed an expansion that increased seating capacity by 80 percent. (Courtesy of St. Teresa Catholic Church.)

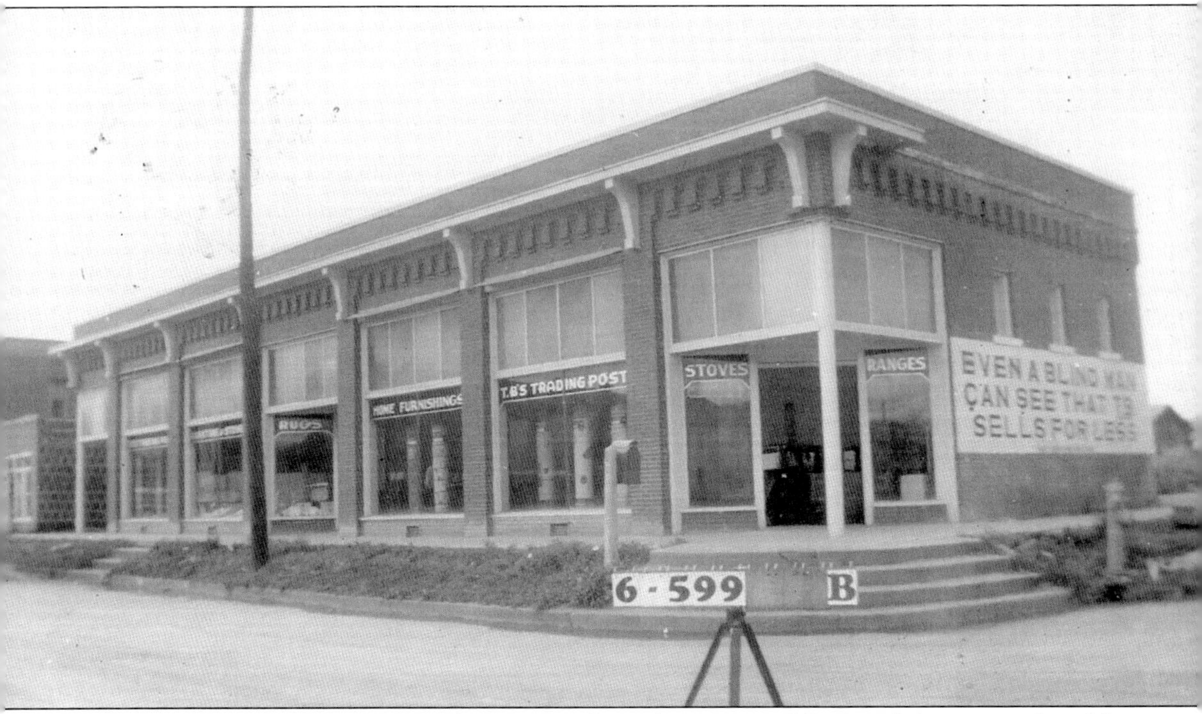

The building pictured here at the corner of Ninth Street and Railroad Avenue is the oldest standing building in downtown Leeds. It was built between 1883 and 1887 and has been restored to its former glory. Located at the center of the early town near the Southern Railway Depot, the building housed Leeds's first post office in 1889. In the 1930s, T.B. Whitmire owned the building, which housed T.B.'s Trading Post. The oldest street in downtown Leeds, Ninth Street has also been the starting point for parades in Leeds. Through the years, Leeds has been a sister city to Leeds, England. During America's bicentennial celebration, a parade recognized a top official who was visiting from Leeds, England. This ambassador came to the city to commend Leeds, Alabama, for its accomplishments. A permanent display of his gifts to the city can be seen in the Leeds Jane Culbreth Library. (BL.)

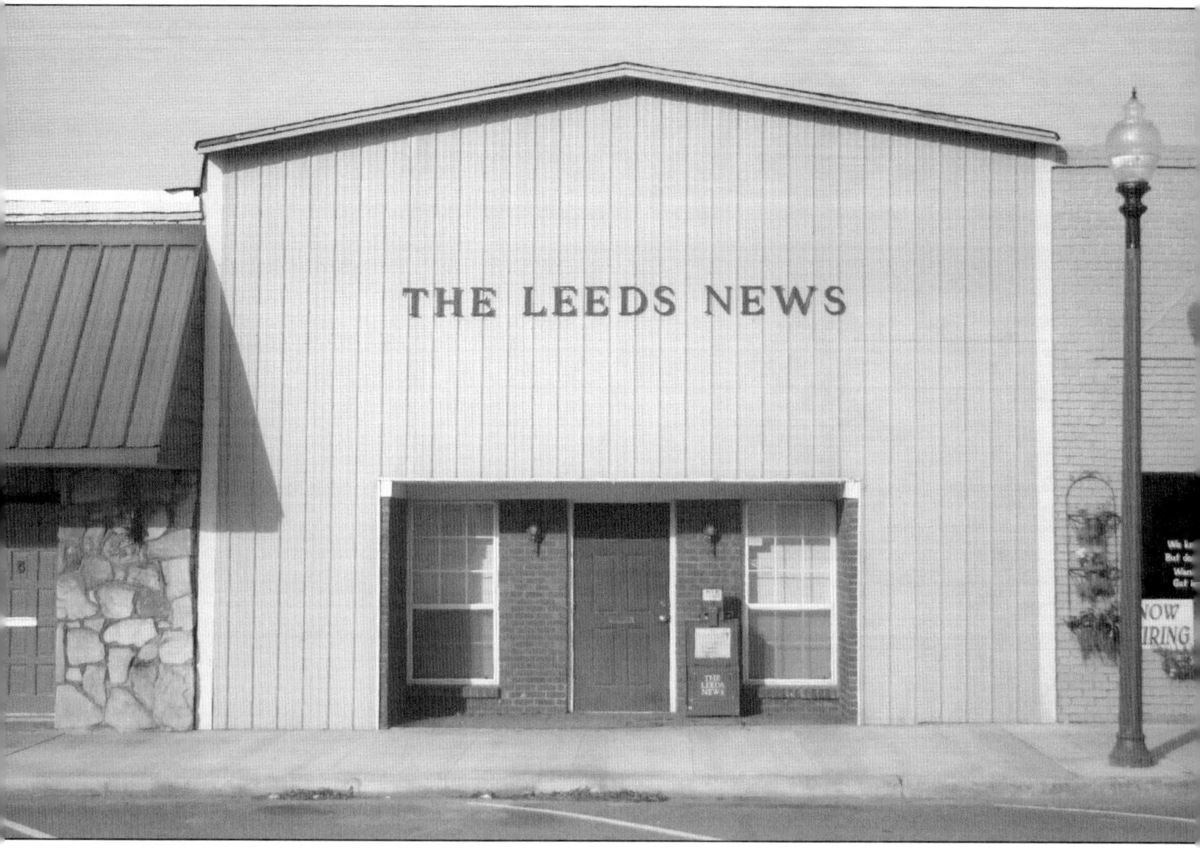

Bernice Lee Goodson became the editor of *The Leeds News* in 1939 and continued to publish it until 1946. Bob Bryan purchased the newspaper in March 1973 from Ethel Blair. Her husband, Edmund Blair, had published *The Leeds News* and the *St. Clair News Aegis* for more than 35 years before his death. A collection of issues of *The Leeds News* from 1939 to 1976 is on microfilm at Samford University Library in the Special Collections Department. On August 31, 2011, the newspaper ceased publication. At the time, the city of Leeds and the Leeds Scenic Byway team, along with volunteers from Leeds High School and the Woman's Literary Club of Leeds, were well into a project to sort and secure the archives at the city records building. Shortly after the *St. Clair News Aegis* absorbed *The Leeds News* and took the office to Pell City in September 2011, this group of volunteers found a collection of *The Leeds News* newspapers dating from the 1930s.

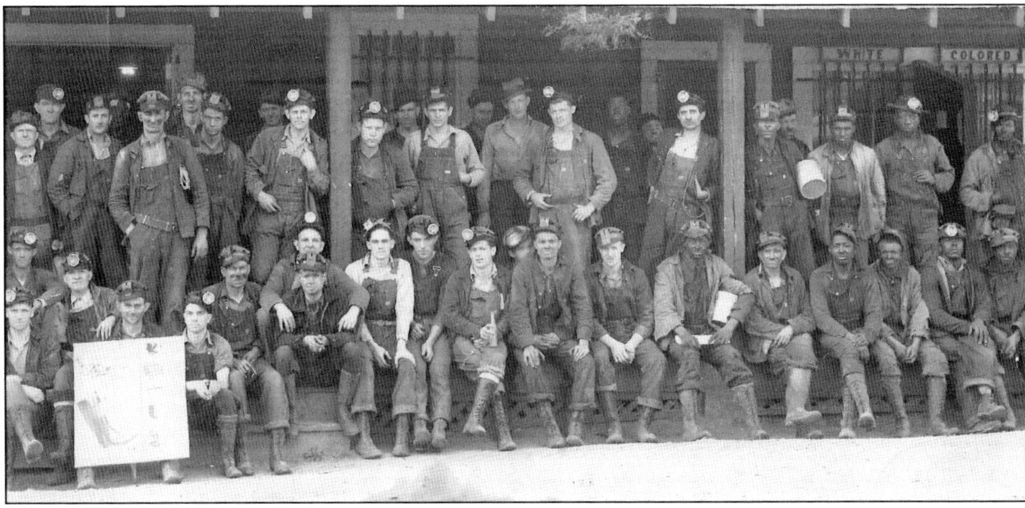

Coal miners employed at the Red Diamond Mine pose for a photograph on the porch of the commissary of the Red Diamond Mine in Leeds around 1938. The mine, company store, and company-owned houses were once located near what is now the intersection of Interstate 20 and US Highway 78. The mines in Leeds, Red Diamond and Henry Ellen, contributed to the local economy during the Great Depression. (LHS.)

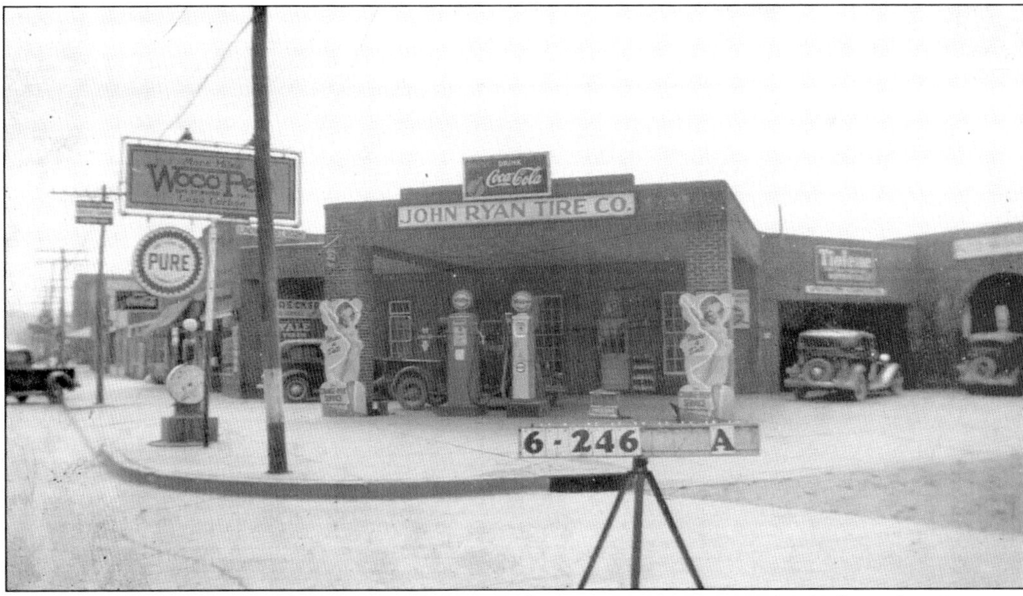

John Ryan Tire Company, shown in 1939, was a full-service gas station in the Idaburg development. Some industries remained open in Leeds during the Great Depression, and people with jobs depended on storeowners and gas stations for their basic needs, including food, clothing, and transportation. As a result, businesses such as Ryan's were also able to remain open. (BL.)

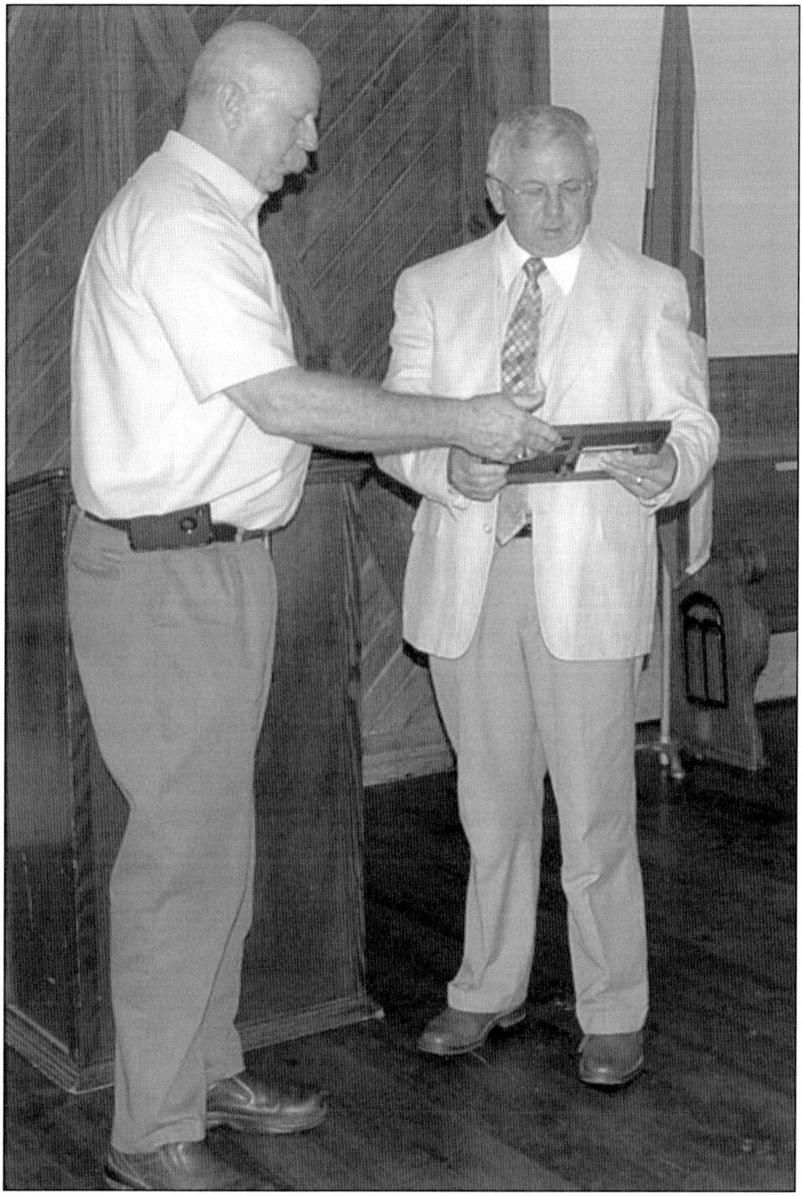

Leeds Historical Society has drawn its presidents from local and state leaders since it was founded in 1998. Here, Frank Little passes the Leeds Historical Society presidency to Dickie Drake. He held the post for a year before his brother, state representative Owen Drake, died, leaving a vacant seat in the Alabama House of Representatives. Dickie Drake ran for the seat and became the second Drake from Leeds to be seated in Alabama's legislative body. Two other Leeds natives, Sonny Moore and Jim McClendon, also served as state representatives. Both Drake brothers were retired from the US Air Force. As a state legislator, Dickie Drake faced the challenge of governing during an economic downturn and high unemployment among his constituents with guarded optimism. A chance to carry out work that Owen Drake had begun motivated Dickie Drake to run. Prior to his retirement from the military, Dickie Drake held the rank of chief master sergeant in the US Air Force and served as an in-flight refueling program manager in the Bosnian-Kosovo conflict, the Gulf War, the Iraq War, and the Afghanistan War.

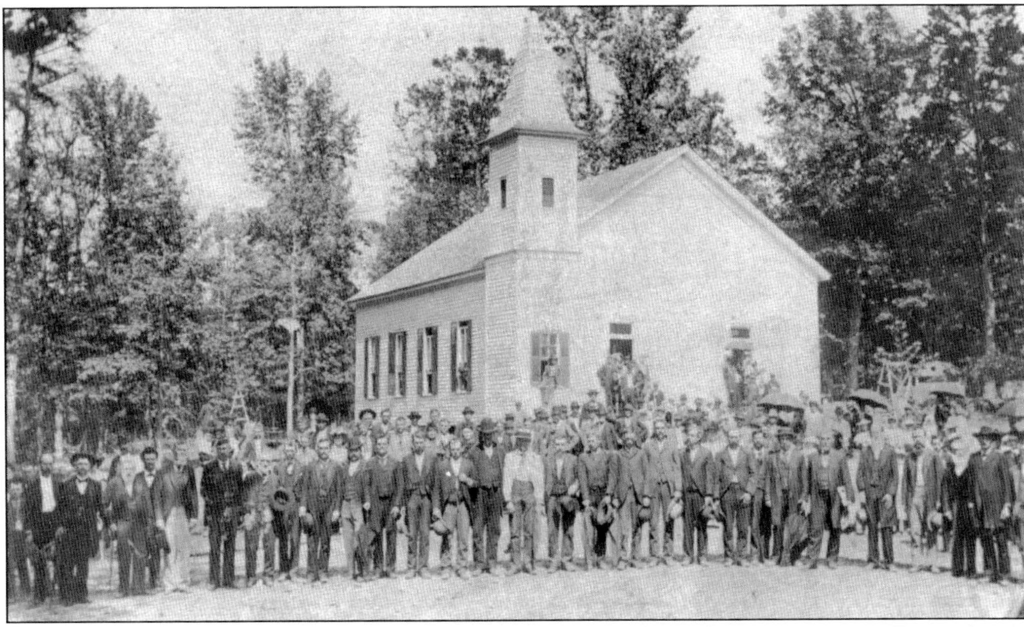

Mount Hebron Baptist Church was founded 75 days before Alabama became a state on December 14, 1819. The building pictured here, with congregation members, is a 1930s version of the structure built in 1922. It is the fifth church structure the congregation built. The record books of Mount Hebron are preserved in the Special Collections Room at Samford University in Birmingham. (BM.)

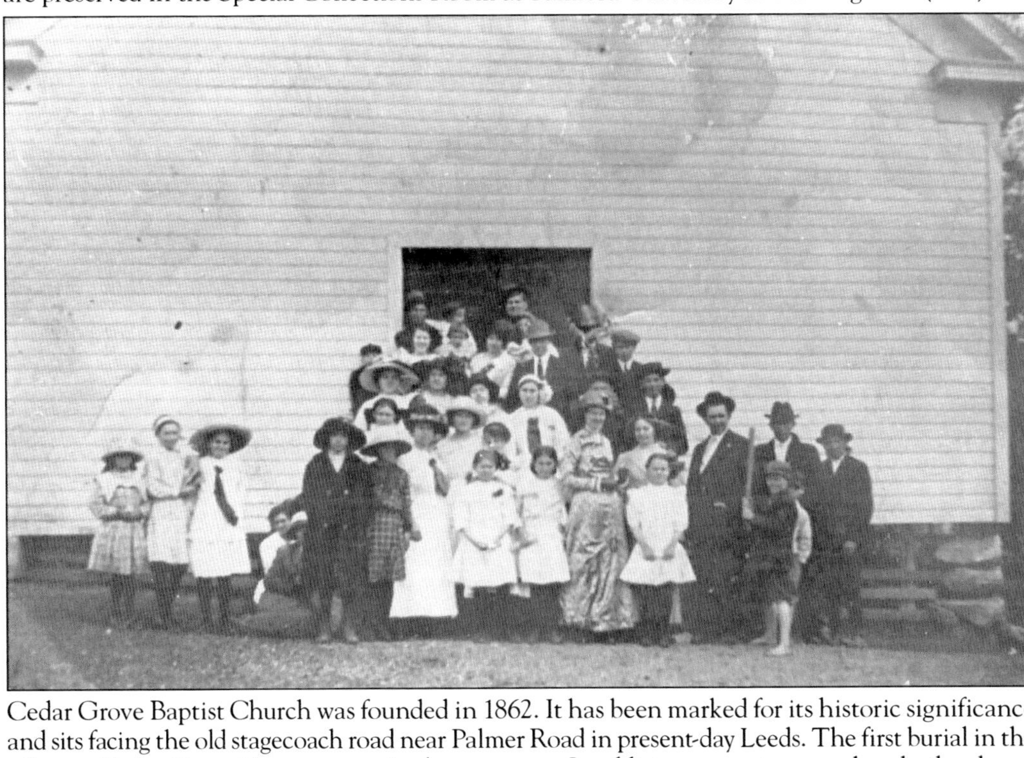

Cedar Grove Baptist Church was founded in 1862. It has been marked for its historic significance and sits facing the old stagecoach road near Palmer Road in present-day Leeds. The first burial in the adjacent Cedar Grove Cemetery was in the same year. In addition to serving as a church, the chapel also served as one of the first schools in the valley and as a hospital during the Civil War. (LL.)

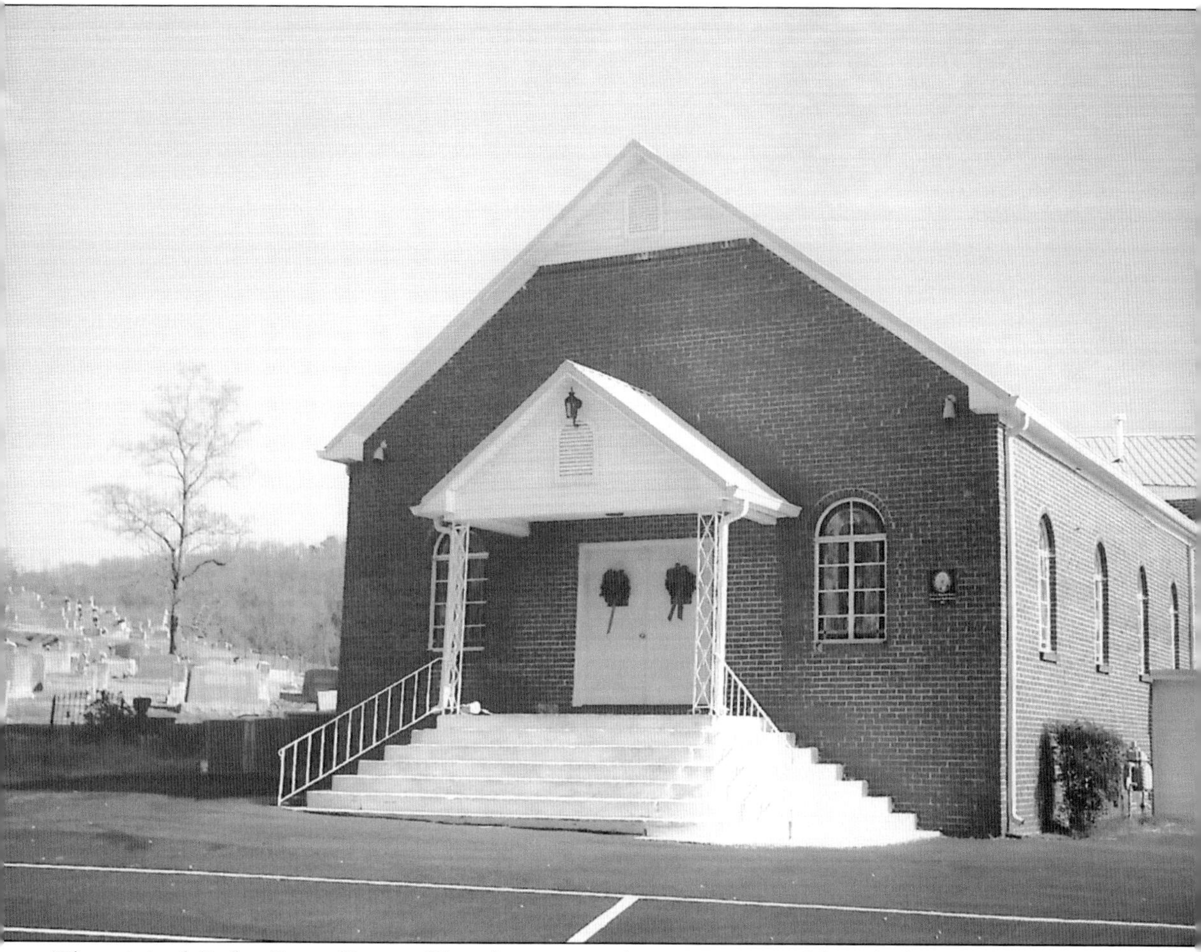

The original Cedar Grove Baptist Church retains its basic structure, although the wood exterior has been bricked and a foyer added to the front. Inside are handmade cedar pews crafted from trees cut down on the property. The original congregation met in a log cabin. On July 8, 1862, Hezekiah Moor deeded a portion of land to the church, recorded and described in Book E of the St. Clair County Probate Court: "Beginning at Red Oak on the south side of main road, and north of the church house, running thence twenty rods to a red oak and thence southwest twenty rods to a post oak, thence west to the main road, thence up the main road to the beginning corner, and a way to the spring east of south from the church direct one rod in width." The land would be used for permanent church grounds including a cemetery, both named Cedar Grove.

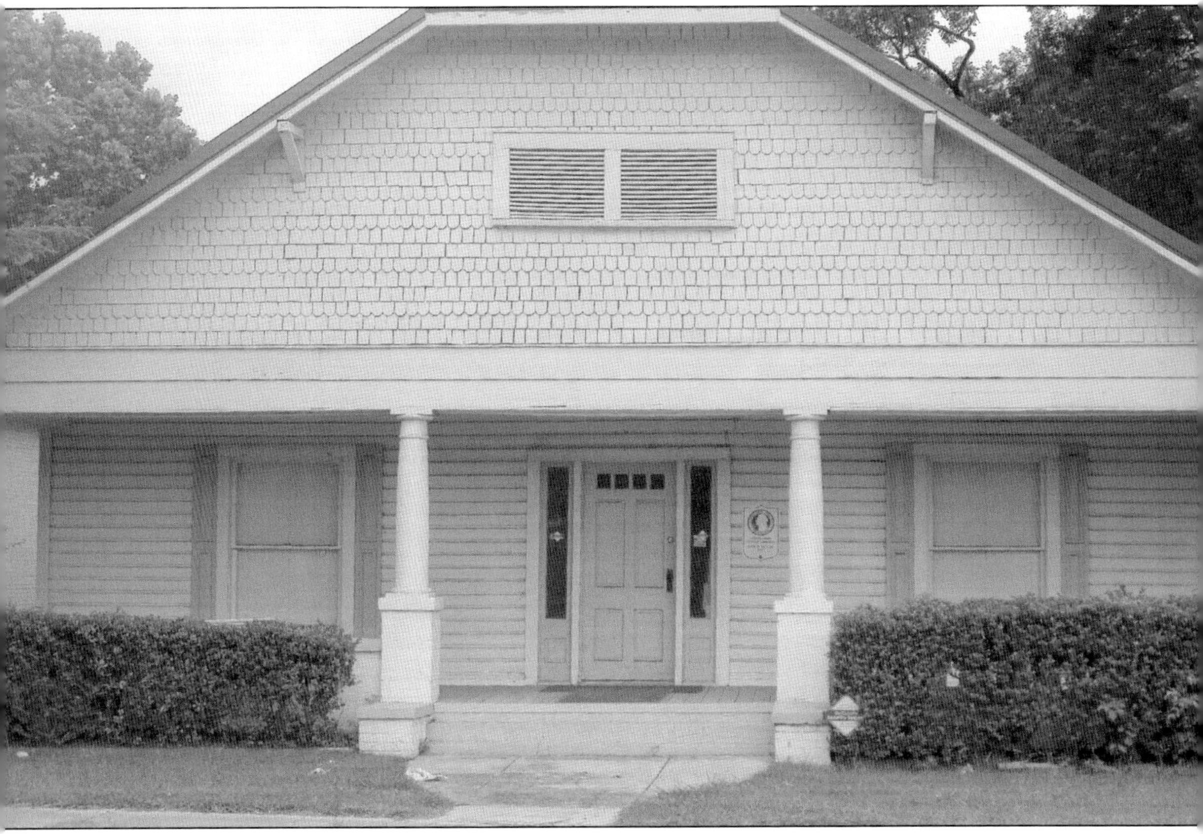

J. Wallace Lewis, often called Mr. Chero-Cola in his time, built his "pretty bungalow" in 1920. He came to Leeds with very little capital and built what became a prosperous Coca-Cola distributorship. But his first "big yellow" Chero-Cola truck lent what the *Leeds Progressive Review* called "an air of cosmopolitanism" to the town. The house was restored and remains on Ashville Road (US Highway 411) near the railroad trestle. The *Leeds Progressive Review* of Saturday, April 24, 1920, shares the enthusiasm for persistence and energy in a businessman: "Mr. Lewis is an example of that which a young man can accomplish by grit, grace, and energy. Coming to Leeds . . . years ago . . . he located on the Little Cahaba River which flows through Leeds and his pretty bungalow faces the highway [US 411]." The Cahaba is immediately outside the door of the building next to the Lewis house, which is on the site of the original Chero-Cola buildings.

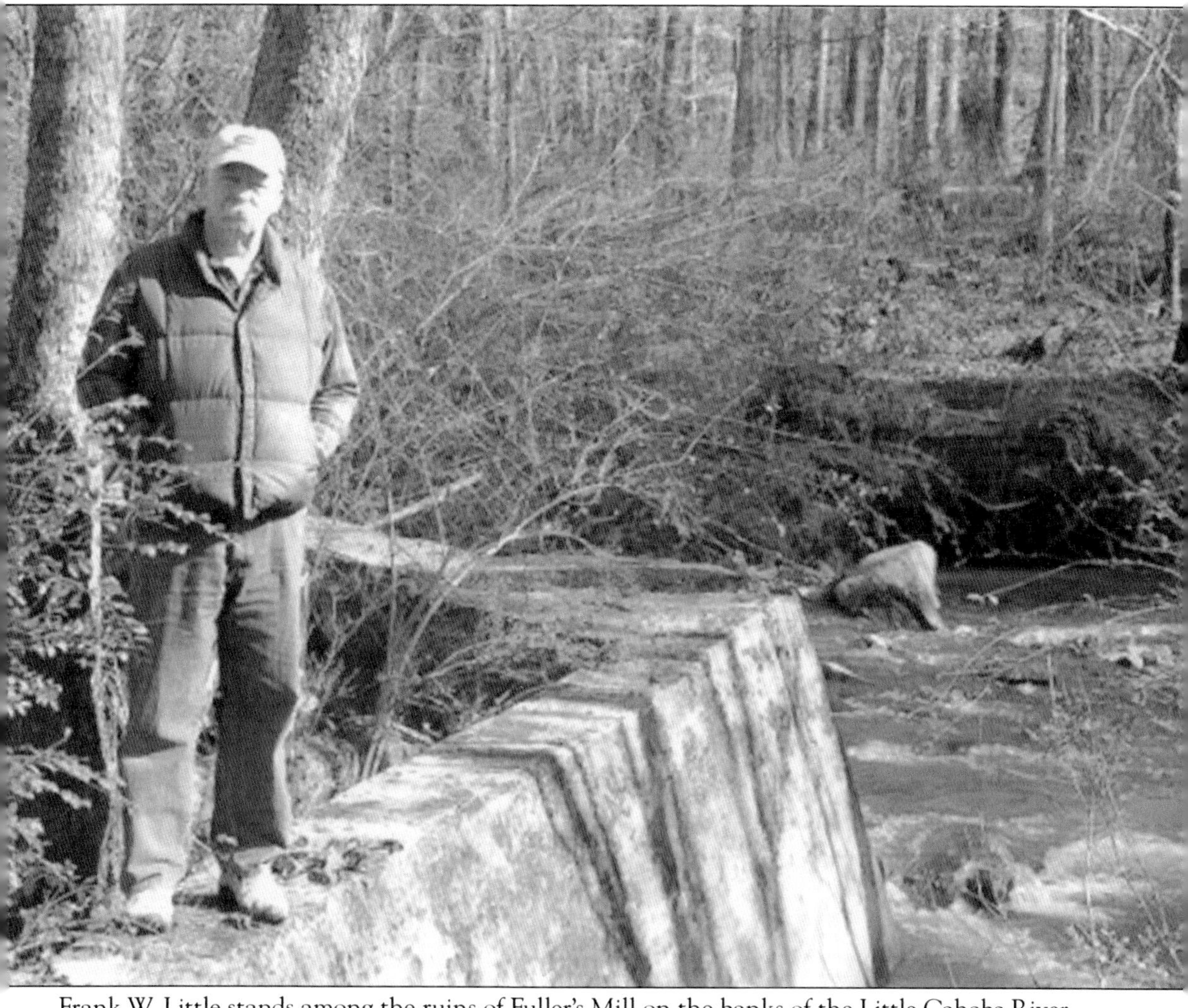

Frank W. Little stands among the ruins of Fuller's Mill on the banks of the Little Cahaba River, which was built and operated almost 200 years ago by his ancestor Henry Little. Frank not only has Henry Little's blood coursing through his veins, he also shares his ancestor's pioneer spirit. A decorated veteran of the Vietnam War, this Leeds native has held leadership positions in local civic organizations, such as the Leeds Masonic Lodge No. 446. He also served as president of the Leeds Historical Society. In 2010, the Fuller's Mill property was deeded to the historical society by Jimmy Moore. The society is working to clear the property so that the ruins of the mill can be seen from Alabama Highway 119. Frank's ancestors, along with the other founders of Leeds, left generations of local descendants who have understood the Scots-Irish ethic of sleeping after the work is done. (Courtesy of Frank Little.)